PRIDE OF SMALL NATIONS

PRIDE OF SMALL NATIONS

THE CAUCASUS AND POST-SOVIET DISORDER

Suzanne Goldenberg

Zed Books Ltd
LONDON AND NEW JERSEY

Pride of Small Nations was first published by
Zed Books Ltd, 7 Cynthia Street, London N1 9JF, UK,
and 165 First Avenue, Atlantic Highlands, New Jersey
07716, USA, in 1994

Copyright © Suzanne Goldenberg, 1994

Cover designed by Andrew Corbett
Set in Monotype Bembo by Ewan Smith
Map by Jenny Ridley
Printed and bound in the United Kingdom
by Biddles Ltd, Guildford and King's Lynn

The right of Suzanne Goldenberg to be identified
as the author of this book has been asserted by her
in accordance with the Copyright, Designs and
Patents Act, 1988.

A catalogue record for this book is available
from the British Library

US CIP data is available from the Library of Congress

ISBN 1 85649 237 0 cased
ISBN 1 85649 238 9 limp

For Jassy
meri jaan

Contents

Acknowledgements

This book would never have been possible without the immense generosity and kindness shown to guests by the peoples of the Caucasus. I am indebted to many people who offered their friendship and their help during a time of scarcity and danger.

I am grateful to the *Guardian* for granting me the leave of absence during which I initially became interested in the Caucasus, and to my colleagues in the foreign department who forgave my distraction during the process of writing the book. Without the encouragement of Michael Simmons I might never have had the courage to start it. Jonathan Steele offered advice when I was in the region and made helpful comments on the manuscript.

John Wright and George Hewitt of the London School of Oriental and African Studies and Jonathan Aves of the London School of Economics were generous with their time and expertise. I would also like to thank Solmaz Dabiri of the BBC, Michael Dwyer, Paulette Farsides, Mark Smith of the Royal United Service Institute, and Anna Zelkina of St Antony's College, Oxford for their suggestions on chapters.

Factsheet

North Caucasus

Chechnya

Head of government: General Dzhokhar Dudayev
Capital: Grozny

Ingushetia

Head of government: General Ruslan Aushev
Capital: Nazran

Population of Checheno-Ingushetia (separate figures unavailable): 1,338,023.
  Chechens 55 per cent; Russians 22 per cent; Ingush 12 per cent;
  Armenians 1 per cent; Ukrainians 1 per cent; others 9 per cent
Religion: Sunni Muslim

Daghestan

Head of government: Magomed Ali Magomedov
Capital: Makhachkala
Population 1,802,188. Avars 27 per cent; Dargins 16 per cent; Kumyks 13
  per cent; Lezgins 11 per cent; Russians 9 per cent; Laks 5 per cent;
  Tabasarans 4 per cent; Azerbaijanis 4 per cent; Chechens 3 per cent;
  others 6 per cent
Religion: Sunni Muslim

North Ossetia

Head of government: Akhsarbek Galazov
Capital: Vladikavkaz
Population: 632,428. Ossetians 53 per cent; Russians 30 per cent; Ingush 5
  per cent; Armenians 2 per cent; Georgians 2 per cent; Ukrainians 2 per
  cent; others 6 per cent
Religion: Sunni Muslim/Orthodox

Kabardino-Balkar Republic

Head of government: Valery Kokov
Capital: Nalchik
Population: 753,531. Kabardians 48 per cent; Russians 32 per cent; Balkars 9
per cent; Ukrainians 2 per cent; Ossetians 1 per cent; Germans 1 per
cent; others 6 per cent
Religion: mixed

Karachai-Cherkess Republic

Head of government: P. Shevotsukov
Capital: Cherkessk
Population: 414,000. Russians 42.5 per cent; Karachai 31 per cent; Cherkess
9.6 per cent; Abasin 6.5 per cent; Nogai 3 per cent as well as Ukrainians,
Ossetians, Tatars, Armenians, Greeks, Belarussians, Kabardians
Religion: mixed

Adygeya Republic

Head of government: V. Savelyev
Capital: Maykop
Population: 432,000. Russians 68 per cent; Adygs 22 per cent; Ukrainians 3
per cent as well as Belarussians, Tatars, Germans, Greeks and Gypsies
Religion: mixed

Georgia

Head of government: Eduard Shevardnadze
Surface area: 69,700 square kilometres
Capital: Tbilisi (population 1,268,000)
Population: 5,395,841. Georgians 70 per cent; Armenians 8 per cent;
Azerbaijanis 6 per cent; Russians 6 per cent; Ossetians 3 per cent;
Abkhazians 1.7 per cent; others 5 per cent.
Religion: Georgian Orthodox

Armenia

Head of government: Levon Ter-Petrosian
Surface area: 29,800 square kilometres
Capital: Yerevan (population 1,202,000)
Population: 3,304,453. Armenians 94 per cent; Azerbaijanis 3 per cent;
Russians 2 per cent; others 2 per cent
Religion: Armenian Apostolic and Catholic Churches

Azerbaijan

Head of government: Heydar Aliyev
Capital: Baku (population 1,780,000)
Surface area: 86,600 square kilometres
Population: 7,019,739. Azerbaijanis 83 per cent; Armenians 6 per cent;
   Russians 6 per cent; Lezgins 2 per cent; others 4 per cent.
Religion: Shia Muslim

(All population figures are from the 1989 census.)

Chronology

1801: Georgia annexed by Russian empire.

1813: Russia wins most of present-day Azerbaijan from Iran.

1828: Capture of what is now Armenia.

1864: Russia's conquest of north Caucasus is complete.

1915: Between one and 1.5 million Armenians are killed in Ottoman Turkey, through execution and forced death marches.

1918: Georgia breaks away from fledgling Trans-Caucasian republic on 26 May to declare independence, leaving Azerbaijan and Armenia with no choice but to follow suit.

February 1921: Bolshevik forces complete their victory over the Caucasian states by invading Georgia.

1922: The Trans-Caucasus Federation becomes part of the Union of Soviet Socialist Republics.

1985

10 March: Mikhail Gorbachev becomes first secretary of the Communist Party of the Soviet Union.

1987

January: Perestroika, or restructuring policy, launched.

1988

21 February: Hundreds of thousands demonstrate in Yerevan demanding annexation of Nagorno-Karabakh.

26-28 February: Anti-Armenian pogroms in Sumgait, Azerbaijan; official death toll is thirty-two.

7 December: Armenian earthquake.

1989

9 April: Nineteen demonstrators killed in clashes with Soviet troops at protest in Tbilisi.

July: Eighteen killed and more than 200 hurt in ethnic riots in Abkhazia.

November: Clashes between Georgian nationalists and Ossetians in Tskhinvali, capital of South Ossetia.

December: Armenian parliament votes to unite with Nagorno-Karabakh.

1990

13 January: Azeri mobs turn on Armenians in Baku.

19 January: Soviet troops attack Popular Front protesters; 160 Azeris believed killed. Soviet troops sent into South Ossetia.

23 August: Armenia declares intention to secede.

October: Zviad Gamsakhurdia's Round Table-Free Georgia wins parliamentary election.

11 December: Georgian parliament removes autonomous status of South Ossetia.

1991

February: Armenia decides to hold referendum on independence.

17 March: Referendum on Gorbachev's proposed treaty to preserve Soviet Union. Georgia boycotts, but Ossetians and Abkhazians take part.

31 March: Georgia holds referendum on independence.

9 April: Georgian parliament votes to secede from Soviet Union.

May: Gamsakhurdia elected Georgian president.

19 August: Failed putsch in Moscow against Mikhail Gorbachev.

30 August: Azerbaijan declares independence.

23 September: Following referendum, Armenian parliament declares independence.

16 October: Levon Ter-Petrosian elected as Armenian president.

27 October: General Dzhokhar Dudayev elected in Chechnya.

27 November: Chechnya declares independence.

8 December: Formation of Commonwealth of Independent States (CIS).

25 December: Mikhail Gorbachev stands down as Soviet president.

1992

6 January: Zviad Gamsakhurdia toppled in a coup.

19 January: South Ossetia votes in referendum to join Russian federation.

28 February: Eduard Shevardnadze returns to Georgia.

Early March: Reports of Armenian massacre of Azeris at Khojali in Nagorno-Karabakh.

6 March: Ayaz Mutalibov toppled.

7 June: Abulfaz Elchibey elected President of Azerbaijan.

Mid-June: Peacekeeping force established in South Ossetia.

14 August: Georgian forces invade Abkhazia.

11 October: Georgian parliamentary elections. Shevardnadze becomes chairman of parliament.

Mid-November: Clashes between Ingush and Ossetians in North Ossetia. State of emergency declared in parts of North Ossetia.

1993

4 June: Clashes in Gyandzha, Azerbaijan, between government troops and rebels led by Suret Husseinov.

Early June: Azerbaijan, Armenia and Karabakh Armenians sign peace accord.

18 June: President Abulfaz Elchibey flees to Nakhichevan.

Early July: Heydar Aliyev consolidates position as Azerbaijani leader.

23 July: Agdam, the Azerbaijani town serving as a staging post in the war over Nagorno-Karabakh, falls to Armenian forces.

27 July: Abkhazians and Georgians sign Sochi peace agreement to end war.

August: Armenian forces capture the Azerbaijani towns of Jebrail and Fizuli, forcing tens of thousands of Azeris to flee over the Araxes river into Iran.

29 August: Referendum in Azerbaijan rejects return of Abulfaz Elchibey.

Mid-September: Supporters of Zviad Gamsakhurdia step up rebellion in western Georgia; Gamsakhurdia returns from exile.

24 September: Azerbaijan applies to join CIS.

27 September: Sukhumi falls.

3 October: Heydar Aliyev elected Azerbaijani president.

8 October: Georgia applies to join CIS.

6 November: Georgian government forces, freed up by Russian army protection of bridges and key installations, drive Gamsakhurdia rebels from their last stronghold.

31 December: Zviad Gamsakhurdia dies in mysterious circumstances; there are confused reports of murder, suicide and a fatal illness.

Further Reading

Altstadt, Audrey (1992), *The Azerbaijani Turks: Power and Identity under Russian Rule*, Hoover Institution Press, Stanford, California.

Bremmer, Ian and Taras, Ray (1993), *Nations and Politics in the Soviet Successor States*, Cambridge University Press.

Broxup, Marie Bennigsen (ed.) (1992), *The North Caucasus Barrier: The Russian Advance towards the Muslim World*, Hurst & Co, London.

Conquest, Robert (1978), *The Nation Killers: The Soviet deportation of nationalities*, Macmillan, London.

Kazamzadeh, Firuz (1951), *The Struggle for Transcaucasia, 1917–1921*, Templar Press, New York.

Lermontov, Mikhail (1966), *A Hero of our Time*, trans. Paul Foote, Penguin Books, London.

Mandelstam, Osip (1933), *Journey to Armenia*, Redstone Press, London.

Nahaylo, Bohdan and Swoboda, Viktor (1990), *Soviet Disunion: A history of the nationalities problem in the USSR*, Hamish Hamilton, London.

Nasmyth, Peter. (1992), *Georgia: a Rebel in the Caucasus*, Cassell, London.

Suny, Ronald Grigor (1972), *The Baku Commune 1917–1923. Class and Nationality in the Russian Revolution*, Princeton University Press.

Suny, Ronald Grigor (1989), *The Making of the Georgian Nation*, I.B. Tauris, London.

Tolstoy, Leo (1977), *'Hadji Murat' in Master and Man and Other Stories*, trans. Paul Foote, Penguin Books, London.

Walker, Christopher (1990), *Armenia. The Survival of a Nation*, Routledge, London.

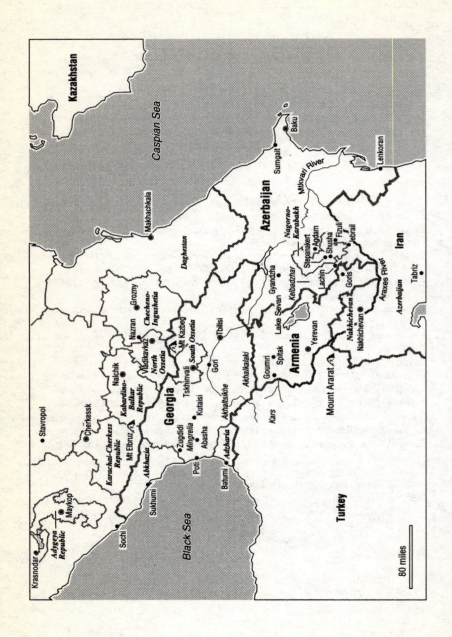

1

Introduction

Far away on the horizon groups of dancing stars wove wondrous patterns, fading one by one as the pale light of dawn spread over the deep
violet sky and lit up the virgin snow on the steep mountain slopes. Dark
mysterious chasms yawned on either side of us. Wreaths of mist coiled
and twisted like snakes, sliding down the folds of neighbouring cliffs into
the abyss, as though they sensed and feared the approach of day. There
was peace in heaven and on earth. It was like the heart of a man at
morning prayer.[1]

The Caucasus cast a spell over early travellers. It banished the ennui
of the drawing room of 19th-century St Petersburg for the writer of
the above passage, the poet Mikhail Lermontov. He was enchanted by
the Caucasus, by the jagged mountain peaks higher than the Alps, and
by the 'blood snows', the glaciers tinged crimson by iron oxides.
Lermontov perceived a nobility in the simplicity of the Cossack way
of life and in the codes of honour of the mountain tribesmen. He met
his death in the Caucasus at the age of 26 in a duel over a trivial insult
from a fellow officer.

Beauty and danger. The mountain chain that stretches eastwards for
700 miles from the Black Sea to the Caspian marks the furthest reaches
of Europe and the frontier between the Muslim and Christian worlds.
The region includes Mount Elbruz (which at 18,480 feet is higher
than Mont Blanc), the desolate treeless landscape of Armenia, the lush
vineyards of Georgia, the oil fields of Azerbaijan, the remote villages
of Daghestan, and the workaday black soil of southern Russia's bread
basket.

I first travelled in the Caucasus in the heady and uncertain days of
the winter of 1991–2. In December 1991, Mikhail Gorbachev acknowledged the failure of his attempts to negotiate a new treaty preserving the union and stepped down as Soviet president. His departure
removed the last, and artificial, barrier to the dissolution of an unhappy union, and the peoples of the Caucasus reached out and grabbed
for independence with both hands.

For the contemporary traveller, the fascination and danger lay in the welter of political struggles, banditry, territorial rivalries, economic disruption and ethnic violence that was to characterise the first years of independence of Armenia, Georgia, and Azerbaijan, and the nationalist stirring of the smaller ethnic groups which live in the autonomous republics within Russia. An old proverb became a popular adage for journalists covering the region: 'When shall blood cease to flow in the mountains? When sugar cane grows in the snow.'

After seventy years of isolation, the region had all the unpredictability of a frontier. At times it was impossible to resist the notion that the period of imperial struggle had returned. War had rendered useless many of the conveniences of the 20th century. In Yerevan, families turned their backs on gas-starved central heating and built precarious-looking wood-burning stoves from scrap metal. Horsecarts replaced automobiles when petrol vanished. Women with little interest in cooking pickled every vegetable they could coax into life on their balconies.

One evening, I joined an Armenian family in Nagorno-Karabakh around the gas jet that served as their single source of light and heat. My host rolled tobacco, which he had grown and dried himself, in strips of newspaper. In a low voice at first, he spoke about the war in the enclave as the site of the final clash between the Muslim world and Christendom: a mountainous Armageddon. The firelight, his apocalyptic vision, the misery of his existence – all made it conceivable for a moment that the Crusades were being re-enacted in the Caucasus.

The three main nations of these new border lands, Georgia, Armenia and Azerbaijan, have been known collectively as the Trans-Caucasus. But the term has now been discarded as being too closely identified with Russian rule. After all, the region is only on the far side of the Caucasus from the Russian vantage point. Of the three, Georgia, on the southern foothills of the Caucasus range, shares the longest frontier with Russia. It also borders Turkey, and Armenia and Azerbaijan to the south. To the west, Georgia's Black Sea coast marks the only subtropical climate zone in the former Soviet Union. At the time of the 1989 census, Georgia had a population of 5.4 million, 70 per cent of whom were ethnic Georgians. Although the Ossetian and Abkhazian minorities were allocated autonomous territories within Georgia during the Soviet period, their share of the overall population is relatively small – 3 per cent and less than 2 per cent respectively. The Adzhars, or Georgian Muslims, also constitute an autonomous region. Georgian, the official language, is a non Indo-European language with a unique alphabet. The country is a little bigger than the Republic of Ireland, measuring 69,700 square kilometres, and includes areas afflicted by earthquake activity.

Azerbaijan, on the western coast of the Caspian Sea, is the largest country in the region. It shares a frontier with Armenia to the west, Daghestan to the north, and Iran to the south as well as Georgia. About the size of Portugal and covering 86,600 square kilometres, it includes within its domains the disputed enclave of Nagorno-Karabakh, which is mainly populated by Armenians, and Nakhichevan, which is separated from the rest of the country by Armenia. At the time of the 1989 census, Russians and Armenians made up about 6 per cent each of Azerbaijan's population of 7 million, but worsening ethnic conflict has led to mass migration from the republic. The Azerbaijani language, originally Persian, was heavily influenced over the years by Turkic-speaking settlers from the east.

Mountainous and earthquake-prone, Armenia is the smallest country of the three – about the size of Belgium, at 29,800 square kilometres. It has no outlet to the sea, but is wedged between Turkey and Iran to the south, Georgia to the north and Azerbaijan to the east. Armenia is the most ethnically homogenous of the three republics: at the time of the 1989 census more than 93 per cent of the population of 3.3 million was Armenian. But there are significant numbers of Armenians elsewhere in the former Soviet Union, particularly in Georgia, as well as in the US, France and the Middle East. The Armenian language is the sole member of a distinctive group within the Indo-European family and has its own script.

The Soviet census of 1989 recognised nineteen native national groups in the autonomous republics of Russia's northern Caucasus. There are dozens more ethnic groups, making it one of the most linguistically and ethnically various regions in the world. Geography contributed to the diversity: the mountain terrain isolated population groups, and preserved a multiplicity of dialects that would otherwise have disappeared.

However, the peoples of the north Caucasus can generally be divided into four: the Circassian, or, as they call themselves, Adyg tribes of the north-west and Black Sea coast, including the Adygs, Cherkess, and Kabardians; the indigenous Caucasian nations like the Chechens or Ingush; the descendants of locals and the Turkic-speaking invaders of the 13th century like the Karachai, Balkar and Kumyks; and the Iranian-speakers like the Ossetians, as well as a few much smaller ethnic groups.

The Chechens are the most numerous nationality with a population of 950,000; the numbers of some of the other recognised ethnic groups have dwindled to below 20,000. Daghestan is the largest autonomous republic, combining ten national groups, while the other larger nationalities have territories of their own or share with one other nation.

The turbulence that now engulfs the Caucasus has been a constant companion to an ancient and famously complicated history. The Caucasus has for millennia been at the periphery of competing empires. Greek, Roman, Byzantine, Arab and Mongol armies all passed through before the region was carved up by the Ottoman and Persian empires in the 16th century. Russia made its first foray into the Caucasus at around the same time, by sea from the eastern shores of the Caspian. However, its initial advances southwards were tentative and sporadic. Only in 1864 could Russia say with confidence that it was master of the Caucasus.

Although their kingdoms were nearly always vassal states to larger and more powerful empires, the Georgians and Armenians retained distinctive cultures. Both peoples are intensely proud of their antiquity, and of their embrace of the Church soon after the dawn of the Christian era. But although Christianity was to prove a source of inner strength through centuries of foreign invasion, it seldom brought the two nations together against a common enemy. The Armenian Church grew up independently of the Greek Church. The Georgians, however, are Orthodox.

Arab invaders brought Islam to the region. In the 8th century the new religion took root in Azerbaijan, which had previously had Zoroastrian and Christian kingdoms, but it was 1,000 years before Islam established itself among the north Caucasian peoples. While the Azerbaijanis of today are Shia Muslim, the north Caucasians are Sunni, with their own strong mystical traditions. Nowhere is Islam as strong as in the Middle East and there are remnants of pagan practices particularly among the Abkhazians, who live in north-western Georgia along the Black Sea coast.

The three main cities of the Caucasus are a reflection of this history of upheaval and change. Tbilisi, the 1,500-year-old Georgian city, is the most graceful. It was sacked repeatedly, pillaged as recently as 1921 by the Red Army, and little remains from the golden age of the late 12th century. The crumbling but still beautiful buildings on the eastern bank of the Mtkvari river were built by Armenians in the 19th century. They serve as a reminder of the days when Tbilisi was the hub of Armenian intellectual activity.

Baku, the Azerbaijani capital, shares Tbilisi's cosmopolitan past. Although the oil rigs are far from the city centre, they have an invisible presence in the pastel mansions that relieve the uniformity of Soviet architecture. Their extravagance was a product of the intense competition between the industrial barons of Russia, Germany, France and Britain after oil was discovered in the late 19th century. As in Tbilisi, Armenians made up the core of Baku's skilled workers, and reaped the benefits of the oil rush. The sudden wealth largely excluded the Azerbaijanis, creating a sense of deprivation that still lingers.

Yerevan, the Armenian capital, grew even more rapidly than Baku, but it was a process based on loss rather than on the accumulation of wealth. The population of the provincial town more than doubled to over one million people in the space of twenty years, swelled by refugees from the pogroms of the Ottoman empire. The Ottoman campaign of persecution against the Christian minority reached its apogee in the massacres and forced marches of 1915.

The Armenian tragedy provides the most brutal illustration of the way in which the three main Caucasian nations were subjected to the imperial imperative at the beginning of this century. All three countries were briefly independent in the period between the Bolshevik revolution and the consolidation of Soviet rule, but the experience of statehood was a disaster.

Thrust into independence by the collapse of the Tsarist empire, the weak and inexperienced governments were beset by infighting between communists and nationalists, ethnic violence, poverty and famine, as well as by foreign intrigues, notably British and Turkish. Despite appeals for foreign support, the fledgeling governments were unable to resist the Bolshevik forces and were annexed by the Red Army. The independence of the mountain peoples of the north Caucasus was even more illusory; some of the worst fighting between the Red and White armies took place in the north Caucasus.

The policy of foreign states towards the three republics was crucial in their defeat by Bolshevik forces. Although – apart from Azerbaijan's oil – the region boasts few natural resources, it was considered an important bulwark for Russia against Turkey and Iran, and against the greater Muslim world beyond. In the post-Soviet order, the Caucasus has proved much more of a filter than a barrier. It is still an important arena for Iran and Turkey, but the emphasis is more on building new economic alliances and trade routes in a region that, despite its current instability, offers an entry to the markets of Europe and the West.

Russia's perception of the region has been coloured by the long and bitter wars fought over the north Caucasus. The guerrilla struggle led by the warrior-priest Imam Shamil assumed a place in the Russian imagination parallel to the position of the Khyber Pass and the north-west frontiers of colonial India for the British. Contemporary travellers to the region were struck by the vengeance wreaked against the Caucasians.

'The Circassians hate us. We have forced them out of their free and spacious pasture lands; their auls (villages) are in ruins, whole tribes have been annihilated', Pushkin wrote after a journey through the mountains to Armenia and Turkey in 1829.[2] But he remained hopeful of integrating the warlike tribes into Russian society: 'The influence of luxury may favour their taming; the samovar would be an important innovation.'[3]

The duration and savagery of the Caucasian wars also brought this remote and inaccessible region to the attention of the rest of the world. They were a relief to 19th-century Britain and France, which had viewed Russia's advance into the Caucasus with trepidation. The Tsarist preoccupation with its enemies on the southern flank kept Russia out of the race for colonies in the Middle East and Asia. 'All accounts of war in the Caucasus which have reached Europe have been obscure and almost resembled fairy tales', wrote a German traveller to the area in 1875. 'Stories were told of proud mountaineers who inspired by the love of freedom and independence disputed with the Russians at the price of their blood, every inch of their native soil.' Such stories, wrote Lieutenant Baron Max Von Thielmann

> induced half of Europe during the time of the Crimean war to believe that it only required a little more active assistance on the part of the allies to have incited every man in the Caucasus to openly revolt and drive the Russians back into the steppes.[4]

But although Russia saluted the bravery of its opponents in the literature of Pushkin, Lermontov and Tolstoy, it continued to view its neighbours from the position of a colonial power, creating a sense of suspicion of the other that has become ingrained. Amid the economic hardships in the Russian cities of the north today, Caucasians are seen as untrustworthy market traders and the ruthless dons of a proliferating criminal mafia.

During the years that followed the Soviet annexation of their republics, the Caucasian nationalities suffered alongside Russians the reign of terror of Joseph Dzhugashvili, or Stalin. Stalin and his equally sadistic acolyte, Lavrentii Beria, remain Georgia's most famous sons, but they showed no mercy to their native region. Stalin's ascent from obscurity to superpower leader brought purges of intellectuals in Georgia, Armenia, and Azerbaijan, and mass deportations and expropriations of the Meskhetian Turks of Georgia, and the Chechens and three other nationalities of the north Caucasus.

What distinguished the Caucasians from the other non-Russian republics was the strength of their national feeling. Languages and traditions were jealously guarded despite attempts at Russification and secularisation, which were at their most zealous in the northern Caucasus, and the fabric of society remained largely intact. Fewer Russians settled in the Caucasus than in other parts of the former Soviet Union.

And even judging only by the rates of mixed marriage in the republics, the spread of secularism and education did little to dilute old affiliations. The incidence of intermarriage in the Caucasus was 4 per cent compared to rates approaching 20 per cent in the Baltics and Ukraine. In public life as well, national sentiments were never entirely forgotten. The Chechens continued throughout this century to rise militarily against what they regarded as an alien and infidel rule, and there was dissident activity in Georgia and Armenia throughout the Brezhnev era (1964–82).

Perestroika, and the opportunities it offered for greater autonomy, was greeted enthusiastically in the Caucasus. The Georgians moved swiftly to assert their right to sovereignty, and the Armenians launched a campaign for unity with the enclave of Nagorno-Karabakh. But in 1988 the resumption of political activity on an openly national basis led to violence.

Since independence in 1991, the political and economic prospects of all three states have been compromised by nationalist, ethnic and territorial conflict. The warfare that has become endemic to the Caucasus has been made materially possible by the disarray that accompanied the demobilisation of the former Soviet Army. The region is awash with weaponry and with willing mercenaries among the unemployed and homeless soldiers of the old order. The security threat this poses goes beyond the small-scale fighting of some of the ethnic conflicts, challenging the governability of the Caucasus in ways that impinge on Russia as well as on Iran and Turkey.

In hurtling towards independence, the Georgian national movement was unable to find a popular consensus over what form of government should prevail. Confusion over the political agenda allowed for the development of a politics in which nationalism and personality took centre stage. Ethnic chauvinism made life increasingly uncomfortable for the small but strategically placed Ossetian and Abkhazian minorities, and provoked corresponding nationalist movements which have turned into warfare. The resulting combination of political and ethnic disputes now threatens Georgia's territorial integrity.

In Azerbaijan, the struggle between the old communist regime and nationalists was played out only after the state became independent, a reflection of its rather late development of a distinct political consciousness. Now Azerbaijan must redefine its relationship with Russia and confront the task of nation-building at a time when its national identity and boundaries are insecure.

Armenia has benefited from the most stable post-Soviet government in the region, a result of the active role the diaspora has played in keeping political pluralism alive. But the gap in understanding of the Armenian reality between the large overseas community and locals carries with it certain tensions.

Nagorno-Karabakh, an Armenian-populated enclave within Azerbaijan, was the object of Armenia's first national stirrings. Since 1988, the Armenian campaign for unification has descended into the bloodiest and most intractable of the post-Soviet conflicts. The situation in Nagorno-Karabakh provides the most extreme example of the inherent dangers when the conflicts contained during the Soviet period become active once again. It also demonstrates the resistance of ethnic and territorial disputes to peaceful solutions and outside mediation.

Other ethnic and territorial conflicts loom in the northern Caucasus, where the first national stirrings have begun among the small nations that are still formally part of Russia. The Chechens, the most forward-looking nation, have re-examined and then set aside the persecutions of the past, devoting their energies to sustaining the independent state declared in November 1991. But the past is still a central issue for the Karachai and Balkar, whose rediscovery of the deportations of their people during the Second World War is central to the development of a national consciousness. Still others remain prisoners of their history: the Adygs, or Circassians, condemned to obscurity by their dwindling population; the North Ossetians, left exposed by their old alliances with Moscow; and the Russians and Cossacks, forced to confront their new status in a changing society.

The outlook for the nations on either side of the Caucasian range is uncertain. But despite an often grim prognosis, the current tensions cannot entirely extinguish the wealth of the Caucasian traditions and languages, the delights of its scenery, and the almost embarrassing generosity of its people. Nineteenth-century travellers were captivated by their journeys through the heart of the region. Then as now, there was really only one route to choose: through the Daryal pass connecting Georgia to Russia. Almost to a man, they found it a magical experience, exulting in their first glimpse of the great Kazbeg mountain which guards the Georgian side of the border. Nowadays, the average travel time for the 125-mile journey between Tbilisi and Vladikavkaz in North Ossetia is four hours.

My reasons for following their route during my months of travel through the Caucasus were entirely prosaic. I had waited in vain for an entire day at a Russian army base, putting my faith in the assurances of a kindly officer that the skies would clear and that I would fly by helicopter to Vladikavkaz. I spent much of the next equally grey and overcast day at Tbilisi airport, where the Aeroflot ground crew could offer no guarantees that fuel could be found for any of the flights scheduled that day. And so I decided to go by road.

There had been heavy snows earlier that week and avalanches had closed the route, but now I was told the way was clear. Few drivers wished to chance the journey; reports of highway robbery had made people wary of travelling. But eventually one came foward in a car so old and rickety that it seemed a miracle when we reached the city limits. He assembled what looked like a series of Hoover attachments to blow air on the windscreen to prevent it from fogging and we drove towards the mountains. It began to snow, quite heavily. We drove on.

As the road began to climb, we formed a convoy of other foolish and impatient travellers, cutting a slow passage through banks of snow that reached 10 feet in height. Every so often, one car would be trapped in a drift, its wheels spinning uselessly until other passengers in the convoy alighted to push it on its way. There were several such halts, and passengers were traded from vehicle to vehicle on the grounds that an even distribution of weight would help everybody to travel quicker. People shared out dumplings and bottles of Georgian red wine.

Six hours later and still many miles short of Vladikavkaz, even the most intrepid of drivers began to lose heart. There were increasingly acrimonious discussions about whose turn it was to get out and push. My driver had become hysterical, convinced that we would never get through and were bound to freeze to death in the night. For distraction, I turned to the two Georgian men who had been allocated space in our car from another vehicle.

'So what brings you to Vladikavkaz, business or pleasure?'

'Business', the taller one replied. 'I am going to buy opium and my friend has escaped from prison.'

Just then, the moon escaped from behind a patch of cloud and the first car in the line lurched free from the snow. The driver was cheered. 'Well, English,' he said, stabbing through the window at the moon. 'Very romantic, isn't it.'

Well, yes.

Notes

1. Lermontov, Mikhail (1966), *A Hero of our Time*, trans. Paul Foote, Penguin Books, London, p. 43.

2. Pushkin, Alexander (1974), *Journey to Erzerum*, trans. Birgitta Ingemanson, Ardis, London, p. 23.

3. Ibid., p. 24.

4. Thielmann, Max Guido Franz Von (1875), *Journey in the Caucasus, Persia and Turkey in Asia*, trans. Charles Hereage, John Murray, London, p. 24.

2

Histories: Ancient and Modern

History is a dangerous thing in the Caucasus. Disasters, betrayals, or rare moments of stability remain close to the surface no matter how remote in time. At the beginning of nearly every interview, I would be interrupted and admonished: 'First you must understand our history.' Inevitably, the account that followed would be at odds with the version I had just heard.

It was impossible not to be confused. In ancient times, the Caucasus mountain range served as a barrier between the northern Eurasian steppes and the more advanced civilisations of southern Mesopotamia and Anatolia. But along its east-west axis, the situation was far more fluid. The course of the Araxes river, which now delineates the southern border of Armenia and Azerbaijan, was a main trading route between the Mediterranean and the Orient. There was a parallel northern path to Central Asia, India and China by way of the Black Sea, Georgia and northern Azerbaijan. Along both those routes, the traffic has been two-way. For the West, the passage across the Caucasus meant access to the fabled riches of the East; for the Asian invaders who traversed the isthmus it was an entry point to Europe. The strategic location of the Caucasus has almost always assumed a value far larger than the silks and spices, and latterly the oil and mines, which it possesses. Its awkward position on the invasion and trade paths between two continents has determined its eventful history.

For much of this history, the Caucasus has been swept up in the struggles of competing powers. The region has generally been on the edges of empire; in fact, the dividing line between great powers has often run right through the Caucasus. But far from allowing the Caucasus to develop as a sleepy backwater, its position on the periphery has been hotly contested. The entire region has been exposed to attack far more often than had it been near the centre and the main garrisons of empire. Invaders would test their strength by prising off just a little corner of the empire; the reigning power would consider whether its loss justified a larger, more bruising confrontation. From time immemorial until well after the First World War, this dynamic was fundamentally unaltered. Although reduced at times to a side-show, the Caucasus was still deemed important enough to the out-come of the Great War to merit direct German and British intervention. As ever, the designs of the great powers were disastrous for the local peoples.

The impromptu history lessons I received in the Caucasus did offer a glimpse of this. Whether involving imperial warfare directly or its consequences for smaller nationalities, this history of struggle has shaped the fate of the Caucasus. When I returned to the West, I was shocked by how little published material there was on these dramatic rivalries, and on the Caucasus as a whole. There were plenty of works on Armenia, a fair number on Georgia, but little beyond Raj-style travel memoirs for the north Caucasus. Azerbaijan, in particular, had been almost completely neglected by Western scholars. However, this was in part a consequence of the relatively recent formation of a distinct Azerbaijani national identity. Until the First World War, the people of what would become the Soviet republic of Azerbaijan were referred to variously as Turks, Tatars and Caucasian Muslims (although the term Azerbaijani will be used here consistently to avoid confusion).

The isolation acknowledged by this literary lacuna was also a rela-tively recent phenomenon. The seventy years of Soviet rule had tied the Caucasus firmly to the centre of a single empire, a departure from its traditional position. Add to that the delicacy with which scholars had to approach the study of non-Russian dominions of the Soviet empire and it becomes clear why the study of the Caucasus has been so discouraging. During a time when modern discussion in general was circumscribed, there was a particular sensitivity about subjects which touched on the 'nationality question'. The assumption that the Soviet Union, by incorporating nationally based republics, had neu-tralised demands for self-determination, precluded debate. Certain topics just were not discussed.

Most notable among the pre-perestroika omissions, for its obvious implications, was the brief period of independence experienced by Georgia, Armenia and Azerbaijan between the 1917 revolution and their forcible annexation by the Red Army. There was a deliberate emphasis on more distant eras to detract from uncomfortable episodes during the Russian conquest of the Caucasus. Some of these blank spots were filled in by émigré historians. However, among them were those whose scholarship was compromised by the pursuit of an anti-Soviet agenda.

Perestroika brought the possibility of re-examining past events, but the reclamation of history has been subject to the compulsions of nation-building. Politicians have indiscriminately invoked mythology and fact in the building of coalitions for the new era of multi-party politics. For Georgians and Armenians, there is a strong temptation to glorify a fabled past in preference to the political and economic uncertainties of the present. Sometimes history is inseparable from current post-Soviet disputes. Georgian historians, for example, have dismissed as fiction past works detailing the connections between the Ossetian and Abkhazian kings and medieval Georgia. In their view, the Ossetians arrived in Georgia only 200 years ago – as serfs on the estate of Prince Matchabelli. The implication of this argument is that the Ossetians, as recent and poor arrivals, do not deserve lands of their own in Georgia. In Armenia, a hankering after lost glories has served to reinforce a sense of cultural superiority. Armenians are understandably proud of their alphabet, invented in the 5th century by Saint Mesrop Mashtots. But they use the lack of an Azeri counterpart – the language was transcribed relatively recently and has used Arabic, Cyrillic and Latin scripts – to question their neighbour's right to be considered as a nation.

The smaller ethnic groups are no less guilty of the misrepresentation of history, although their fabrications initially seem less dangerous. The nationalist group Ademon Nykhas has propagated a number of myths about the uncertain origins of the Ossetians in order to establish a pedigree with which to strengthen their present territorial claims. Among the notions peddled by nationalist ideologues is the theory that Ossetians, or their precursors, were lords of an empire that took in Catalonia and Britain. The place names of London and Croydon, like almost all Ossetian settlements in the Caucasus, end in d-o-n – and this is taken as evidence of Ossetian settlement. In Ossetian, London means 'a place where people can stand' and Croydon means 'mill'. Even more poignant are the claims by the Shapsugis, an Adyg or Circassian tribe, that Nefertiti was a Shapsugi queen. Their culture destroyed by the Russian conquest of the Black Sea coast, the once numerous Shapsugi tribe has been reduced to fewer than 10,000 heavily assimilated survivors, and their language is virtually extinct.

The combination of great antiquity, providing ample material for distortions, and bitter present-day conflicts makes it exceedingly difficult to write an honest history of the Caucasus. This chapter hopes merely to provide a sketch of the events and of the loyalties that are helping to shape the future.

Ancient histories

GEORGIA

What was to become the Georgian nation emerged first in the west of the country. After the destruction of the Hittite empire by Assyrian invaders in around 1200 BC, fleeing tribes migrated to what is now south-western Georgia, mixing with ancient ethnic groupings in the region to found the kingdom of Colchis in 600 BC. Other tribes of the Hittite empire later settled to the east of the Surami mountain range, founding the kingdom known as Iberia – which had no connection to Spain – in about 300 BC. The name Georgia did not emerge until more than 1,000 years later, and was a variation of a word applied by Arab and Iranian traders: Gurjistan. Georgians called their country Sakartvelo, after a mythical founding father.

The ancient geographical dislocation between Iberia and Colchis helped lead to the emergence of three distinct linguistic strands from the prototype Georgian language: Mingrelian/Laz in western Georgia and around the Black Sea coast, Svan in the north-western mountainous region, and classical Georgian, or Kartvelian, in the eastern Kakheti and Kartli regions. This dialect became the sole Georgian literary language and the basis of Orthodox liturgy.

Even from so remote a period, Georgia was integrated into the Black Sea trading system. Greek colonists established trading centres along the coast at what are now Batumi, Poti, and Sukhumi in the 7th century BC. They were aware of, and admired, the rich vineyards and fertile lands of the Iberian kingdom, while recoiling from the strange customs of the peoples of Colchis. Those early contacts have been immortalised in Greek mythology. The rock to which Prometheus was chained after he attempted to steal fire from heaven is said to be Georgia's Mount Kazbeg, while Jason and the Argonauts' quest for the Golden Fleece in Colchis is believed to refer to ancient methods of panning for gold. In the 20th century, the Black Sea Greeks, reinforced in numbers by refugees from the Ottoman empire, were dispersed and deported by Stalin.

Before the advent of Christianity, both Colchis and Iberia were centres of active and varied religious life, encompassing Zoroastrianism from Persia as well as the Greek creeds. Georgia's conversion to Christianity in about 330 AD – roughly thirty years after Armenia – is ascribed to a slave from Cappadocia called Nino. She possessed healing powers, curing the Iberian queen and winning her trust. The new religion spread quickly in western Georgia. In the 5th century, the Georgian Church won autonomy within Greek Orthodoxy, a status maintained except for a brief period at the end of the Tsarist era.

To further the spread of religious life, a Georgian script was created and the first literary work appeared; *The Torture of Shushanik* describes the martyrdom of an Armenian princess at the hands of her apostate husband, the Georgian prince Vakhtang Gorgasali. At around the same time, feudal structures similar to those in Europe began to emerge, setting in motion a rivalry between the king and his appointed governors and the hereditary clan leaders that was to fatally weaken Georgia.

During the 6th century, Georgia became caught up in the struggle between the Byzantine and the Iranian empires for domination of the Caucasus. By 510 AD, the Iberian kings, who by then ruled western Georgia as well, were so weakened that Iran was able to abolish the monarchy and assert direct control over internal affairs. With the Georgian monarchy in abeyance, the Church began to assume more importance as a national symbol.

From this time onwards, internal disarray and great power competition deprived Georgia of all but brief periods of independence. Georgian rule in Tbilisi resumed only at the end of the 11th century under David the Builder, scion of a mixed Armenian/Georgian dynasty. After his restoration, the Bagratid line reigned over Georgian kingdoms of varying size and autonomy for more than 800 years. Under his stewardship (1089-1125), Georgia won the protection of the Byzantine emperor, and the two wings of the kingdom were united. Its domains extended into Armenia, Daghestan, Ossetia and Abkhazia. David's great-granddaughter, Queen Tamar, expanded Georgia's dominions further still. Under her rule, Georgia absorbed the town of Trabzon, now in Turkey, and sent raiders into Tabriz in Iran. She presided over a flowering of Georgian culture. Shota Rustaveli's epic *Knight in a Panther Skin*, about an Indian prince searching for his kidnapped betrothed in Arabia, was written during her rule.

The Mongol invasions which followed Queen Tamar's rule – eight in less than twenty years – brought an end to Georgia's golden age. When the Byzantine empire collapsed in 1453, Georgia was isolated from western Christendom. Inside Georgia, the united kingdom had fragmented into Kartli and Kakheti in the east, and Imereti to the west of the Surami range. Five princely families took advantage of the disarray to set up principalities of their own in Mingrelia and Abkhazia and other areas in western Georgia.

ARMENIA

The Armenians are descended from ancient Indo-European tribes who inhabited eastern Anatolia from prehistoric times and call their land Hayastan, perhaps after the legendary ancestor Haik. The first kingdom to be established within the borders of present-day Armenia was that of Erubuni, with its capital just outside Yerevan, in the 8th century BC. Succeeding kingdoms became part of the Persian empire until the rule of King Tigran II (95–55 BC).

Through a series of military victories over Rome, Parthia (Persia) and the Seleucids, Tigran united all the territories inhabited by Armenians to weld together a kingdom stretching from the Caspian Sea to the Mediterranean. His reign represented the apogee of Armenian power; after his death Armenia reverted to its position as a semi-autonomous state on the borders of two empires.

Most famous as the world's oldest Christian nation, the Armenians were converted by St Grigory the Illuminator in 301 AD. Christianity developed independently of Rome and Constantinople, a break confirmed in a 5th-century schism in the Church, which left Armenia outside the Byzantine fold. The development of a distinctive script in the 5th century enabled the Bible and other works to be translated into Armenian, strengthening an identity that was to provide succour through centuries of warfare and repression.

The distinguishing feature of Armenia's history has been the carve-up of its land by competing powers, a pattern set in motion in 387 AD when the country was divided between Rome and Persia. In 640 AD, the Arabs replaced the Persians in the eastern half of Armenia. From then on, the Armenian kings struggled to steer their country between the Muslim invaders and absorption by the larger Byzantine empire. There was a brief flowering of the Armenian kingdom of Ani, now well inside Turkey, during the 9th and 10th centuries. As in Georgia, this short-lived autonomous regime was presided over by the Armenian/Georgian Bagratid dynasty. However, the Armenian Bagratid rulers failed to make accommodation with their Byzantine overlords. The Byzantines set the Armenian princes against each other, and so destabilised the kingdom that they were able to gobble it up in 1045 AD. Twenty years later, the Byzantine rulers of Ani themselves were conquered by the Seljuk Turks, a disaster that was compounded in the 13th century by the first of the Mongol invasions.

But while Caucasian Armenia entered into a dark period with the Turkish and Mongol invasions, a new Armenian kingdom was flourishing at Cilicia on the Mediterranean Sea in an area that is now part of Syria. An ally of the Crusaders, Cilicia became a main entrepôt for East–West trade, exporting spices, perfumes and silks to Europe for three centuries. But amid repeated assaults from Seljuk and Mamluk invaders, and internal struggle between the Catholic and Armenian Apostolic churches, it fell apart in the 14th century.

By 1502, meanwhile, the Safavid shahs of Persia had conquered much of Armenia from the Mongols. Although the Mongol over-lordship had destroyed the Armenian nobility through heavy taxation and land confiscation, a new class began to emerge and prosper under the Safavids. The Armenians were granted a monopoly of the Persian silk trade, a privilege used by merchants to extend their contacts with Russia. By the end of the 17th century, the Armenians had cornered the Russian market in silk, and had set up silk farms on the banks of the Terek river in the north Caucasus.

AZERBAIJAN

One of the most interesting details about Caucasian history is the emergence of a third Christian culture – after Armenia and Georgia – in what became Muslim Azerbaijan. The existence of the kingdom overturns the comon perception that there is little to distinguish the Azeri nation from the Turks. Azerbaijan was never a part of the Ottoman empire, and although local rulers enjoyed relative autonomy it was always a part of a wider Iranian domain.

The borders of Caucasian Albania, or Arran as it was called by the Persians, originally extended along the western shore of the Caspian as far north as the town of Derbent in Daghestan. There is no connection between this ancient, vanished kingdom and the Balkan country of the same name. Even earlier, that portion of Azerbaijan that lies to the south of the Araxes river had been the birthplace of Zoroastrianism, the religion that is the source of ancient Persian culture. Azerbaijan in fact means 'land of fire'.

Caucasian Albania's inhabitants, a mixture of sedentary Iranian tribes and mountaineers, were believed to have been converted to the Armenian church in the 4th century. This initial contact was strengthened when, in the 5th century, the Albanian kingdom began to expand westwards towards Armenia. The seat of the Albanian Church was also transferred from Derbent.

The Armenian script was adopted for the Albanian language and eventually replaced it altogether, leaving only a few church inscriptions in northern Azerbaijan as evidence of its existence. The Caucasian Albanians were tolerated by the Persian Sassanid overlords, who had established vassal states in the region in the 4th century. But their culture, and that of the Zoroastrian creed in the south, disappeared after the Arab conquest of the 7th century Islamicised the region. The Arab rulers brought Azerbaijan more firmly into their orbit than the Sassanids had done. Large numbers of troops were stationed in Azerbaijan, and a powerful administration, headed by local governors, was built up.

By the 10th century, the local Arab-sponsored dynasties were waning and Azerbaijan became disturbed, making it vulnerable to Turkic invasions from the east. The wave of Turkic settlers that accompanied the invasions gradually began to supplant the Persian identity. In the 14th century, the distinctive Azeri Turkic language emerged. But the hybrid identity persisted, with Azerbaijanis adopting Shia Islam at the end of the 15th century. Azerbaijan's status as an Iranian possession remained strong under the Safavid dynasty, whose capital was at Tabriz in southern Azerbaijan. The Safavids, who were themselves Turkic, divided Caucasian Azerbaijan into a number of khanates which were ruled by hereditary tribal chieftains or directly appointed rulers. The khans' influence varied according to the size of their territory and the relative strength of the reigning Safavid Shah. The leading khanates were Baku or Shirvan, Shekhi, which was famed for its silks, Gyandzha, Derbent in what is now Daghestan, and Karabakh, which occupied a much larger swathe of territory than today. The last years of the Safavid dynasty saw a flourishing of Azeri Turkic as a literary language, embracing the national poet Nizami of Gyandzha and others.

Great power rivalry

From the 16th century onwards, the Caucasus became one of the arenas for Ottoman–Safavid rivalry. The struggle was a continuation of the competition between earlier powers – Greek and Persian, Roman and Parthian, Byzantine and Sassanid – and a common doomsday scenario has it recreated in the successor states of the bygone empires, Iran and Turkey.

The competition between the two powers stabilised in 1555, when the Caucasus was partitioned along a north-south axis. Arran or Azerbaijan remained almost entirely within the Iranian domain, but Georgia was divided along the traditional lines of the eastern and western kingdoms. Western Georgia, including Imereti, Abkhazia and Mingrelia, was ceded to Turkey, giving the latter, with its Balkan possessions, exclusive control over the Black Sea. The most prosperous provinces of eastern Georgia, Kartli and Kakheti, went to Iran. In 1639 Armenia was partitioned, with four-fifths ceded to Turkey, and the remaining one-fifth to the Safavid empire.

These divisions were rarely peaceable. There were frequent though short-lived Ottoman incursions into Azerbaijan, and Persian expeditions into western Armenia, but the rivalry was at its most intense in Georgia and eastern Armenia. Whenever one power sensed that its opponent was diverted elsewhere or weakened through internal power struggles, the other would try to increase its share of Georgian terri-

tory, leaving devastation in its wake. During this period Georgia became impoverished, and its population fell by nearly half. Imperial
slave-traders preyed on the population; from the north marauding
Daghestani tribes looted merchant caravans and livestock.

During the 18th century, the Iranian empire entered into a period
of chaos which allowed its vassal states a measure of autonomy. The
Safavid dynasty's weakness had not gone unnoticed in Russia. Two
hundred years earlier, the Russians had seen in Ivan the Terrible's
conquest of the Astrakhan khanate on the northern shore of the Caspian
Sea (1556) the possibility of opening the Volga river as a trade route.
Travelling down the Volga to Astrakhan, across the Caspian Sea by
boat, and then up the Terek river inland, a Russian expedition had
built a fort in the Caucasus at Terki in the 1550s, but there had been
no further expansion. In 1722, sensing a new opportunity, Peter the
Great dispatched a force southwards. The expedition landed at Derbent
after travelling by sea from Astrakhan. From there, the troops moved
on to capture the khanate of Baku. But the expansion was short-lived;
ten years later Russia was forced to withdraw when a more powerful
dynasty took charge in Persia.

Russia's increasing presence was welcomed by Georgia, where it
was seen as a counter-balancing force to the Ottoman–Persian rivalry.
In 1783, Irakli II (1744–98) persuaded Russia to enter into an alliance
intended to protect Georgia from its Persian overlords as well as the
raiders from the mountains to the north. The Treaty of Georgievsk
committed Russia to the defence of Georgia by permanently station-
ing two battalions of Cossacks on its soil. However, it ruled out Russian
influence in Georgian internal affairs and guaranteed the autonomy of
the Georgian church and monarchy, and the rights of traders and
noblemen.

Georgian hopes of Russian protection were soon frustrated. Four
years after the signing of the Treaty of Georgievsk, following the
outbreak of the second Russian–Turkish war, Russia withdrew its
forces. In 1795, the Persian monarchy was able to reassert its control
after a crippling battle of succession and the forces of Agha Moham-
med Khan Qajar, aided by the khanate of Gyandzha, marched on
Tbilisi. Catherine II ignored the appeals for help from her Georgian
ally, although she sent a fleet into the Caspian Sea to take Derbent and
Baku. Tbilisi was sacked and pillaged.

However, Irakli's son, Giorgi, continued the campaign to secure
Georgia's future. Beset by squabbling among Georgia's bloated nobility, Daghestani raids, and poverty, Giorgi agreed to the annexation of
his country, securing only a promise that the Georgian royal family
would be protected. Tsar Alexander I formally annexed eastern Geor-

gia in 1801. The annexation of Georgia was not entirely smooth. There was discontent at the flouting of a promise to allow the Georgian ruling family to remain intact, and measures to reduce the autonomy of the Georgian Church led to a popular uprising in Kakheti in 1812.

But Russia was secure enough to turn its attentions to the remaining territories held by Qajar Iran. In 1804, the first Russian–Persian war broke out for control of the khanates of Azerbaijan. In 1813, after a further period of warfare, the Treaty of Gulistan was signed confirming Russia's possession of eastern and western Georgia and Daghestan as well as the khanates of Baku, Shirvan, Gyandzha and Karabakh. All warships but Russia's were banned from the Caspian Sea, securing the Tsarist hold on the region.

In 1826, emboldened by confusion over the Decembrist rising in Russia in the previous year, Persian forces attacked Georgia and Karabakh. They were routed and pursued by the Russians into Yerevan and Tabriz. The treaty ending that conflict in 1828 fixed the frontier between Russia and Iran at the river Araxes, a border that has remained stable to this day. In addition to the division of Azerbaijan, the treaty of Turkmanchai also ceded Yerevan and Nakhichevan to Russia, and required Persia to pay 20 million roubles as an indemnity payment. The Russian annexation was greeted with relief by Armenians living in Karabakh, who had appealed to Russia for protection as early as 1789. It was a sign that the Armenians now believed themselves secure that 60,000 migrated to Russia from Persia, and that many settled in Karabakh.[1]

Simultaneous with its campaigns against Iran, Russia began to expand into territories on the Black Sea that were controlled by Turkey. In the first decade of the 19th century, Russia took Mingrelia, Guria and Abkhazia under its protection. Although the Tsarist forces were welcomed by the feudal Georgian rulers, in reality the principalities were to have little experience of Russian supervision or assistance for the next fifty years. Mingrelia was not annexed until 1867.

The capture of Turkey's coastal territories and of the strategic Iranian fortress at Yerevan (both in 1828) guaranteed Russia a permanent presence in the Caucasus. But it did not entirely rule out Iranian and Turkish involvement in the region. Although Iran adjusted to the loss of its Caucasian possessions, Turkey was never reconciled to its defeat. For the next fifty years, it played a destabilising role, engaging in warfare directly or by proxy through local protégés. The Ottomans sponsored several risings in the Black Sea involving the Mingrelians, Circassians and Abkhazians, as well as in the high mountains. While Russia was absorbed in the war for the mountain fastnesses, Turkey attempted to chip away at the empire from the south, capturing the Mingrelian capital of Zugdidi in 1855 and attempting to spark a revolt in western Georgia and in Svanetia. The Russian empire resorted to power games too, inciting the largely Shia Azerbaijanis to volunteer on the Turkish front against the largely Sunni Ottoman forces. This period of intermittent conflict did not end until 1878 when the Treaty of Berlin gave Russia Batumi, in what is now south-western Georgia, as well as Ardahan and Kars, historically Armenian territory. The treaty compelled the Turkish sultan to protect Armenians still within his domains, but these safeguards were to prove illusory.

North Caucasus: exile and loss

By 1828, Russia had secured its hold on the former Iranian and Turkish territories of the Trans-Caucasus. Tsar Nicholas I, altogether a harsher ruler than his brother Alexander I, turned his attention to the mountainous and inaccessible north Caucasus which separated Russia from its new possessions. Russia was anxious that the new possessions would begin to pay for themselves, and wanted a secure route through the mountains as a conduit for trade with Persia.

From the beginning of the 19th century, when the campaign for the Caucasus began in earnest, there were two theatres of war, 140 miles apart. In between lived the Kabardian, Karachai, and Ossetian people who by the 19th century were either in alliance with Russians or, at any rate, were not hostile. Their compliance had been won by assiduous cultivation of the local aristocracy including the contracting of marriage alliances between Russian royalty and native princesses. The western theatre involved Circassian or Adygeyan territory between the Black Sea and the Kuban river, and the eastern the lands of the Chechens and Daghestanis between the Terek and the Mtkvari.

It was in the eastern theatre that the fiercest fighting took place, in battles that captured the popular imagination in Russia and the West. The Chechens and Daghestanis united around a series of warrior priests who declared a holy war against the infidel invaders. The most famous of these religious warriors was Imam Shamil, an ethnic Avar from Daghestan, who led a mainly Chechen army for more than thirty years. Shamil, like his forebears, was a follower of a Sufi brotherhood, the Naqshbandi, a mystical current of Islam originating in Central Asia. He combined a military jihad with the egalitarian traditions of a mountain society.

Two strategies dominated Russia's conduct of the war. There was the gradualist approach of the 'Caucasian line', credited to General Alexei Yermolov, which involved the construction of a chain of fortresses. The first three fortresses were built between 1818 and 1820 in the delta formed by the Sunja and Terek rivers: Groznaya ('Menacing'), Bnezapnaya ('Sudden') and Burnaya ('Stormy'). Although costly and slow to construct, the line was intended to consolidate Russia's hold on the region by establishing Cossack farming garrisons and expelling the local population. However, it became clear that despite the deployment of as many as 250,000 men, Russia could not guarantee the safety of its soldiers from snipers even a step outside the fortresses.

That led to the second strategy: 'pacification', a system of reprisal so brutal that it shocked the Russian writers of the day. Entire villages were ravaged as punishment for the deaths of Russian soldiers. There were frequent massacres of women and children, and deportation of men to Siberia. Nor was the guerrilla leader himself spared the excesses of the Tsarist campaigns. Shamil's eldest son, Jamaluddin, was taken hostage in 1839 and held in St Petersburg for more than ten years until his father could redeem him. The son, so thoroughly assimilated that he had a commission in the Russian army, had grown unused to mountain life, and died soon after his return.

The wars also devastated the countryside, disrupting farming as peasants fled deeper into the mountains to escape the terror. The thick forests which had covered Chechnya and Daghestan and provided shelter to Shamil's guerrillas were burnt down, never to be restored. After more than thirty years of warfare and an economic blockade, the combination of the two strategies exhausted the Chechens and Daghestanis. Shamil was run to ground at last in the village of Gnib in 1859, ending the holy war in the eastern theatre. He was held in such esteem as an opponent that he was made a prisoner rather than executed, a fact which only added to his stature in the West. Shamil spent the rest of his life with his family in the Russian towns of Kazan and Kaluga. After years of pleading, he was finally allowed to visit Mecca in 1871, where he died after completing the *haj* pilgrimage.

After Shamil's capture the rebellion was concentrated along the Black Sea coast, where 'pacification' was no less savage. Entire tribes vanished, and half a million Circassians, or Adygs as they call themselves, went into exile. Burning their villages behind them, the Circassians fled by sea to Turkey and the Balkans, later to become dispersed and assimilated throughout the Ottoman empire. Another 30,000 perished in a smallpox epidemic. Today, only scattered communities of Circassians remain in Jordan, in Israel's Galilee valley and in other parts of the Middle East of what had once been the most numerous Muslim nation in the north Caucasus.

In the eastern Caucasus, sporadic rebellions continued for the rest

of the Tsarist era, and inevitably the Chechens figured in the leadership. The Russian–Turkish war of 1877–8 provided the first opportunity for revolt, while memories of Shamil were still fresh in people's
minds. The perpetual unrest led the Russians to resort frequently to
repression. Each revolt was put down with high casualties, and punished with mass deportations. Although the harsh measures did not
break the Chechens, they did lead thousands to seek a better life
outside the empire. Between 1895 and 1905, 10,000 Chechens left for
Jordan, Syria and Iraq. Local disturbances following the revolution of
1905 brought further persecution, and thousands of Chechens were
banished to Siberia.

Tsarist rule

Russia's early administration of the Caucasus was a directionless affair,
obscured as it was by military compulsions and brutality, until the
appointment of Prince Mikhail Vorontsov as viceroy in 1845. The area
was too diverse and too far removed from St Petersburg for a unified
policy, and it suffered from the uneven calibre and temperament of the
Russian officials sent to administer it. On the whole, Russian policy
had consisted of neglect in the hope that it would encourage assimilation. Vorontsov, in contrast, was sent to the Caucasus with the direct
aim of transferring the region from military to civil administration. He
set out to overhaul a corrupt and inefficient regime with the express
purpose of making the Caucasus an integral part of the Russian empire.

The Trans-Caucasus was carved into four provinces within the
Russian empire – Baku, Yerevan, Elizavetopol (Gyandzha) and the
headquarters at Tbilisi. The divisions were intended to obliterate all
traces of Persian administration. Yerevan province, consolidating the
Yerevan and Nakhichevan khanates, became a quasi-Armenia within
the Russian empire.[2] Baku province, along the eastern shore of the
Caspian, took in the khanates of Baku, Kuba and Shekhi and, initially,
the khanate of Karabakh, before it was put under the jurisdiction of
Elizavetopol. It is important to note that at this stage the peoples of
the khanates were not known as Azerbaijanis, and were referred to
variously as Tatars, Turks or Muslims. They were also not a homogenous population, but included mountain peoples and other Iranian
groups as well as Armenians. Armenians made up a large share of the
population in Tbilisi province, which was subdivided into a western
and eastern district.

Vorontsov's innovation was to appoint locals to administrative positions and to newly established provincial courts and councils. He also
allowed Georgians to conduct a review of their legal codes to see

which should be preserved in Russian law – the committee of aristocrats saw fit to jettison most of the statutes – and to assess which families were genuine members of the nobility. He embarked on a flurry of reconstruction projects in Tbilisi and other decaying cities, and tried to encourage trade by improving roads and launching steamship lines. He also invested in libraries and gymnasia, or high schools, which were scarce in Georgia. The schools were intended to train the children of the aristocratic and merchant classes for service in the empire, but there was a nod to local sentiment in the teaching of Georgian, Armenian and Turkish history.

This enlightened imperialism established Vorontsov as easily the most popular viceroy in a chain of inept and discourteous Russian representatives. The inclusive nature of his approach endeared him to the aristocratic classes, who made up a disproportionate share of Georgian society. The emerging Armenian merchant class also benefited from imperial efforts to spur trade in the region by lowering tariff rates. But for all his liberalism, Vorontsov did not ease a policy of discrimination against Muslims, who suffered restrictions in education and other areas of public life. In all his measures, there was a common thread which was to inform future developments in the Caucasus. Whether building schools or encouraging enterprise, Vorontsov favoured Georgians over Armenians, and Armenians over Azerbaijanis. The peoples of the north Caucasus were seen as out-and-out savages, unworthy of upliftment.

National awakening

GEORGIA

Although Vorontsov thought he was breeding loyal subjects of Russia by taking more locals into his administration, his liberal approach provided the climate in which emancipation movements could develop. The first cultural movement, which was led by the gentry, surfaced in Georgia, but as the years passed all of the peoples of the Caucasus became influenced by the campaigns for civil rights taking place in Russia – limited as these were to the élite. Although Georgia and Armenia had been saved from destruction by their incorporation into the Russian empire, there was still support for demands for reform of the absolute monarchy. The subject assumed greater urgency after 1881. The new Tsar, Alexander III (1881–94), departed from the relatively benevolent rule of his predecessor and launched a campaign of persecution against all non-Russians in his dominion.

In Georgia, the latter half of the 19th century brought a flowering of literature and painting, and the beginnings of a café society in

Tbilisi. At its centre was Ilia Chavchavadze, the aristocratic founder of the influential *Iveria* newspaper, who argued for greater cultural freedoms and full civil rights for Georgians within the Russian empire. In the countryside, meanwhile, the ideas of the Narodnaya Volya, or People's Will movement, which had been been transplanted from Russia, took root.

Romantic and Slavophile and largely from aristocratic backgrounds, the Narodniks believed that Russia, feudal, backward and agrarian, could avoid the evils of profit-seeking industrial society. It could achieve a socialist order of its own based on a primeval community of land. All that was needed for Russia's socialist salvation was the abolition of serfdom and autocracy. They idealised the peasantry and believed that, rather than the industrial proletariat, it would be the leading class, the creative force of the revolution. In 1881, Narodnik conspirators assassinated Tsar Alexander II.

The ideas of the agrarian socialists had a natural appeal for the Georgians, isolated as they were from Europe. The Narodnaya Volya movement grew particularly quickly in the west of the country, where rural poverty was greatest. Although serfdom was abolished in Georgia in the 1860s, many peasants were still enslaved by a practice known as 'temporary obligation' in which they continued to work for their masters to raise the payment to redeem a piece of land. Between them the peasants, who made up more than 80 per cent of Georgian society, owned 6 per cent of the land.[3]

But although largely still a rural society, there were the beginnings of industrialisation in Georgia and an inchoate working class in the factories of Tbilisi and the tobacco plants and oil terminal at Batumi. It was here that the ideas of the Russian Social Democratic Workers Party first gained hold before eventually supplanting the Narodnik movement. The most important exponent of these new ideas in Georgia was Noe Zhordania, a disillusioned seminarian from a modest family in Guria.

Zhordania had studied in Warsaw and, after a period of exile in Europe, returned to Georgia in 1897, convinced from his exposure to Western ideas that the working class rather than the peasantry was crucial to making a revolution. He established a popular newspaper, which was critical of the argument advanced by the intellectuals that meaningful reform could be undertaken within the structures of the empire. Zhordania's party, initially called Mesame Dasi or the Third Group, was especially active in Batumi and Tbilisi. A year later, another disillusioned seminarian, the son of a shoemaker from Gori, drifted to the radical wing of Zhordania's group. He was Joseph Vissarionovich Dzhugashvili: Stalin.

It was the seminary which was the forcing house of Stalin's political radicalism. For years before Stalin's admission in 1894 at the age of 15, the seminary had been viewed by the Russian authorities as a hotbed of sedition. Students smuggled in forbidden works by Darwin and Hugo, while teachers let dangerously liberal ideas circulate. In 1886 Joseph Lagiyev, a student expelled for his anti-Russian attitude, assassinated the principal, and in December 1893, just a few months before Stalin's admission, the students went on strike to demand a course in Georgian literature. Years later, when Stalin recalled publicly the motives for his conversion to socialism, he referred not only to the grinding poverty of his childhood but to the atmosphere of rebellion that prevailed in the seminary. He was brought into Mesame Dasi by schoolfriends a few years older who had been expelled from the seminary; in 1899 he was expelled himself on the grounds that he did not sit his exams.

At around the same time in Russia, there was a debate raging in progressive circles between legal and revolutionary Marxists. When the same discussions filtered south to Georgia, the right-wing, legal strain of Marxism had the upper hand in the Third Group. Stalin joined the left-wing minority. So while Zhordania remained active in his newspaper and in legal politics, Stalin helped the organisers of a railway strike. In May 1901, after the arrest of more senior colleagues, he went underground to live the life of a hunted agitator. Zhordania continued to operate openly. In November, when the Georgian branch of the Russian Social Democratic Workers Party was founded, Stalin was elected to the nine-member steering committee, but moderates like Zhordania were in the ascendancy.

Soon after, Stalin left for Batumi, a town near the Turkish border. The oil pipeline from Baku had just been completed and Batumi was growing in importance as an industrial centre. It needed an energetic organiser although there were indications that Stalin's departure from Tbilisi also resulted from personal antagonisms. He was arrested in Batumi in April 1902 for organising an illegal printing press, and eventually exiled to Siberia. While he was in jail, the divisions between Bolshevism and Menshevism had become more acute. Although Georgian revolutionaries were overwhelmingly Menshevik, soon after his reappearance in Tbilisi in February 1904 Stalin plumped for Lenin and Bolshevism.

Later that year, a strike broke out among the oil workers of Baku, and Stalin left for the port city. Although he was not there long enough to have led the strike, he is believed to have carried some weight with the workers who, in December, forced the industrialists to sign the first ever collective bargaining agreement in Russia. A few weeks later, on 8 January 1905, came Bloody Sunday, and Stalin returned to Georgia. Within days, much of the province was up in arms in protest at the shooting of 150 demonstrators who, singing hymns and led by a priest, had tried to present a petition to the Tsar at the Winter Palace in St Petersburg. Revolutionary activists organised strikes in all the main cities of Georgia. Factories were idle and trains were blockaded. Roaming gangs of peasants seized farmland by force, occasionally after killing the local landlord. When Cossack troops invaded a meeting of priests and beat up those present, even the most conservative and Russophile aristocrats joined the uproar.

In an effort to restore stability, the government imposed martial law while embarking on a parallel programme of appeasement by holding out the offer of reforms. These efforts were compromised by continuing Cossack violence and acts of hooliganism by the reactionary Black Hundreds gangs. Finally, after nearly a year of unrest, the revolutionaries were overwhelmed in December 1905. Stalin and others at the centre of the protests in Georgia fled to Baku, where there was more support for the Bolsheviks. He was to stay there, organising the workers in the melting-pot of the oil industry, with another Georgian, Sergo Ordzhonikidze.

Stalin's departure left Zhordania and his followers in a prime position in Georgia when the Tsar agreed to limited reform by convening a national Duma, or parliament. Georgia's was the only Social Democratic party to ignore a boycott of the Duma elections and Zhordania's wing of the Third Group dominated the slate of candidates returned to the 1906 assembly. At the head of the parliamentary delegation was Zhordania himself. Their triumph was short-lived. The Tsar dissolved the Duma in July 1906 after declaring most of its proposed electoral reforms inadmissible. Deputies who protested against the dissolution were banned from further Dumas for life. Zhordania went underground to avoid arrest.

ARMENIA

The repression of Alexander III tempered the pro-Russian feeling that had distinguished Armenians since their accession to the Russian empire. Pro-Russian sentiment, already strong when the first Armenian territories entered the Russian empire in 1828, had intensified as life under Ottoman rule became increasingly hazardous. The economic situation in the six eastern provinces of Turkey had become precarious, with Kurds and newly arrived Circassian refugees competing for land against Armenian peasants. As the situation worsened in Turkish Armenia, the Armenians of the Caucasus had grown more prosperous and more Russified under the relatively benign rule of Alexander II. Increasingly, they began to regard themselves as Europeans, and to identify with the other Christian peoples of the Ottoman empire who were beginning to gain their freedom. The competition between European powers in the Balkans led the Armenians to speculate about a future as an autonomous region within Russia.

Then in the closing years of the 19th century, the Russian regime began to retreat from some of the freedoms that the eastern Armenians had enjoyed over their brethren living under Ottoman rule. In 1885, Armenian schools and churches, which had flourished for fifty years in the Caucasus, were closed and Armenian charitable institutions attacked. Armenians were forbidden to learn other languages – specifically Russian, which was the key to advancement.

As with the Georgians, the repressive measures helped to advance the ideas of the Narodnaya Volya among the Armenians who formed the backbone of the working class in Tbilisi and Baku. Some Armenians gravitated towards branches of the Russian Social Democratic Workers Party. But the majority was preoccupied with the plight of their poorer and less-educated kin in Turkey, who were suffering far greater repression. These concerns were reflected in the organisations that began to emerge in Caucasia, as well as in Turkey and other parts of Europe. The most significant was the Dashnaktsutiun, or Armenian Revolutionary Federation, founded in Tbilisi in 1890. Although based in Tsarist Russia, the Dashnaks, who were a highly disciplined conspiratorial organisation, operated almost exclusively in Turkish Armenia, sending groups of armed men across the border on guerrilla raids. Yet despite this element of armed struggle, the Dashnaks still envisaged a future for Armenians within Turkey. Armenians would control all internal economic and political affairs, while deferring to Turkey on currency, external defences and foreign policy. They supported a similar arrangement in Russian Armenia. The socialist element of the Dashnak programme became more pronounced only after 1907, when the organisation joined the Second International. It espoused freedom of speech, separation of church and state, a minimum wage and an eight-hour working day.

AZERBAIJAN

The process of modernisation for the Azerbaijanis, the least urbanised community in the Caucasus, was slower and more uneven than for Georgians and Armenians and only really started with the beginning of the Baku oil rush in 1870. From then on, Baku was a boom town. Until 1884 it had no railway, and oil was shipped out by way of the

Volga to the Baltic Sea. However, the industry grew regardless, with the number of workers rising from 1,200 in 1883 to 27,000 in 1901. By 1898, Baku's output had surpassed that of the entire American oil industry. In the meantime, it had also produced the world's first oil-tanker and the first oil pipeline, which was made of wood. But relatively little of the wealth of the boom years went into the pockets of local Azerbaijanis.

As Russia had not yet fully embraced the industrial era, foreign firms initially supplied much of the capital for developing the industry. The largest among them was the Nobel company. Robert Nobel, brother of the more famous Alfred – the explosives manufacturer – had arrived in Baku in 1875 to buy wood to make rifle butts. He stayed and set up a refinery. Within thirty years, the Nobel company had become one of the biggest oil firms in the world and was a symbol of the Baku boom. However, British investment was significant and there were also French, German, Belgian and Dutch firms competing for oil leases. But even after local firms began to enter into the industry, Azerbaijani entrepreneurs had only a small share of leases on the oil fields, compared to Armenians and Russians. By 1900, Armenians owned 29 per cent of the industries in Baku and Muslims, including Lezgins and Tatars as well as Azerbaijanis, owned 18 per cent.[4] However, Azerbaijanis owned half of the Caspian Sea merchant fleet, and half of the oil tankers.

Employment in the industry directly, as with ownership, worked against the Azerbaijanis. Armenians, many from the underdeveloped mountainous Karabakh region, and other foreigners moved into the best jobs, with Azerbaijanis and other Muslims supplying largely unskilled labour. Several wealthy Armenians also hired Dashnaks as private bodyguards, and as collection agencies and strikebreakers before the party programme became overtly socialist.[5]

The correspondence between class and ethnicity was crucial to the development of the city and the tensions that ensued.

> This bustling industrial city was hardly a melting pot. Ethnic communities tended to live their separate lives in distinct neighbourhoods and the differences in their economic status perpetuated and accentuated barriers of culture, religion and language.[6]

Notwithstanding the unequal creation of wealth by the oil boom, a nascent intelligentsia had begun to emerge in Baku from the 1880s. Still strongly pro-Russian, the intelligentsia sought to improve the position of Muslims within the empire. It began to preach the virtues of education and secularisation and to petition the government to broaden opportunities for Muslims. A disproportionate number of the intelligentsia belonged to the Sunni minority, and this factor was perhaps responsible for their efforts to establish the supremacy of Azeri Turkish over Persian.

The juxtaposition of the revolutions against Russian and Persian Qajar autocracy in 1905, and the overthrow of the Turkish Sultan in 1908, provided a further stimulus for Azerbaijani enlightenment. It also highlighted the choices facing Azerbaijan in its search for identity: pan-Islam, and the struggle for a better future for all Muslims living in Russia; Pan-Turkism and Pan-Azerbaijanism and the pursuit of ties with the Turkic and Iranian civilisations that had shaped its heritage, or the pursuit of an exclusively local Azerbaijani course.

The 1905 revolution in Iran was viewed with interest in Baku. The large number of Iranians working in the oil industry had helped maintain a sense of connection with Iranian or southern Azerbaijan. Some 800 local men crossed the border to join the fighting in Tabriz. Many of them were allied with the Baku branch of the Russian Social Democratic Workers Party, Hemmat, which was formed in 1904. Despite its Azeri name, Hemmat was in fact the product of Georgian and Armenian revolutionaries, including Stalin and the Armenian leader, Stepan Shaumian.

The unrest that seized the Caucasus in 1905 after Bloody Sunday also had a radicalising effect. It exacerbated the friction that had been building up between rival economic communities. When, in February, a Muslim was murdered by a Dashnak unit, Azerbaijani resentment erupted. For three days, police stood by as Azerbaijani thugs burnt and looted Armenian sections of Baku. During the summer months, there were clashes in Yerevan, Gyandzha, Tbilisi, Nakhichevan, and Shusha in Nagorno-Karabakh. In Baku, Armenian-owned shops were destroyed and Armenian-owned oil fields set alight. The death-toll after months of violence was estimated to be as high as 10,000. However, despite the appalling level of casualties, the participation of highly organised Armenian Dashnak fighting units ruled out comparisons with the persecution of Armenians in Ottoman Turkey. 'The Dashnaktsutiun as a party bears a major portion of responsibility for it was often the leading force in perpetrating the massacres.'[7]

In the aftermath of the disturbances, a new, radical group – Difai – emerged in Gyandzha. While warning the Armenians that it would respond with force to further attacks, it decried the violence and blamed it on the divisive effects of Russian rule. The Difai party emphasised the Azeris' Muslim identity. Its leaders envisaged a broadly based Islamic state within the Russian empire, including Daghestan as well as Baku, Gyandzha, and Yerevan province. This vision of a community transcending national and ethnic boundaries was not so different from the traditional Islamic view, and the party had tacit support from the Shia mullahs.

The establishment of a constitutional regime in Turkey in July 1908 also affected the way Azerbaijanis saw themselves. The new government, dominated by the Committee for Union and Progress, believed in an ethnic empire that would unite the Turkic peoples of Russian Central Asia and China under Istanbul's rule. It encouraged links with Azerbaijan, and many intellectuals visited Istanbul. They were impressed by the progress made by the Young Turks, comparing Turkey favourably to the backward state of southern Azerbaijan. By 1913, the intelligentsia's vague notions of identity were more firmly grounded. Rather than Caucasian Muslims, they began to see themselves as Azeri Turks, a shift made apparent in the founding of the Musavut (Equality) party. The Musavut absorbed many of the elements of the Difai party and some of Hemmat. On the eve of the revolution, it was the most popular party among Azerbaijanis, although it did not enjoy the virtual monopoly of the Dashnaks among the Armenians, or Zhordania's Social Democrats in Georgia. Its power base was in Gyandzha rather than the cosmopolitan Baku.

The embers of empire

When the Great War broke out in 1914, the peoples of the Caucasus became pawns in the imperialist ambitions of both the Ottoman and Russian empires, with horrific consequences. The Armenian genocide, when between one and 1.5 million people were executed or died on death marches organised by the Turkish authorities, is the best-known case, and because of its scale is beyond comparison. But there were other tragedies. Like the disaster that befell the Armenians, they resulted from the suspicion in which minorities were held by the fading imperial powers. Atrocities were not the exclusive preserve of the Turkish forces on the Caucasian front. In 1915, the same year as the Armenian massacres, Russian forces ravaged the Chorokhi valley of south-western Georgia, leaving alive only 7,000 of its 52,000 inhabitants. The attack was a reprisal for the participation of Georgian Muslim irregulars in a doomed Turkish raid on Batumi.[8]

The pro-Russian stance of the Armenians in the Trans-Caucasus had left their brethren exposed. In the villages of eastern Anatolia, the Armenians were subjected to increasing Turkish persecution from 1895. Although thousands of Armenians signed up to serve in the Turkish forces after war broke out, their loyalty was under scrutiny. The Turkish Armenians were further compromised by the intense interest taken in the progress of the war by their Caucasian kin. Soon after war was declared, the Armenian Catholicos wrote to the Russian Viceroy and to the Tsar asking them not to forget the 'Armenian question'. The church leader appealed for the unification of Armenian lands in a single province that would be independent of Turkey and under Russian protection. In the spring of 1915, Dashnak envoys visited Britain and France to lobby for an autonomous Armenia – including the territory of Cilicia on the Mediterranean – within the Ottoman empire.

Russia, which openly coveted Turkish Armenia, was eager to exploit this loyalty. It had declared an interest in the six eastern provinces of Turkey in secret discussions with Britain and France on plans for the carve-up of the Ottoman empire after its defeat. To this end, Russia created a special role for the Armenians on the Caucasian front. Unlike the Georgians, who served in ordinary units, and the Azerbaijanis, who were excluded from service because they were Muslim and therefore regarded as unreliable, the Armenians were encouraged to form their own battalions. The Armenian volunteer battalions were in action until 1916. The authorities also subsidised independent Armenian military activity by channelling 200,000 roubles to the Dashnaks for use in mounting operations and uprisings in Turkish Armenia.

The Turkish revenge came swiftly. Throughout the winter months of 1915, Armenian soldiers in the Turkish army were taken aside in batches of 50-100, arrested and summarily shot. On 24 April 1915, some 600 leading Armenian intellectuals were arrested and murdered in Constantinople. With the Christian minority now leaderless and without defenders, the authorities moved against the bulk of the community in the villages. In large-scale operations, they were dragged from their homes and ordered to march to new settlements, allegedly near Aleppo in Syria. They were given no time to pack or prepare, and were forbidden to sell their property to get money for their journey. Those Armenians who were not killed outright were set upon by Kurdish irregulars and brigands en route, or died of thirst and disease in desert conditions. When the Russian forces moved into what had been the Armenian heartland in Van, Mush and Bitlis between September 1915 and March 1916 they encountered empty towns, the ruins of churches, and corpses decomposing by the roadside. The genocide had virtually eliminated the Armenians from their historical homeland in eastern Armenia, leaving them only the small, barren territory in the Russian Caucasus. The holocaust was to become the ruling factor of Armenian political life in the Caucasus, which received hundreds of thousands of refugees, and in the diaspora beyond. In the diaspora, there has been a continuing struggle for the modern Turkish state finally to acknowledge that the massacres did take place.

By the spring of 1917 the war, and food and fuel shortages, had placed an insupportable burden on the government of Tsar Nicholas II. In March, the Petrograd garrison mutinied, the Duma refused to obey the orders of the Tsar and a provisional government was formed. The revolt initially had the broad support of all social classes. But by the summer, differences began to emerge in Russia – as in the Caucasus – over what form of revolution was more appropriate for relatively backward societies. Although it was hoped that the conflict could be resolved between the Menshevik position that Russia was not ready for a movement beyond a bourgeois-democratic revolution, and more radical demands for workers' power, any such prospect disintegrated in November 1917 when the Bolsheviks seized and consolidated their hold on power.

Aside from an island of support for the Bolsheviks in Baku, the Caucasus remained solidly Menshevik even after the defeat of their faction in Russia. The three main parties – the Armenian Dashnaks, the Azerbaijani Musavists and Zhordania's Social Democrats – considered the Bolshevik government in Russia illegitimate and irresponsible. Their rejection of the new regime necessitated a debate on a form of regional government for the Caucasus. None of the main political parties was prepared to move towards separation, but the need to create a united regional authority resulted in the formation of a provisional government in December 1917. A month later, the demoralised Russian forces were evacuated from the borderlands of the Caucasus. In March 1918, the Brest-Litovsk treaty negotiated by the Bolsheviks signed away Kars, Ardahan and Batumi to the Turks, as well as the districts of Akhaltsikhe and Akhalkalaki, inside Georgia but populated mainly by Armenians. The two retreats, military and diplomatic, left the poorly equipped Georgian and Armenian units to face the enemy alone.

In Azerbaijan, meanwhile, there was an uneasy coexistence between the Musavist government in Gyandzha and the Bolshevik-controlled Baku Soviet, headed by Shaumian. Life in the oil town was rapidly becoming intolerable, with spiralling inflation and the reluctance of peasants to bring their food to the market presenting a real prospect of famine. The old economic resentments resurfaced as the Bolsheviks tried to discredit the Musavut among the Russians and Armenians by linking it to ethnic violence. Initially, the Dashnaks remained neutral. In March 1918, as the situation deteriorated, the well-armed and equipped Baku Soviet demanded that the Menshevik-dominated city council submit to its authority. The Musavists agreed, but before the message of their surrender could be conveyed, street-fighting erupted. The Dashnaks weighed in on the side of the Bolsheviks as the battles disintegrated into anti-Azeri pogroms. About 30,000 people were killed. The Bolsheviks, now the outright rulers of Baku, seized control of the local Duma. They combined the workers' and administrative council into a single authority, called the Baku Commune, and promptly nationalised the oil industry in the name of their party colleagues in Moscow.

In April 1918, the new regional parliament of the Trans-Caucasus was unsure of what to do next. The Mensheviks were still hoping that the Bolsheviks would give up power voluntarily. When the Bolsheviks abandoned plans to take part in the all-Russia constitutional assembly called by the Kerensky government, the Mensheviks were forced to act. Under pressure from the Turkish military to separate Trans-Caucasia from Russia in return for diplomatic recognition – and, implicitly, peace – the government of the Trans-Caucasus voted to declare independence. The move was supported fully by the Musavists, who saw the Turkish leverage as a relief from the Christian overlordship most evident in Baku, but only haltingly by the Armenian Dashnaks and Georgian Mensheviks. Their disagreement was a further sign of the abiding ethnic divisions in the region. In any case, the fragile Democratic Federative Republic of Trans-Caucasia lasted only five weeks. While officially recognising the new republic, the Turks advanced across the border, taking the fortresses of Kars and Batumi, and invading Yerevan province. Their drive towards Baku was greeted with enthusiasm by the Georgian Adzhars and other Muslims.

Zhordania, realising that the embryonic republic was doomed, began to consider seriously German offers of assistance. For although they were allies in the war, German and Turkish ambitions were not identical. The Germans were suspicious of Turkish moves in the Caucasus and would have preferred the Turks to concentrate their troops against the British in the Arab provinces of the Ottoman empire. After secret negotiations at the Black Sea port of Poti, the two nations signed a treaty under which Germany was awarded free use of Georgia's railways and Black Sea ports for its troops, as well as valuable mining concessions. In return, Germany extended diplomatic recognition to the new republic and pledged to protect its borders from the Turks.

Reassured by protectorate status, Georgia declared independence on 26 May 1918 and a new flag, deep red with a black and white stripe on the edge, was unfurled over the former viceroy's palace in Tbilisi. Azerbaijan issued its own proclamation a day later. Armenia, impoverished and overwhelmed still by the massacres in Turkish Armenia, reluctantly followed suit on 29 May. From the outset, the Armenian republic was the most fragile. At the time of the declaration of independence, the Dashnak leadership was still in Tbilisi and Baku, as was the majority of the Caucasian Armenian population. Of the 700,000 Armenians living in Yerevan district, half were refugees from Turkish Armenia.

The threat posed by Turkey dominated the first few months of independence. In June, Georgia was forced to concede the loss of Akhalkalaki and Akhaltsikhe in return for Ottoman recognition. Armenia gave up Nakhichevan. As the Turks approached Baku, Shaumian wavered over whether to ask for assistance from British forces based in Iran. His own forces were deployed in northern Azerbaijan in an ill-conceived operation against the Musavist power base in Gyandzha. Finally, in August, with the Turkish forces almost within sight, Shaumian and the other leaders of the Baku commune embarked by sea for Astrakhan, a safe Bolshevik port on the Caspian. Their ship was apprehended and turned around, and the commissars were jailed.

The Armenians and Russians who succeeded Shaumian invited British troops to Baku. On 17 August 1918, General Dunsterville arrived with a small force of 1,000 men. However, he realised that his force would be useless against a far superior Turkish army, and one month later he withdrew. On 15 September, the Turks occupied Baku and within twenty-four hours took their revenge on local and refugee Armenians for the March pogroms. Nearly 10,000 Armenians died at the hands of the Turks and their Azerbaijani cohorts. Stepan Shaumian and other top Bolsheviks escaped the city once again, but the ship's crew refused to make for Astrakhan. The Bolsheviks were taken to Krasnovodsk, which was held by a right-wing government of Social Revolutionaries. All twenty-six were shot. The order to execute the commissars was known to a British army captain in the area, Reginald Teague-Jones. His decision not to inform his commanding officer, or otherwise act to have the men saved, tarnished Britain's reputation in the Soviet Union for years.

Within a month, however, the course of the war altered dramatically. Although the outlook for a Central Powers victory had seemed bright when Georgia became a protectorate, in October 1918 the Turks sued for peace and, in November, the Germans signed the armistice ending the war. The Turkish and German troops were withdrawn from Azerbaijan and Georgia. Their departure, coupled with the disarray in Russia, left a power vacuum in the Caucasus.

In November 1918, following negotiations with the new Musavist administration, a more permanent British force arrived in Baku. Britain was intent on securing control of Baku's oil for the Entente, and on squeezing Bolshevik energy supplies. It also hoped that by encouraging unity, it could transform the Caucasus states into an effective barrier to Soviet expansion, as well as a base for its own operations against the Russian Bolsheviks. The British occupation of Georgia was restricted to Batumi and its oil terminal. Both nations were ambivalent about the arrival of the troops. The British felt they could not trust a country that had so easily sought an alliance with Germany, and it rankled with the Georgians that, despite their formal invitation to Britain to intercede, they really had no choice in the matter.

Armenia, however, was delighted at the prospect of British intervention. Throughout the war, Armenia had put its hopes in Western assistance and expressions of sympathy. It believed that the Americans too supported the creation of an independent Armenian homeland. In Washington, the documented account of the Ottoman persecution by the ambassador to Turkey, Henry Morgenthau, had created a genuine sympathy for the plight of the Armenians. President Woodrow Wilson made statements of support for an Armenian homeland, although these were never translated into action. This conviction that help would arrive belied the precariousness of Armenia's actual situation. It had a rampantly hostile enemy on its southern border in the shape of the Turks, and was by far the poorest of the three republics. Yerevan province, or the new Armenian homeland, had no cities of any importance and little industry to support a huge refugee population and stave off growing hunger. But an unswerving faith in imminent statehood led some Dashnak radicals to pursue irredentist claims, for the old destroyed homeland within Turkey and for lands claimed by Georgia, as the successor to Tbilisi province.

In November 1918, Dashnak irregulars attacked Akhalkalaki and other Armenian-populated districts in southern Georgia. These border regions had been juggled back and forth between Turkey and Russia for much of the 19th century before reverting to Georgia after Turkey's forced withdrawal at the end of the war. Although it had been a mixed Georgian and Turkish Muslim area, its Armenian population had grown rapidly, swelled by refugees. Some of the Dashnaks attempted to march on Tbilisi after the attack on Akhalkalaki. They were repulsed, and outraged Georgian mobs went on the rampage against Armenians in the capital. In the mountains of Nagorno-Karabakh, meanwhile, there were constant skirmishes between Armenian peasants and Azerbaijani herders over grazing lands. The lack of clear frontiers between the two states disturbed the Armenians, who felt as threatened by the Azerbaijanis as they did by the Turks.

Armenia's relations with its neighbours disintegrated still further when Yerevan entered into an alliance with the reactionary General Anton Denikin. In 1919 Denikin's Volunteer Army was at the height of its powers, and the Red Army at its nadir. But despite a mutual

opposition to the Bolsheviks, Denikin's colonial outlook and his in-
sistence on a return to Russia's pre-war boundaries ruled out co-
operation with the Caucasian peoples. With the First World War at an
end, Denikin's Volunteer Army presented the most potent threat to
Azerbaijan and Georgia. In the north Caucasus, his troops had been
responsible for the fall of the Turkish-sponsored independent emirate
established in 1917.

Amid this atmosphere of upheaval, all three governments did attempt a degree of normality. Elections were held on the basis of universal suffrage, and duly returned Musavists in Azerbaijan, Dashnaks
in Armenia, and Mensheviks in Georgia. Georgia introduced limited
land reform, and nationalised resources like the manganese mines,
ports and railways. In Azerbaijan, laws restricting trade unions were
repealed, and the working day reduced to eight hours. The first university in the Caucasus was opened at Tbilisi. However, even these
small steps were compromised by the failings of an inexperienced
leadership. The Georgian government's social-democratic principles
were tested by a rise in ethnic chauvinism, the brunt of which was
borne by the Russian working classes and by minorities. Scandal
overtook the government in Azerbaijan, where the prime minister
was forced to resign after a member of his cabinet was caught selling
oil at below market prices to Georgian businessmen. In Armenia, the
ruling Dashnaks used strong-arm tactics to silence their opponents.
Theirs was a party dictatorship disguised as a democracy.

But it was the fighting among the Trans-Caucasian nations themselves that proved most dangerous. In the end, it destroyed any prospect of Entente support for independence. The violence tarnished the
cause of independence at the same time as it demonstrated an inability
to provide a viable resistance to Soviet expansion. That weakness rendered the Caucasus useless as far as the interests of the Entente were
concerned. The three new states were not widely recognised and they
were not admitted to the League of Nations. In January 1920, Azerbaijan
and Georgia were told at the Paris Peace Conference that, although
the allies had recognised their *de facto* independence, there was no
intention of sending support troops to the Caucasus. Britain removed
its forces from Azerbaijan in August 1919, and from Batumi in July
1920, despite the threat from the approaching Bolsheviks and the re-
surgent Turks.

Meanwhile, in all three states, Bolshevik activity, and the potential
for disruption through strikes and armed clashes, was on the increase.
At the outset, the Armenian Communist Party, founded by refugees
from Turkey in 1917, had been so weak that it was considered a fiction.
But by the end of 1919, it had gained supporters in Yerevan and other

towns. In Baku, communist activity resumed in early 1919 although not by the Russian Communist Party of the ill-fated Baku Commune, but by the indigenous Hemmat. In Tbilisi, there had always been a Bolshevik presence.

In April 1920, the Eleventh Red Army, having defeated Denikin's White Army and overcome mountaineers and Cossacks in the north Caucasus, was massing along Azerbaijan's northern border. It had about 70,000 men, commanded by Sergo Ordzhonikidze, a Georgian communist. On 27 April, the Musavut government was given an ultimatum to resign. With Azeri forces tied down in Karabakh, there was little prospect of resistance, and the Azerbaijani Duma transferred power to the communists.

Encouraged by the Bolshevik victory in Azerbaijan, Armenian communists, assisted by Red Army units, staged an uprising in Kars. It was put down by the Dashnaks with incredible brutality, devastating the Armenian Communist Party to such a degree that Georgians were forced to take over the leadership. In September 1920, Kars was again the scene of fighting when Turkish forces attacked and captured the historic fortress. A desperate Dashnak government was forced into a humiliating armistice with the Turks. The treaty not only required Armenia to give up its claims to the historic homeland, but to relinquish control of its sole railway line to the Turks. It was with relief that the majority of Armenians greeted the Red Army forces that crossed the border from Azerbaijan on 29 November 1920.

In Georgia, meanwhile, the fall of the Musavut government in Azerbaijan had prompted Zhordania to sign a friendship treaty with Russia in May 1920. It secured recognition of independence in return for a secret accord that would allow Bolsheviks to operate unhindered in Georgia. However, preparations were already underway for its annexation. Later that month, local Bolsheviks seized the military academy in Tbilisi, as a Russian-sponsored Ossetian force crossed the border from the north. Both attacks failed, with the deaths of at least 5,000 Ossetians. But the days of an independent Georgia were numbered. In February 1921, the Red Army penetrated the southern borders of Georgia from Azerbaijan and Armenia. Zhordania fled to Kutaisi and, after Red Army troops pursued him to the western Georgian town, to Istanbul.

With Georgia's collapse, the brief experience of statehood for the Caucasian peoples was over. However, it had made it painfully clear that the independence of the Caucasus was an accident. Lasting only as long as Russia was too weak to re-establish control, the experiment was fatally weakened by the failure to unite ethnic groups and classes against a common threat. The lack of whole-hearted foreign support was also debilitating. Britain's intentions towards the three states were never made clear to them. Despite continued resistance – by guerrilla activity in Armenia's south-west Zangezur district, and by a spontaneous uprising in Georgia – no foreign powers had seen fit to come to the aid of the Caucasian peoples.

As a final indignity, in October 1921, the Bolshevik government signed a new border agreement with Turkey which, although preserving Adzharia and Batumi, signed away Kars, Ardahan and other historic tracts of land. This treaty also bound the Bolsheviks to establish the two autonomous republics of Adzharia and Nakhichevan, which remain a potential source of instability today. Throughout the life of the Soviet Union, Adzharia was the only autonomous territory awarded on the basis of religion rather than ethnicity. Still, the reasons for making a special case of Adzharia appear straightforward – it had at the time of the war a 90 per cent Georgian Muslim population. The establishment of the Nakhichevan autonomous republic, however, owed much to Turkey's lingering ambitions in the region. The republic, which then still had a small Armenian majority, was allotted to Azerbaijan although separated by Armenian territory, for the express purpose of providing Turkey with a short (12-kilometre) frontier with Azerbaijan.

Consolidation of Soviet power

There was no immediate consensus about the future of the newly annexed republics, leaving their status uncertain for more than a year while debate raged about how best to carry out their social transformation. Stalin, who had been elevated to the position of commissar for nationalities, advocated a hard line against the Mensheviks, sparing no quarter for his native Georgia and his old opponent Zhordania. So did two of his allies: Ordzhonikidze and Sergei Kirov, whose murder in late 1934 was to provide the pretext for the Great Terror. They called for ruthless central control to squeeze out dangerous nationalism. However, Lenin, aware of ethnic sensitivities and anxious that the Soviet government should not appear chauvinistic, urged conciliation with the intelligentsia and the peasantry. He was resistant to the forced incorporation of Georgia into the Soviet Union. Even local communists in Tbilisi and Baku disagreed about whether the republics should enjoy autonomy, or be totally absorbed. Eventually, Lenin grew too ill to restrain Stalin and Ordzhonikidze's centralising impulses.

In December 1922, Georgia, Armenia and Azerbaijan were amalgamated into the single Trans-Caucasian Federated Soviet Socialist Republic, and subordinated to the authority of the Caucasian bureau of the Russian central committee. They would remain in the federation until 1936. The Kavburo, headed by Ordzhonikidze, had operated independently and above the local communist parties since 1920. After the Bolshevik victory, it continued to rely on its own cadres from outside the region. From Baku, it controlled appointments to party positions, the disbursement of aid from Moscow and agrarian policy throughout the region. Among the first, fateful decisions of the Kavburo was the setting of internal boundaries between the republics. In 1923, it awarded Nakhichevan, although it was wholly inside Armenia, to Azerbaijan, and granted Nagorno-Karabakh autonomous status within Azerbaijan. The new boundaries also recognised several pockets of Armenians scattered inside Azerbaijani territory.

The early years after the consolidation of Soviet power saw the banning of Menshevik parties, and the arrest of leading activists. But the second half of the 1920s, as in much of the Soviet Union, was a period of relative stability and gradual economic growth. The real efforts to transform society were delayed until 1928, and the adoption of the first Five Year Plan. When voluntary collectivisation of agriculture failed to make significant progress, forced collectivisation was imposed in 1930. The peasants of Caucasia were much poorer than those in Russia, and had much smaller holdings. But there was no recognition of this gap, and no firm definition of who constituted a *kulak*, or rich peasant, who was seen as anathema to communism. Consequently, collectivisation was carried out with little regard for local conditions or sensitivities. So great was the opposition to collectivisation in some areas of the Caucasus that it led to famine and armed resistance. In the Kuban river region of the north Caucasus, whole Cossack villages were dispossessed. There were guerrilla attacks and peasant uprisings in Adzharia and Armenia. Even in areas with little direct confrontation, peasants slaughtered their livestock as a means of resistance. The persecution of kulaks led to widespread hunger, so severe that acts of cannibalism took place in the highly fertile 'black soil' regions of Krasnodar and Stavropol. Armenia also suffered famine until 1934.

Forced collectivisation coincided with a clampdown on 'old practices'; in the Caucasus that meant religion, specifically Islam. In 1928, the party launched an anti-Islamic campaign that had far-reaching effects on both Sunnis and Shias. It cut off Azerbaijanis from their Shia shrines in Iran and Iraq, and in 1935 removed an important medium of communication for the disparate Sunni nationalities of the north Caucasus by denouncing Arabic as a reactionary and clerical language, and banning its use. Gradually, mosques and other religious institutions were closed, leaving the Caucasus without a single theological seminary. Even large cities like Baku were reduced to having only one or two mosques, obliging Shias and Sunnis to worship together.

Yet these years were seen as an interlude. Despite poor harvests and a slump in the rate of industrial growth, the early 1930s were a respite between the catastrophe of collectivisation and the bloody terror of the purges. Although much has been made of Stalin's Georgian roots and the Caucasian origins of his closest allies, Ordzhonikidze and the other notorious Georgian, Lavrentii Beria, it is generally thought that the purges, arrests and executions of the late 1930s were visited more harshly on the peoples of the Caucasus than elsewhere. In the Soviet Union as a whole, millions of people fell victim to the madness, which reached its height between 1936 and 1938. While the purges resulted in the expulsion of an average of 9 per cent of party members throughout the Soviet Union, in the Caucasus the proportion was nearly 19 per cent, and as high as 22 per cent in Azerbaijan.[9]

There was a pattern to the arrests, showcase trials and executions, or, for the more fortunate, imprisonment. The first victims were those who had been members of governments during the brief period of independence; then party activists from that era; non-party intelligentsia, for writers were seen as the keepers of the national conscience; and finally communists who had joined the Bolsheviks relatively late. Within the government and Communist Party, those attacked ranged from the most senior officials to lowly village representatives. Western scholars are divided on explanations for the purges. Some have interpreted the terror as a product of Stalin's paranoia, as a terrible, necessary alternative to popular support, or as the dictator's struggle to assert authority over the periphery. The latter explanation has some credibility, especially if one considers that the shock of the purges destroyed any hope for several years of a local elite consolidating a power base from which to challenge Stalin.

In Armenia, the beginning of the purges was signalled by spectacular arrests. The first secretary of the Communist Party, Aghasi Khandzhian, was shot in the office of Beria, then Trans-Caucasian party chief, in 1936. Hundreds of Armenians, including high government officials, were charged with his murder. More than 3,500 government officials were believed to have perished in 1936 alone, and even their replacements were later liquidated. The national poet, Yeghishe Charents, was put in jail, where he died in 1937. The most celebrated Georgian victim was Budu Mdivani, the Bolshevik whom Lenin had supported against Stalin in the debate over the supremacy of the Kavburo in political decision making. He was also a former premier of Soviet Georgia. Accused of terrorism, espionage, and contacts with émigré Mensheviks, he, his wife and their four sons all perished. Among writers, the poet Titsian Tabidze, a friend of Boris Pasternak, was arrested and executed. The news of his death in 1937 caused fellow poet Paulo Iashvili to shoot himself in the building of the Writers' Union. The north Caucasus was also unspared. In July 1937, there was a 'super purge' of Chechens and Ingush, with 14,000 arrested in a single night. Eventually 100,000 people were seized in Checheno-Ingushetia, from high-ranking levels in the party and government down to the villagers.

In this way, throughout the Caucasus, the combination of forced collectivisation and purges eliminated early sources of opposition to the communists. At the same time, the region, largely agricultural at the time of the revolution, made significant economic advances. After Stalin's death in 1953, the excesses of his era, as well as the heavy losses suffered by Caucasian soldiers in the Red Army during the Second World War, necessitated a massive recruitment drive to replenish the party and government bureaucracy. This search for new personnel to build up local political structures was crucial to the preservation and renewal of national consciousness in the region. It was justified under a policy called *korenizatsia*.

The nationality question

Korenizatsia means 'indigenisation'. Although as a policy it was unevenly applied it contributed to one of the most important, and least understood, legacies of Soviet rule in the Caucasus – the way in which it helped to instil a separate ethnic consciousness. The effects of Soviet rule on ethnic identity went beyond the provision of secure external boundaries, stable administration, and economic development that were lacking in the brief experience of independence. The structure of the Soviet Union, which for the first time linked ethnicity, territory and administration, inherently strengthened national identity. For Muslim nations, with no history of separate statehood, the creation of a designated national territory assumed special importance. The experience of seventy years of Soviet rule, when the Azerbaijanis were officially acknowledged as a specific nationality, rather than Turks, Tatars or Muslims, helped to clarify their sense of identity. For the nations of the north Caucasus, their inclusion in designated autonomous regions was a step towards consolidating an ethnic identity undercut by tribal, clan and village allegiances.

Behind this vision of a Soviet federation was *korenizatsia*, an idea first espoused by Lenin, who thought it crucial to winning the nationalities over to the revolution. At one level, *korenizatsia* encouraged the development of local languages and culture. Its implementation in the early 1920s corresponded to an outpouring of literature in national languages, with more works published in Georgian and Armenian than in most other languages. Non-literary languages benefited too. Latin or Arabic scripts were created for several languages of the north Caucasus, although they were abruptly changed to Cyrillic ten years later. Even in the late 1930s, the Trans-Caucasian languages had an exalted status. Despite the Russification campaigns against other republics, Georgian and Armenian were designated as sole official languages in 1938, a protection extended to Azeri in 1956.

However, this relative cultural freedom for the Caucasian peoples could easily be rescinded, a danger underlined by Stalin during the Second World War. During this period, his nationality policy was so extreme as to verge on annihilation. This fate was narrowly avoided by the Meskhetian Turks and by four peoples of the north Caucasus in an episode that will be dealt with more fully elsewhere. The Nazi German advance deep into the north Caucasus had furnished Stalin with a pretext to neutralise the Chechens, the Karachai, Ingush and Balkar peoples, on the grounds that they were a security threat. Between November 1943 and March 1944, about 400,000 people are believed to have been deported by railway boxcar to Kazakhstan and Kirgizia. An additional 100,000 Meskhetians were deported from southern Georgia in November 1944. It was not until four years after Stalin's death in 1953 that the Caucasian nationalities were rehabilitated by Nikita Khrushchev and allowed to return to their homelands. The Meskhetians, however, were forced to remain in exile. But in all cases, the real reason for such horrific punishment remains obscure. One could speculate that Stalin wished to destroy the Chechens, who historically had been the leaders of rebellion in the north Caucasus. All the other deported peoples in the Caucasus were of Turkic origin, lending credence to the theory that Stalin mistrusted Ankara's ambitions in the region and feared a revival of the First World War German–Turkish axis.

During the next ten years or so of Khrushchev's rule, *korenizatsia* became a keystone of policy in the republics. An entire bureaucracy was put at the service of each republic to promote national culture, from local universities to writers' and artists' unions and dance troupes. The cultural renewal was coupled with attempts to increase the proportion of natives in the republican parties and governments by setting targets for recruitment and initiating training programmes. In practical terms, the policy endowed Georgia with the most highly educated population in the Soviet Union, followed by Armenia. Azerbaijanis became the best-educated Muslim population. The smaller nationalities also gained institutes of higher learning, with universities established in Daghestan and the Kabardino-Balkar republic in the 1950s.

The other result of the policy was higher than average levels of membership in the Communist Party. But this had a hidden disadvantage. *Korenizatsia* created in all three republics an entrenched local party elite that consolidated its power through family networks. The absence of real democracy and the close-knit nature of Caucasian society led to ethnic chauvinism and corruption. Despite the largesse shown towards the majority culture, there were few facilities for minorities, a factor that contributed to an Armenian sense of grievance in underdeveloped Nagorno-Karabakh, for example. In Daghestan a rigid system of quotas, intended to ensure a balanced representation from all ethnic groups, backfired. Instead of obliterating national grievances, the quota system heightened them by focusing attention on the ethnicity of every official.

Nor did the attempts at co-option during the Khrushchev and Brezhnev eras entirely satisfy the aspirations of the major nationalities. A second, clandestine nationalism existed outside the officially sanctioned expressions of culture. Much of the dissident nationalist activity in Georgia and Armenia focused on perceived threats to the church, language and tradition. In Georgia, from the 1960s Zviad Gamsakhurdia became one of the best-known dissidents in the Soviet Union; in Armenia there were constant attempts by students to found alternative organisations to the Communist Party. Demands for recognition of the genocide and the reclamation of lost lands were at the heart of underground political activity in Armenia. In 1966, the National Unification Party called for an independent state which would include Karabakh, Nakhichevan, and Turkish-controlled Western Armenia.

The late 1960s also coincided with Moscow's attempts to reform the corrupt and chauvinistic time-servers who had risen to top positions in the Caucasus under Khrushchev's policy of decentralisation. Eduard Shevardnadze in Georgia, and Heydar Aliyev in Azerbaijan, purged thousands of corrupt officials and black-market businesses. Although the pair were eventually forced to concede their defeat by the scale of corruption, in both cases their lengthy terms as party first secretaries were a springboard to a career in Moscow. Their Armenian counterpart, Karen Demirjian, became ensnared by the local patronage networks, but both Shevardnadze and Aliyev have returned to power amid outpourings of nostalgia for the uncomplicated stability and relative prosperity of the 1970s.

When Mikhail Gorbachev began to initiate his reforms in the mid-1980s, the Caucasus proved the most volatile of Soviet regions. The explosion of ethnic violence revealed decisively to the Soviet leader the perils of ignoring the 'nationality question'. The first agitation to lead to territorial and ethnic conflict was the demand of the Armenian majority of Nagorno-Karabakh to secede from Azerbaijan. The campaign resulted in anti-Armenian pogroms in the industrial city of Sumgait (February 1988) and Baku (January 1990). In Georgia, the anxieties aroused by the Abkhazian minority's demands for more power were behind the watershed April 1989 demonstration in which nineteen people were killed by Soviet troops, and the outbreak of war in South Ossetia in 1990.

But although nationalist activity did so much to undermine perestroika, it had little effect on the collapse of the Soviet Union – that was determined by events in Moscow. In the late 1980s, Armenians still believed that Moscow had a constructive role to play in Nagorno-Karabakh, and few Azerbaijani nationalists thought of outright independence. Even the most radical of Georgian nationalists did not believe that independence was imminent. However, by August 1991, the failed putsch against Gorbachev had changed the situation irrevocably. Azerbaijan, where the Popular Front had been so brutally suppressed in 1990, felt compelled to break with Moscow, declaring independence on 30 August. It was the last Caucasian republic to come to such a conclusion. Armenia had declared its intention to secede on 23 August 1990, a decision formalised on 23 September 1991 after a referendum was held. Georgia declared its independence on 9 April 1991.

With the formal dissolution of the Soviet Union at the end of 1991, the three republics received diplomatic recognition, and a number of countries established embassies in their capitals. The trappings of statehood were beginning to emerge, although it remained to be seen whether this would be on a more lasting and productive basis than the first experiences of independence earlier this century. The post-Soviet leaders referred frequently to this earlier independent era as a means of bestowing legitimacy on their governments. Left unstated was the concern that a similar combination of ethnic discord, local warfare, and superpower rivalry could prove as fatal to the Caucasian republics in the future as it did soon after the First World War.

Notes

1. Walker, Christopher (1990), *Armenia. The Survival of a Nation*, Routledge, London, p. 54.

2. Ibid., p. 48.

3. Lang, David Marshall (1962), *A Modern History of Georgia*, Weidenfeld and Nicolson, London, p. 132.

4. Swietochowski, Tadeusz (1985), *Russian Azerbaijan 1905–1920. The Shaping of a National Identity in a Muslim Community*, Cambridge University Press, p. 39.

5. Suny, Ronald Grigor (1972), *The Baku Commune 1917–1923. Class and Nationality in the Russian Revolution*, Princeton University Press, p. 16.

6. Swietochowski, Tadeusz, p. 21.

7. Kazamzadeh, Firuz (1951), *The Struggle for Transcaucasia, 1917–1921*, Templar Press, New York, p. 72.

8. Lang, David Marshall, p. 185.

9. Suny, Ronald Grigor (1989), *The Making of the Georgian Nation*, I.B. Tauris, London. p. 271.

3

The Unsteady Return to the World Community

Although the civil wars and economic upheavals are familiar, the crippling lack of international support for Georgian, Armenian and Azerbaijani independence after the First World War has few parallels today. Then, all three states were catapulted into independence by war and revolution before it had been formed as an ideal, or voiced as a demand. It was decades before self-determination would be a widely recognised principle, and the three nations struggled in vain for international acceptance only to be denied admittance to the League of Nations. Although Azerbaijan and Georgia found protectors in Turkey and Germany, their fortunes were so weakened by war that they were unable to resist the Bolshevik advance. Britain, another interested party, withdrew when it became evident that the Caucasian countries were of little use in its campaign to contain Bolshevism. The Caucasus was annexed by the Soviet empire.

By 1991 the Soviet Union had dissolved, and in part because of the nationalist forces set in motion by Georgia, Armenia and Azerbaijan. They were not, as before, peripheral to the empire's collapse. And the international community, though initially wary, was far more receptive to their demands for statehood. All three states were fully recognised by the international community, albeit after some delay for Georgia at the height of its civil war. Within four months of the dissolution of the Soviet Union, they had been accepted as members of the United Nations, the International Monetary Fund, and the Council for Security and Co-operation in Europe. The United States and Britain, along with European and Asian countries, opened embassies in Yerevan, Baku and Tbilisi.

But this initial flurry of diplomatic activity has yet to result in a wholesale incorporation of the Caucasus into the world community. As the fledgling democracies of Eastern Europe had so painfully discovered, there is little scope for capitalising on Western expressions of goodwill during a global recession. The even newer states of the Caucasus, still not considered fully European, had even less claim on the attention of richer nations. The Caucasus is too small, too unfamiliar, and too liable to conflict to attract the interest of states which do not directly border on the region. The Armenians do influence opinion in France and the United States, their two centres of cultural life in the diaspora. But they are an exception. Unlike the Jewish, Baltic and Ukrainian immigrant communities, which were active during the Soviet era in keeping alive the issue of national rights, the peoples of the Caucasus rarely figured on Western political agendas. A scarcity of funds and trained diplomats has limited their presence abroad in the post-Soviet order. Although all three states converted their republican missions in Moscow into embassies, they have very few representatives further afield.

The conflicts of the Caucasus, though devastating, are confined to a relatively small geographical area. Except for Nagorno-Karabakh, they do not immediately appear to have broad international implications. The United Nations and the Conference on Security and Co-operation in Europe have been confounded by the ferocity of the combatants in Karabakh and in Abkhazia. At the same time, the resulting political uncertainty has forestalled major policy initiatives on the part of the West. In terms of global finance, the Caucasus lacks the certain oil wealth of Central Asia which has spurred American, Japanese and German entrepeneurs to visit the region. However, the potential for developing Azerbaijan's offshore oil fields has attracted British and American interest, and Britain has become one of the main purchasers of Azeri petrochemicals.

But although the battle for influence in the Caucasus cannot compare in scope to the intrigues of the First World War, it has still been keenly fought by the traditional rivals: Turkey, Iran and Russia. The competition has kept cartographers in work, with recently published maps showing hugely bloated versions of Turkey extending all the way into Central Asia, and an Armenia thrusting hundreds of kilometres westwards into Anatolia. Both Turkey and Iran's policies are based on an expectation that the Commonwealth of Independent States (CIS) will not endure. Although the Caucasus remains bound to Russia by infrastructure and the distribution network of the old command system, Ankara and Tehran hope to create new economic and security partnerships in the region. These designs have been complicated by Azerbaijan's withdrawal from and later return to the CIS, and Georgia's reluctant entry.

By emerging as an active foreign player in the Caucasus, Turkey hopes to increase its stature in the West, and ease its acceptance into

European institutions. The European Community's evident reluctance to admit Turkey as a member and its declining utility to the West as a Nato ally since the end of the Cold War have forced the Turkish government to seek new ways of establishing itself as a valued part of Europe. Azerbaijan, along with the Muslim states of Central Asia, has been central to Turkey's designs of reaffirming the country's historic role as a bridge between east and west. As a counterpoint to Turkey's ambitions, Iran has tried to marshal events so as to promote the Caspian Sea region as the focus of a new, geographically determined commonwealth. Because of its historic connections as the most enduring colonial power in the Caucasus, it has also been more assiduous in cultivating relations with Armenia and Georgia,

Moscow's influence in the region remains undiminished and, some Georgians and Azerbaijanis would argue, as malevolent as ever. There has been a subtle shift away from Russia's traditional Armenian allies towards Azerbaijan (especially after the rise to power of Heydar Aliyev), and its relations with Georgia have deteriorated. Russia's actions in the north Caucasus appear to be based on its reluctance to relinquish control over the non-Russians within its dominions.

Turkey's 'lost cousins'

Turkey signalled its intent towards the Caucasus in November 1991, when it became the first nation to support the independence of any of the former Soviet republics outside of the three Baltic states by recognising Azerbaijan. Its activities in the region have remained focused on Azerbaijan, although it tried to break away from the traditional hostility that has characterised relations between Armenians and Turks. Within Turkey, there has been a realignment towards the east following what is perceived as an apparent rejection by European states. There is a deep feeling of responsibility towards the Muslim republics, or as the Turkish press regularly describes them 'the lost cousins of the east'. Of all the Turkic-speaking republics, Turkey has felt the closest to Azerbaijan. Although Azerbaijan was never a part of the Ottoman empire, and Azeris are nominally Shia Muslims while the Turks are Sunnis, Turkey has claimed close linguistic, cultural and ethnic links to Azerbaijan.

But despite this careful cultivation of the notion of a wider Turkic community, Turkish officials have stated that they have no intention of creating a political or military alliance between Turkey and the young Muslim republics. Tempting as it may seem to consider Azerbaijan as the bridgehead for Ankara's expansion into Central Asia, pan-Turkism has not enjoyed official support since the founding of the modern

Turkish republic in 1923. Ankara has repeatedly ruled out the possibility of a revived Turkic empire. However, Turkish relegation of the ideology to the fringes of right-wing debate may change dramatically. Turks have been deeply affected by the plight of the Bosnian Muslims, and Western inertia over their suffering at the hands of the Serbs has increased the Turks' own feelings of insecurity in Christian Europe. Amid the stirrings of sympathy and Muslim solidarity that have accompanied the war in the former Yugoslavia, the collapse of the Soviet Union suddenly made pan-Turkism a more viable prospect. Certainly Iran and Armenia have been sceptical of claims that pan-Turkism is dead. 'Nobody should be uneasy when we call them brothers. What else can we call them when our language, ethnic roots, religion and blood is the same?' the then Turkish prime minister and later president, Suleyman Demirel, said in May 1992.[1] His remark was typical of the official Turkish approach to the Caucasus and Central Asia: overstating a shared cultural heritage while seeking to allay fears of a revived empire.

Aside from accentuating cultural similarities, the thinking behind Turkey's overtures was that the Caucasus could benefit from Ankara's experience of building a market economy. Local commentators, by extolling Turkey's economy, secular outlook, and rudimentary democracy, created the notion of the 'Turkish model' of development, and presented it as a desirable route for Azerbaijan to follow. The implication was that an alternative model exists only in Iran, promising fundamentalism, isolation from the West, a less vibrant economy and instability for the entire region. However, critics of Ankara's approach have pointed out that there is little to distinguish Turkey's mixed economy and pro-Western alignment from Egypt or Pakistan, and that there may be no such thing as a specifically Turkish model. The Turkish literacy rate and level of development in the south-east, in particular, lag far behind those of Azerbaijan.

There have been a number of symbolic steps to encourage a sense of unity with Azerbaijan. In January 1992, Prime Minister Demirel, and the then chairman of Nakhichevan's parliament, Heydar Aliyev, inaugurated a bridge between the enclave and Turkey, and officially changed its name from Bridge of Longing to Bridge of Hope. Turkey then sent several truckloads of medicine and aid over the Araxes into Nakhichevan. Other important connections were made about the same time, when the Teletas firm secured a $2.3 million contract to supply radio equipment for rural areas in Azerbaijan, and the Netas company, itself a subsidiary of the Canadian firm Northern Telecom, undertook to upgrade Baku's rickety old telephone exchange.

Since then, Turkey has consciously sought to reinforce a sense of ethnic solidarity. In April 1992, it began to broadcast several hours a day of Turkish satellite television programming to Azerbaijan, complete with subtitles to acclimatise Azeris to the differences in standard Turkish, as well as to the Latin script. When the Baku government decided to scrap the Cyrillic script and return to the Latin alphabet in early 1992, Turkey responded by sending printing presses, typewriters and thousands of books in Turkish to Azerbaijan. It has funded hundreds of Azeris studying at its secondary schools and universities, and set up crash courses for would-be diplomats.

All of these initiatives were greeted enthusiastically in the Turkish press, and embraced by the private sector. Even before the start of the satellite broadcasts, two Turkish papers, both right-wing and Islamic, began to print special Azerbaijani editions. The Turkish Airlines flights beween Istanbul and Baku were often booked solid by businessmen, and there was a great deal of interest in government efforts to increase trade contacts through regular high-profile exchanges. In April 1992, Demirel included dozens of businessmen among his 140-member entourage for his first tour of the Muslim republics, including Azerbaijan.

In the international arena, Turkey included Azerbaijan in two world bodies. The Black Sea Economic Co-operation Project, which was Turkey's brainchild, is the only one to include all three Caucasian republics. The other is a loose grouping of Soviet Muslim republics, of which Azerbaijan is a member by virtue of its shared Turkic heritage with Central Asia. Aside from its three member states from the Caucasus, the Black Sea group inaugurated in Istanbul in June 1992 included Russia, Ukraine and Moldova, Bulgaria, Romania, Greece and Albania. Not all of these states have a Black Sea coastline. The deliberate inclusion of Greece, with which Turkey has had uneasy relations, reflected Ankara's hope that as the countries became more interdependent economically, they would search more energetically for peaceful solutions to outstanding disputes. Armenia was included for similar reasons.

In Turkey, the Black Sea project has been described as an important outlet for the Caucasus towards Europe. At its inception, it was seen as a step towards a common market with co-operation in transport, mining and communications and the exchange of economic and commercial information. Turkey hoped to benefit directly by creating a market for its agricultural surplus and its well-established consumer goods industry in the former Soviet Union. This hard-edged practicality also saw Russia and Azerbaijan as important new sources of oil and gas. But critics of Black Sea co-operation wondered how real a part it could play in promoting a secure and stable environment given the disputes between Armenia and Azerbaijan, Greece and Turkey, and Russia and Ukraine. In addition, none of the countries aside from Greece and Turkey are in a strong economic position. All are undergoing serious dislocation, output has been falling in the 1990s, and they have only basic communications and transport links.

Within the other new grouping of Turkic Muslim states, Azerbaijan has been accorded a prime position because of Baku's history as a trading centre, and an impression that it has been the most interested in moving swiftly towards market reform. A poll of 1,500 Turkish businessmen who had visited all the Muslim republics found Azerbaijan the most eager to free the economy and approve joint business ventures; it was also the state least subject to religious constraints.[2] The first summit of Turkic republics was held in Ankara in November 1992. It included all the Muslim republics of the former Soviet Union except for Tajikistan, whose people are Farsi-speaking. However, the effectiveness of the Turkic summit was immediately undermined by the reluctance of Central Asian republics to join an explicitly political body. They made it clear that they retained an allegiance to Russia, and would not jeopardise this primary relationship by forming new partnerships. Kazakhstan's president, Nursultan Nazarbayev, refused to endorse any statements concerning the Bosnian Muslims or Turkish Cypriots, issues where Turkey had hoped for support. He feared such actions could potentially antagonise America and Russia, which feels a connection to the Serbs because of a shared Orthodox heritage. Kazakhstan also ruled out any support for Azerbaijan in Nagorno-Karabakh, with Nazarbayev insisting that the Turkic states remain studiously neutral.

Azerbaijan did not openly share Nazarbayev's doubts, but his intervention revealed to the pan-Turks in Baku the resistance from their brethren within the former Soviet Union to any attempts to revive Turkestan, or a great Turkic empire. The single statement issued from the summit was careful to incorporate some of Nazarbayev's reservations. While stressing the 'special bonds' between the Muslim republics and Turkey, it emphasised that any future co-operation would be 'on the basis of principles of independence, sovereignty, respect for territorial integrity and non-interference in each other's affairs'.[3] There was no mention of Cyprus or the Bosnian Muslims. The summit was a disappointment to Turkey, which has earmarked large sums for export/import credits in the region, including $150 million for Azerbaijan. But despite mixed results initially in the Black Sea and Turkic alliances, Turkey was determined to continue its efforts in the former Soviet Union. This was because Ankara believed the West would be interested in drawing on its expertise in the region. As Erol Manisali, the director of the Centre for Ethnic and Middle Eastern Studies at Istanbul University, explained:

> Such a policy does not constitute an obstacle to the development of Turkey–European Community relations. On the contrary, enhancing Turkey's influence in the region will aid the development of economic and political relations between Turkey and the EC. The EC, which does not want, politically, to admit Turkey to membership, will be forced, although Turkey will remain outside the Community, to rely on it for support.[4]

Should Azerbaijan fail to develop as a secular democracy with a market economy, Ankara feels that this will reflect badly on its own achievements. Mindful of its massive foreign debt and balance of payments deficit, as well as its soaring inflation, Turkey has been aware that it is unable to invest on a large scale in the region. As an alternative, it has actively sought European Community and American financial backing for its initiatives. In February 1992, Demirel visited Washington to propose co-operation between the US and Turkey in foreign policy. He envisaged a joint US–Turkish committee to co-ordinate policy in Azerbaijan, as well as in Central Asia. Turkey also tried to interest the US and Japan in a project of the United Nations Development Programme to send volunteers to Azerbaijan and Central Asia. These would be mainly technical experts in the fields of law, banking, telecommunications and agriculture. However, despite initial optimism, Western investment in Azerbaijan through Turkey was not immediately forthcoming, with some indications that the US and EC countries would get involved only directly.

Even while seeing the Caucasus and Central Asia as an important eventual outlet to the West, Turkey has been careful to preserve good relations with Russia and Iran, its two other rivals in the region. In addition to the Black Sea project, Ankara redoubled its efforts to improve ties with Moscow by expanding trade. In November 1992 it concluded the first arms deal between Russia and a Nato member, spending $75 million on helicopters, armoured carriers and other equipment. It was equally anxious to avoid confrontation with Iran, another important export market and a main transit route to Central Asia.

Old hatreds: Turkey and Armenia

The challenge for Turkey and Armenia has been to transcend the collective memory of the 1915 massacres. Yerevan has been forced to seek an accommodation with the Armenians' worst enemy, and Ankara has had to suffer frequent reminders of a dark era in Turkish history for which it disclaims responsibility. From the outset of independence, Turkish officials were acutely aware of the influence of the Armenian diaspora, and did not want Ankara to be seen as actively hostile to Yerevan. In the 1970s, Armenian lobby groups in Washington began to cultivate supporters in the US Congress who pressed for official recognition of the Ottoman persecution of the Armenians. Although these efforts caused occasional awkwardness between Turkey and America, they did not really damage their close association. But following Armenia's independence, Turkey began to be more jealous of its warm relations with the United States. Ankara believed that Armenia, if it were isolated from its neighbours, would be trapped into the same role that Israel plays in the Middle East. Although within Armenia there has been a degree of relish at the comparison, Turkey feared that the creation of a Western outpost with virtually unconditional US support would worsen regional conflict and instability. Ankara also feared that the war in Nagorno-Karabakh might be converted from a territorial dispute into a wider Christian–Muslim conflict. Such a religious polarisation would be particularly difficult for officially secular Turkey.

Armenia's President Levon Ter-Petrosian shared Turkey's desire to leave behind the distrust and bloodshed of the Ottoman empire. Landlocked and surrounded by unreliable (Georgia) or hostile (Azerbaijan) neighbours, Armenia realised that it had to improve relations with Turkey to secure a land route to the West. But although Turkey extended early recognition to Armenia, there were several obstacles to establishing diplomatic relations. A number of these barriers were legal and historic, and a consequence of irredentist claims to territory now inside Turkey. When the Armenian parliament declared independence in August 1990, it stopped short of demanding the return of previously Armenian lands. However, five months later parliament declared that Armenia no longer recognised the existing frontiers, established in 1921 by the Treaty of Kars. The treaty, concluded by the Turks and Bolsheviks after the fall of the independent Armenian republic, signed away portions of what is considered historic Armenia, and this has rankled with radical nationalists ever since. Following the vote in parliament, Turkey declared that it would not open diplomatic relations with Armenia unless Yerevan respected the existing frontiers. It has also bridled at Armenia's efforts to have the modern republic acknowledge the events of 1915. Armenia's declaration of independence incorporated the demand that Ankara recognise, and apologise for, the Ottoman genocide.

This bitter historic legacy formed a backdrop to the groundswell of popular support in Turkey for the Azerbaijani side in the war over

Nagorno-Karabakh. The force of this domestic opinion has led the government to abandon its initial protestations of neutrality in the conflict and to become openly supportive of Azerbaijan in the diplomatic arena. Popular opinion has been deeply stirred by the conflict although, according to both Turkish and Azerbaijani officials, there has been no military aid for Nagorno-Karabakh. A number of Azerbaijani officers have been trained in Turkey, as have Bulgarian, Romanian and Albanian soldiers, but the Turkish government has resisted pressure to take a larger direct military role in the conflict. In March 1992, reports of Armenian atrocities committed after the capture of the Muslim village of Khojali led to large anti-Armenian demonstrations. Hundreds of thousands of people joined the protests, which spread to several cities in Turkey, and raised a clamour for Ankara to wade into the conflict on Azerbaijan's behalf. Among the protesting voices was that of the late President Turgut Ozal who suggested that Turkey 'should frighten the Armenians a little'. His remarks were immediately condemned by Demirel, but they were widely reported. For Armenians, Ozal's comments confirmed their suspicion that Ankara would be hard-pressed to remain neutral in the conflict. The pressure on Turkey to intervene in Karabakh continued throughout 1993 as Armenian forces seized up to 20 per cent of Azeri territory outside the enclave. Tansu Ciller, the new prime minister, repeatedly used international forums to warn Armenia against the perils of aggression.

Armenia's Ter-Petrosian had a similarly difficult time in balancing nationalistic and expansionist sentiment against foreign policy needs. The Dashnaktsutiun party, which formed the government in Nagorno-Karabakh and the official opposition in the mainland, has also been one of the most powerful parties in the Armenian diaspora. It took a much harder position against Turkey than Ter-Petrosian was willing to pursue. Officially, the Dashnak constitution has yet to renounce claims to Kars and other north-eastern areas of Turkey. In the Armenian government, the friction between the two positions resulted in the sacking of Armenia's American-born foreign minister, Raffi Hovannisian, in October 1992.

But despite such difficulties and the friction that marked the early stage of relations between independent Armenia and Turkey, there was continued striving for a rapprochement. In early 1993, Yerevan signalled that it would relinquish its claims to Kars and other areas of north-eastern Turkey and recognise its existing frontiers. In February 1993, following a visit to Turkey by two of Ter-Petrosian's most senior advisers, Ankara announced that it would send fuel and food to Armenia. A few months earlier, Turkey had allowed the passage of 35,000 tons of wheat in EC food aid to Armenia. Although it charged Armenia commercial rates for carriage, the decision was an important concession to German and French demands that Turkey allow its territory to be used for the trans-shipment of aid. And even in the face of such demands, it was still an act of political courage. The original agreement, under which Turkey would have supplied 300 million kilowatt hours of electricity to Armenia to help it survive the Azerbaijani blockade, had been signed in November 1992. But Azerbaijan and opposition MPs protested at the deal, and Turkey was forced to cancel the contract in January 1993. Demirel explained:

> It's a very sensitive issue ... We are very much against hurting Azerbaijan but when your neighbour (Armenia) says I am dying of hunger you cannot tell her to die. These people are without fuel and energy under severe winter conditions.[5]

Subsequently, Turkey allowed further relief supplies to be sent by rail through its territory to Armenia. However, even this relenting on aid was not to last. Humanitarian assistance to Armenia, whether Turkish or European, has been regularly imperilled by Ankara's anger over the war. Just weeks after Turkey sent the first aid to Armenia, it announced it would close the border to aid convoys following a new Armenian offensive in March 1993 on territory of Azerbaijan proper to the west of the enclave. Relations declined even more drastically as the fighting continued and tens of thousands of Azerbaijanis were driven out of their homes.

Although Turkish activity in the Caucasus has been overwhelmingly directed towards Azerbaijan and to a lesser extent to rescuing relations with Armenia, there have been attempts to develop ties with Georgia. One positive step was the adoption of a law in Turkey to allow for the immigration of Meskhetian Turks, who have not been allowed to return to Georgia since they were deported to Central Asia during the Second World War. The Meskhetians, originally from the Turkish–Georgian border area, adopted Islam and Turkish language and customs during the long years of Ottoman rule. The other contact with Georgia has been mainly unofficial. Unlike Turkey's border with Armenia, where rail links have been cut periodically as a protest over Nagorno-Karabakh, the Georgian–Turkish border has remained open, and relatively porous. A tremendous number of small traders have visited Turkey to sell cheap goods for hard currency, and Georgians have been foremost among them. In 1992, Turkey received an estimated three million visitors from eastern Europe and the former Soviet Union; most of them were suitcase traders.[6] Despite the instability in Georgia because of the war with Abkhazian secessionists, ferries have continued to cross the Black Sea to Turkey from the port of Poti. Although Turkey has maintained a wait-and-see attitude towards Georgia so long as it remains unstable, such contacts have helped to maintain a tenuous connection between the two countries.

Another little-reported aspect of Turkey's involvement was religious activity by private organisations. In April 1992, a Turkish religious foundation undertook a programme to build and refurbish mosques in Muslim republics including largely Shia Azerbaijan. It donated $1 million in funding for the training of Muslim clergy from Chechnya and Daghestan in Istanbul, and for the distribution of religious material.

Iran: the 'natural ally'

The Western press has portrayed Iranian and Turkish foreign policy in the Caucasus as a contest between the forces of modernity and of religious obscurantism. There have been plentiful warnings about Iranian-style fundamentalism crossing the Araxes river to find new converts among the Azerbaijanis, who are, after all, nominally Shia Muslim. Yet despite heightened concern about fundamentalism, there have been few signs of a developing Islamic consciousness. After more than seventy years of Soviet rule, Azerbaijan is an overwhelmingly non-religious society. The much-heralded religious revival has been confined to Chechnya and Daghestan where Sunni Muslims dominate, and where there is an old tradition of Islamic politics from the days of the Russian conquest. Iranian scholars have argued that their government, far from promoting Islamic rule, has actually been much more interested in building relations with the Christian states of Armenia and Georgia. They doubt that Tehran would welcome any challengers to its claim to be the world's sole Islamic state.

Azerbaijan, approached by two suitors who were both claiming kinship, appeared initially to favour Turkey. In this, it chose language over religion or ethnicity. The importance of blood ties with Iran and shared customs, like the celebration of the Novruz new year, melted away before the prospect of a stronger connection to Turkey. Azerbaijanis spoke about their brothers, the Turks, and this warm fraternal feeling was reflected in the renaming of government institutions to strengthen a Turkic identity. Later on, when Ankara's promises of economic assistance did not bear fruit, there was real anger against Turkey. Azeris came to see the claims of brotherhood as a potential strait-jacket rather than a support, and regarded with distrust Ankara's objectives in the region.

There was a similar transformation of opinion on an official level.

While Azerbaijan's early leaders favoured Turkey, their successors were more determined to obtain a balance of powers. The first president, the former apparatchik, Ayaz Mutalibov, while keen to preserve and strengthen relations with Moscow, had seen Turkey as his country's most important neighbour. In Febuary 1992, he told me that after Azerbaijan became independent he had had one satellite telephone line installed. That was a hot line to Turkey. Otherwise, there was no change to the outdated and unreliable presidential communications system. 'Turkey and Iran are different,' he said. 'Turkey is a civilised country and we are making our way towards it. We are following the Turkish model.' Mutalibov's successor, the popularly elected Abulfaz Elchibey was even more openly pro-Turkish. The former dissident's rhetoric had for years betrayed pan-Turkic sympathies, which were shared by other leaders of his Popular Front party. Elchibey had a clear vision of a world in which the CIS has withered away, leaving Turkic states to come together as a power in the Middle East and Central Asia. It was not a dream shared by the man who replaced him in June 1993, the former Communist Party boss in Azerbaijan and Soviet politburo member, Heydar Aliyev.

Aliyev's rise to power brought an immediate warming of relations with Iran. They grew so warm, in fact, that conspiracy theorists among Elchibey's disgruntled followers accused Tehran of having worked for their leader's overthrow. While he was parliamentary chairman of Nakhichevan, the border territory cut off from Azerbaijan by Armenia, he had cultivated relations with Tehran, and responded warmly to Iran's offers to ease the effects of Yerevan's blockade. In March 1993, Aliyev visited Tehran and Tabriz to secure a deal to import fuel, food and other goods for the enclave. The Iranian gesture of solidarity to Aliyev was typical of Tehran's efforts in the region. It has extended small but specific offers of energy aid to Georgia, as well as to Armenia. Iranian officials claim that such projects have been more influential than the grand development schemes which Ankara has promised and may be unable to carry through because it lacks the funds.

However, Iran's relations with Azerbaijan are complicated by a reluctance to arouse separatist feelings among its own large ethnic Azeri community. Most analysts believe there is currently little risk of a real secessionist movement developing among the estimated fifteen million Iranian Azerbaijanis. Although less favoured under the Islamic republic than previously, the Azerbaijanis of Iran are still a prosperous community, and enjoy a reputation as quick-witted traders. There have been no signs that they are interested in becoming part of a large independent Azeri state. But such an eventuality cannot be dismissed entirely. In 1945 a Soviet-backed separate republic was declared in

Iranian Azerbaijan. The puppet state was defeated a year later, but only with the backing of the United States.

Iran began to court Soviet Azerbaijan in 1989 after the death of Ayatollah Khomeini. The Iranian president, Ali Akbar Hashemi Rafsanjani, visited Baku following a series of high-level diplomatic exchanges which concluded commercial, trade, travel and cultural agreements. After the dissolution of the Soviet Union, Iran viewed Azerbaijan as an integral part of a new potential regional common-wealth. With little faith in Iranian circles that the CIS would survive, Tehran invited Azerbaijan to join the Economic Co-operation Organisation. Iranian-sponsored, the ECO had been founded with Turkey and Pakistan in 1964. It did not prove effective in building trade alliances, and was barely recognised in the West. But the ECO was revived in 1990 and Tehran hoped that it would become the engine for reducing trade barriers between Muslim states and for encouraging joint ventures. In February 1992, Iran announced that the ECO would found an investment bank to speed development in Azerbaijan and Central Asia. At the same time, the ECO announced a reduction in tariffs on about a hundred commodities in an effort to spur trade. However, the stability of the ECO has been weakened by the competition between Turkey and Iran, and the ambiguity of Ankara's membership. If Turkey were accepted as a full member of the EC, it would be unable to sustain its membership in a rival trade organisation like the ECO.

Iran has also tried to encourage the development of a common market for what it sees as a natural geographic trading area, the Caspian Sea. In February 1992, it founded the Caspian Sea Co-operation Zone comprising Kazakhstan, Russia, and Turkmenistan as well as Azerbaijan. Like the Black Sea group it is primarily an economic organisation, aimed at co-ordinating development of marine resources. By including Russia and Kazakhstan in the group, both of which are well regarded in the West, Iran hopes to gain the support and recognition which had eluded the ECO. Otherwise, the proposed Caspian Zone will be reduced to a formality. However, it incorporates the same problems with dual membership as the ECO. Both Azerbaijan and Russia are members of the Black Sea group, which could lead to conflicts of interest if both organisations are transformed into exclusive clubs which, like the EC, provide preferential trading terms for their members.

In Nagorno-Karabakh, Iran tried to play a neutral role, relying on its relatively peaceful relations with its own Armenian trading community to try to gain the trust of the leaders of independent Armenia. Although its first attempt at brokering a ceasefire in the spring of 1992 ended dismally with the Armenian capture of Shusha, Iran has persisted in trying to end the war. For these efforts, Iran came under attack from militant nationalists in Azerbaijan who accused Tehran of giving arms and funds to the Armenian side. But by August 1993 Iran was forced to warn off Armenia, whose forces occupied a swathe of territory 100-miles wide along its borders. Tehran's anxieties increased as the Armenian forces continued to extend their control over the highlands of south-western Azerbaijan, carving out a security zone dangerously close to its own territory. By the autumn of 1993, the Iranian Red Crescent had set up several camps for refugees in Azerbaijan as the number of people dispossessed by the conflict reached one million.

The CIS: good neighbours or Russian domination?

Outside the Baltic states, which declined to join the Commonwealth of Independent States altogether, the Caucasus demonstrated the most scepticism about the grouping which succeeded the Soviet Union in December 1991. Georgia's erstwhile president, Zviad Gamsakhurdia, was openly hostile to the organisation, and Azerbaijan's dissident leader Abulfaz Elchibey led his country out of the CIS in October 1992, but they were never able to extricate their countries entirely from Russia's grasp. Their decision to stay aloof from the CIS was reversed by their successors, Eduard Shevardnadze and Heydar Aliyev, who committed both countries to the union. Azerbaijan applied to rejoin the CIS in September 1993, and Georgia in October. Only Armenia has been a loyal member, genuinely interested in CIS security and other arrangements. Russo-Georgian friction over Abkhazia and the deployment of former Soviet troops has shown clearly the difficulties of transforming old power networks into a relationship of equal states. In Azerbaijan, Moscow's policies have been dictated by larger security interests as well as control of the country's oil. Protection of Russian nationals has rarely entered into Moscow's calculations. Although there has been a migration of Russians from Azerbaijan since 1990, the Russian communities of Georgia and Armenia are insignificant compared to the numbers in the Baltic states and Central Asia.

Even Elchibey's rejection of the CIS was tinged with caution. While ruling out political union, he tried to encourage economic relations with Russia. In May 1992, two separate Azerbaijani delegations travelled to Moscow for talks with then vice-president Alexander Rutskoi, as well as other senior ministers, to offer reassurance that Baku did not intend to cut itself off from Russia completely. The visit was notable for its timing – soon after the Popular Front came to power – and represented a departure for a movement founded to fight for Azerbaijani independence. The Popular Front had harboured a grievance against Moscow dating from January 1990, when Soviet troops were used to put down a series of its protests in Baku with horrific brutality. The overtures to Moscow two years later were an acknowledgement that no matter how adamantly Baku pursued real independence, and no matter how enthusiastic it was about a Turkic commonwealth, Russia remained an influential neighbour with whom it was politic to pursue good relations. It was a sentiment expressed even by ardent nationalists such as Tamerlane Karayev, erstwhile deputy chairman of the Azerbaijani parliament and a leading member of the Popular Front:

> When building relations with Russia, we must take into account the existing historical and geopolitical realities and they are as follows: Russia is our northern neighbour and a great power. One of the largest Russian communities lives in Azerbaijan. These ties place considerable obligations on us. We must strengthen them, building our relations on a mutually beneficial, equal and just basis. History, politics and economics have made us partners for centuries.[7]

When Elchibey removed Azerbaijan from the CIS (the apparatchik Ayaz Mutalibov had entered the commonwealth without securing parliament's consent) he signed a treaty of security and co-operation, as well as a number of trade and economic agreements with Moscow. In addition to Russia's importance as a trading ally, Azerbaijan cultivated Moscow's friendship as an antidote to what it sees as hostile world opinion. Another factor drawing the two neighbours together was a shared interest in combating Islamic fundamentalism and separatist movements.

Within Russia, there has been extreme concern about the spread of Islamic fundamentalism from Iran, despite a lack of supporting evidence. For the Russians of the north Caucasus, Islam is seen as a real threat to their existence. Amid such fears on an unofficial and popular level, Azerbaijan has been pictured as a reliable bulwark against Islam. According to Russia's ambassador to Baku, Valter Shonia, Islamic fundamentalism 'is something I did not notice in Azerbaijan and consider it quite inappropriate to make a big deal about it. I also disagree with statements that Iran is allegedly concerned about exporting Islam to Azerbaijan.'[8]

While Georgia's treatment of minorities set it on a collision course with Moscow, Azerbaijan and Russia found a common purpose in preventing a secessionist movement by the Lezgin people, whose land lies along the Caspian Sea coasts of both countries. Azerbaijan and Russia both feared the Lezgin campaign for reunification. For Azerbaijan, the Lezgin agitation raised the threat of additional claims to its territory by minority groups; the case of the Armenians in Nagorno-Karabakh provided the most extreme example of the consequences. Russia is concerned that Lezgin militancy could upset the delicate ethnic balance in Daghestan, and destabilise the north Caucasus.

In contrast, Georgian and Russian interests have clashed over the issue of minority rights. The deterioration of relations between Russia and Georgia throughout 1992 and 1993 set Tbilisi apart as the only government in the region not to have come to an accord defining its relationship with Russia – either through the CIS like Armenia, or by means of a bilateral treaty like Azerbaijan. Although Shevardnadze did sign a memorandum of understanding with Russia during a visit to Moscow in August 1993, the goodwill and economic benefits it promised evaporated after the resumption of fighting in Abkhazia.

The friction between the two countries has been remarkable if only because of the diplomatic skills for which Georgia's Eduard Shevardnadze won acclaim in the West as Gorbachev's foreign minister. Shevardnadze presided over a sharp decline in relations with Moscow. Amid the chauvinistic and alarmist rhetoric that he adopted for his speeches to the Georgian parliament, it was difficult to remember that he had once been closely allied to the more democratic forces surrounding Boris Yeltsin. The sources of Georgian–Russian tension lie in the autonomous territories created for minorities within the boundaries of Soviet Georgia. Tbilisi's attempts to contain secessionist movements in two of those republics have collided with Russian interests in the region. In containing the separatist movement in South Ossetia, Tbilisi suppressed a people who were valued allies of Moscow in the north Caucasus. In Abkhazia, which again borders Russia, Tbilisi's policies came into conflict with Moscow in an even more dramatic fashion. While Shevardnadze, with his warm connections in Moscow, had initially appeared a suitable leader from Russia's point of view, the war in Abkhazia was the single most important factor in the sharp worsening of relations. Soon after the Georgian invasion of the Black Sea region in August 1992, Tbilisi accused Russian troops based in the provincial capital Sukhumi of aiding the separatists. The charges escalated as the months wore on, and Shevardnadze blamed Russia directly for the fall of Sukhumi to Abkhazian forces in September 1993.

The dispute illustrated the difficulty for Russia in changing an approach to the region that had remained fairly constant from the days of the Tsarist empire. Russian policy makers proved unable to reconcile themselves to real Georgian and Azerbaijani independence. Although Moscow's relations with Elchibey never descended into the open hostility that characterised the rhetoric employed by Shevardnadze, it was widely suspected in Azerbaijan that Russian conservatives and elements in the military were behind the overthrow of Elchibey and the installation of Aliyev as leader. Elchibey's grand dreams of Turkish co-operation failed to come to fruition because of lack of funds from Ankara, and of enthusiasm from his own people. But Turkey has always been viewed with suspicion in Russia, a legacy of the wars fought in the last century. It has also been argued that Russia would benefit if Azerbaijan became fragmented as a result of internal power struggles and the war in Karabakh. A weak and unstable Azerbaijan would be unable to seize control of its large oil resources, and would be hard-pressed to attract the foreign investment it needs to exploit its potential riches. Within Russian foreign ministry circles, the series of coups in Azerbaijan coincided with a new debate on the desirability of a fed-erated structure comprising Russia and neighbouring republics like Azerbaijan and Georgia. There was also discussion of Azerbaijan's breakdown into statelets along strictly ethnic lines for the small Kurdish, Lezgin, and Talysh minorities.

In Georgia, while Russia's publicly stated desire to protect the Abkhazian and Ossetian minorities is seen as interference in the coun-try's internal affairs, Russia's failure to rein in its troops opposing the Georgian government in Abkhazia is believed to owe much to stra-tegic compulsions. Abkhazia, on the Black Sea, is an important prize for Russia. Ukrainian independence had forced Moscow to cede its influence over a large portion of the Black Sea coastline; hence it has been loath to relinquish much of what remains of its control over the sea to Georgia. Georgian ports, though inferior to Ukraine's, remain an important asset.

Russia's defence minister, Pavel Grachev, spoke of Georgia's strate-gic importance to his country before visiting Russian military bases there in February 1993. Georgian authorities claimed they had not given permission for the visit. He said:

> As for the Russian troops, the armed forces stationed in Batumi and Gudauta, this is a special matter. ... Just imagine the Black Sea coast of the Caucasus and the section where our troops are stationed ... I will only say that this is a strategically important area for the Russian army. We have certain strategic interests there and must take every measure to ensure that our troops remain there; otherwise we will lose the Black Sea.[9]

Not unsurprisingly, Georgia and Ukraine found common cause against Russia in the debate over Black Sea influence. Ukraine had already grown disillusioned with its Slavic neighbour, Belarus, which had signed a security pact with Russia. It was looking for allies, and Georgia offered the bonus of being a fellow Christian nation in the

Turkish-sponsored Black Sea grouping. In April 1993, Shevardnadze visited Kiev to sign a friendship treaty with President Leonid Kravchuk. Each pledged to protect the other against a hostile 'third force' – which could only mean Russia. There were signs of an alliance even before that. In March, an Abkhazian leader accused Kiev of allowing 720 mercenaries from the more nationalistic western Ukraine to fight on the side of the Georgians. The same man also said that there were 380 mercenaries from the North Caucasus fighting on behalf of the Abkhazians.

Armenia's relations with Russia have been far smoother. Despite Russian attempts to improve relations with Azerbaijan, Armenians remain convinced of the fidelity of their historic protector. Such loyalty is extraordinary and imagines a degree of solidarity between two, Christian, nations that has not always figured in Russia's calculations. In Nagorno-Karabakh, Moscow changed sides with bewildering frequency at the end of the Soviet era. While several of Mikhail Gorbachev's advisers were expressing sympathy for the Armenian position in the late 1980s, Red Army troops were actively co-operating with Azerbaijanis in deporting Armenian civilians from the enclave. Despite such betrayals, Yerevan has seemed determined to entrust its security to an independent Russia. While Azerbaijan created its own army in late 1991, and Georgia founded a national guard even earlier, in May 1992 Armenia joined Russia and four Central Asian republics in a CIS defence union.

The military balance

The number of conflicts in the Caucasus, coupled with an economic crisis affecting the former Soviet army, have combined in lethal fashion. After the break-up of the Soviet Union, Russia assumed control of the Red Army. Despite Yeltsin's stated desire to relinquish a costly and dangerous peacekeeping role in Russia's 'near abroad', Moscow has found it difficult to extricate troops from regional disputes. This in turn raised the temperature of negotiations about the future of former Soviet troops and equipment in the Caucasus. It also encouraged local troops, who in an increasingly hostile atmosphere were afraid for their own physical security, to trade in stolen material. The haemorrhaging of weapons and equipment from the dispirited former Soviet army to local paramilitaries has made a mockery of attempts at arms control. The region is awash both with small arms and with larger equipment.

In May 1992, Georgia, Armenia and Azerbaijan were set equal limits on armaments as part of the Conventional Forces in Europe

(CFE) treaty. Officially, each country was allowed 285 tanks, 220 armoured fighting vehicles, 285 guns, 100 combat aircraft and 50 attack helicopters. There are no nuclear weapons in the region. However, according to Western intelligence estimates, all three nations have exceeded their quota. In June 1992, Georgia was believed to possess 850 armoured personnel carriers, 370 tanks and 240 jet fighters. Although Armenia has little air power (there had only been Soviet ground forces there), the two combatants in Nagorno-Karabakh also had more than the CFE limits, with Baku allegedly enjoying a slight superiority. All of the equipment was Red Army stock, much of it stolen by corrupt officers or, in some cases, mercenaries who had defected to local armed formations.

In November 1992, Russia's President Yeltsin became so concerned at the corruption and the loss of Russian army equipment that he called a crisis meeting of generals in Moscow. In large measure, the siphoning off of army resources resulted from economic necessity. In 1992–3, the Russian army planned to demobilise 100,000 men, leaving them without employment or housing. Even many of those who remained in the army faced great insecurity. In Georgia and Azerbaijan, local administrations were actively unfriendly, raising fears about the soldiers' physical security. The troops also went unpaid for months at a time; becoming mercenaries was their only option. In Nagorno-Karabakh former Soviet officers were sighted on both sides: sympathisers as well as outright mercenaries. At the same time, there was an epidemic of theft which led to the transfer of Soviet army stock to local combatants as well as to criminal gangs. Throughout the Caucasus, raids on arms depots became routine events. Aside from directing fresh stocks to the war zones, the raids are one of the main sources of supply for the mafia groups for which the Caucasus has become notorious. As Colonel Valery Simonov complained:

> The district's disintegration has been largely assisted by thieving and corruption at every level from soldier to general. Profiting by the war and the uncontrolled nationalisation of the former Soviet army's property, many have made a pretty fortune ... Today, the Trans-Caucasian military district resembles a big ship amid a raging ocean about to be boarded and pulled asunder.[10]

Although the few thousand Russian troops pulled out of Chechnya with very little difficulty in October 1992, in Georgia and Armenia troop withdrawals have been fraught. The withdrawal of former Soviet troops from Nagorno-Karabakh in March 1992 illustrated the risks of forces getting drawn into local conflicts.

When Regiment 366 of the Seventh Army tried to leave the enclave, ethnic Armenian officers opened up the base at Stepanakert to looters from the Armenian militia before defecting themselves in large numbers. What should have been an orderly withdrawal became a carnival for Armenian militants, who carted off heavy weaponry, binoculars, radios and other equipment, and even an ice hockey game from the mess. Meanwhile, the departing troops came close to a mutiny against the generals who had been flown in by helicopter to oversee the operation, refusing to leave until they were sure they were not going to Azerbaijan.

In Georgia, an agreement was reached in early 1993 that Russian troops would remain until 1 January 1995, and Russian border forces until 1994. Along with Russia and Ukraine, Georgia was to get a share of the Black Sea fleet, but the details were unclear. However, even that seemed uncertain. Finally in October 1993 Shevardnadze agreed to a permanent Russian troop presence in Georgia confined to three bases – at Tbilisi, and at Batumi and Akhalkalaki in the border regions.

The initial withdrawal from Azerbaijan was smooth, with the majority of troops reported to have left in January 1993. However, in June it became evident that several hundred troops had stayed behind at the large Gyandzha base, where they became involved in the uprising that toppled Elchibey. When it was eventually completed, the pullout left Azerbaijan as the only country in the Caucasus responsible for patrolling its own borders. The Caspian Sea flotilla, which is based at Baku, must also be partitioned between Azerbaijan, Turkmenistan and Russia.

There were believed to have been some 62,000 troops in Azerbaijan at the time of the withdrawal. And although estimates are notoriously difficult to confirm, in late 1992 there were approximately 23,000 Russian troops in Armenia and 20,000 in Georgia. All three republics have tried to build up their own armies: Georgia by fusing its powerful Mekhedrioni and other paramilitaries with a National Guard, and Armenia and Azerbaijan by regularising their Karabakh fighting units, and imposing the structures of a professional army.

The moves to rein in the paramilitaries have had little bearing on the other networks that compromise security in the Caucasus: those of the mafia. While much of what Russians define as 'mafia' would amount in Western eyes to little more than the buying and selling of legitimate consumer goods, the uncertain security situation in the Caucasus has provided an atmosphere in which criminality thrives. There is virtually no reliable information on the extent of criminal infiltration of the government and military. What is known is that much of the underworld in Moscow and St Petersburg has been organised along ethnic lines, with distinct gangs of Azeris, Armenians, Chechens and Georgians. During Soviet times, black-market activity was sacrosanct in some parts of the Caucasus because it represented the economics of rebellion: it was seen as an act against the oppressor. That tolerance continues to protect the gun-runners and drug dealers who began to gain in strength after independence.

Aside from guns, drugs and stolen cars from Western Europe, there have been reports of trade in smuggled gold, diamonds, and nuclear materials. Enforcement agencies are concerned that the Caucasus could become a new conduit for drugs from Central Asia, especially Tajikistan, where a potent new strain of opium poppy has been discovered. The gangland-style murder in London of two Chechen emissaries of Chechnya's President Dzhokar Dudayev has heightened awareness of the Soviet mafia, and raised questions about the growth in their activities, especially money-laundering operations.

Nor are the region's civil wars self-contained. Officially, the war in Nagorno-Karabakh has been prosecuted only by local Armenian defence units in the enclave, but its repercussions have been felt throughout the region. The fighting and the severity of the economic blockade of Armenia by Azerbaijan ruled out co-operation between those two states, while Georgia has refrained from trying to mediate in the conflict for fear of alienating one of its neighbours. Georgia has also been too preoccupied with its own conflicts in Abkhazia and South Ossetia. Shevardnadze did not pay his first visit to Azerbaijan until February 1993, nearly a year after he took power, and then only as part of a journey to Tehran where he has had warm relations with the foreign minister, Ali Akbar Velayati, from his own days as a Soviet minister. The delay was an indication of the low priority Georgia has placed on relations with states in the immediate vicinity; it also demonstrated the then Azeri president Elchibey's personal hostility to Shevardnadze as the man who had supplanted the dissident leader Gamsakhurdia as Georgian leader.

In any case, the war between Georgia's two neighbours began to impinge more directly on its own stability despite Tbilisi's reluctance to become drawn into the conflict. The government's balancing act was undermined by the presence of large Armenian and Azerbaijani minorities in its border regions. In early 1993, there were a number of acts of sabotage on Georgian territory against the oil pipeline supplying Armenia. In apparent acts of retaliation, the rail line linking Baku and Tbilisi was blown up, as were a number of important bridges just over the border in Azerbaijan.

As for relations between the three states and the north Caucasus, Georgia's relations with Chechnya were compromised by the breakaway republic's granting of asylum to the fugitive Gamsakhurdia. When Gamsakhurdia first went into exile in January 1992, Azerbaijan, then ruled by the former communist Mutalibov, refused to allow him to cross its territory, while Armenia's former dissident president Ter-Petrosian allowed him to stay. However, the Armenians, visibly nervous about offending the new Georgian regime, made it clear that the invitation was open only for a few days and kept his villa under heavy guard. The involvement of Chechen and Kabardian volunteers in the fighting in Abkhazia has also precluded foreign policy co-operation between Georgia and the north Caucasus. While Armenia has had little to do with the north Caucasus, Azerbaijan has taken a more active role, and has tried to project itself almost as a protector of some of the ethnic groups. In public statements, Elchibey stressed kinship with the Turkic peoples of the north Caucasus. In part, these overtures have been aimed at appeasing north Caucasians resident in Azerbaijan.

Other players: the West

In the world arena, the performances of all three states have been defined by conflict. The maiden speeches to the United Nations of both the Armenian and Azerbaijani foreign ministers in March 1992 concerned the conflict in Nagorno-Karabakh. The then Armenian foreign minister, Raffi Hovannisian, warned of an impending tragedy should the UN fail to address the problem speedily; Azerbaijan's Hussein Aga Sadykhov decried the world's failure to acknowledge the casualties inflicted by Armenia in the conflict. Both the United States and France have demonstrated sympathy for Armenia's position in the enclave. In November 1992, the United States Congress imposed an embargo on aid to Azerbaijan because of its blockade of Armenia. The US later delivered medical aid to the Azeri enclave of Nakhichevan, but through the Azerbaijani Red Crescent rather than through government agencies. France signed a friendship treaty with Armenia in March 1993, and the French singer Charles Aznavour, who is of Armenian origin, has become an unofficial envoy for Yerevan abroad. Aznavour accompanied several aid convoys to Armenia during the harsh winter of 1992–3. His example proved inspirational for another entertainer. The actress and singer Cher, who is partly Armenian, made a lightning visit in early 1993. Following the initial concern about human rights in Georgia under Gamsakhurdia, Western countries also extended humanitarian aid to Georgia, earmarked for Abkhazia as well as Tbilisi.

One of the seemingly unlikely players in the Caucasus has been Israel, which opened embassies in Tbilisi and Baku. The first contacts were forged in early 1989, when Israel sent a forty-man crew to help rescue victims of the massive Armenian earthquake. Israeli charities

remained active in the Leninakan and Spitak disaster zones, while
patients were flown to Tel Aviv for orthopaedic surgery and artificial
limbs. Israel's links with Georgia lie in its historic and once large
Jewish community. The majority of Georgian Jews have now emigrated, mostly to Israel, but have retained their contacts. The Georgian
émigrés have been instrumental in the high volume of 'suitcase trading', and many Tbilisi shops stock Israeli-brand foods and consumer
goods. There are weekly flights between Tbilisi and Tel Aviv on a
British-owned charter carrier. In the political sphere, Abkhazian sources
have accused Israel of channelling arms to Georgia. Shevardnadze also
caused a great deal of mirth in Israel when he invited Tel Aviv to join
the Black Sea Economic Co-operation Council – a geographical impossibility, according to Israel's forces radio. Although Baku also had
a large Jewish community, it was mainly of Russian origin. However,
Israel's ambassador to Russia visited Azerbaijan in early 1993, and
Elchibey expressed interest in developing closer ties with Israel.

But such forays by representatives of states outside the region have
been relatively rare. It remains to be seen how active a role the West
will take in ending the conflicts of the region. In the summer of 1993,
there were encouraging signs on several fronts. The Conference on
Security and Co-operation in Europe (CSCE) induced Armenia,
Azerbaijan and Nagorno-Karabakh to sign a peace agreement that
would require the deployment of CSCE monitors. United Nations
monitors became involved in trying to secure a withdrawal of Georgian forces from Abkhazia in August 1993. In Washington, there were
reports that Clinton administration officials were seriously considering
a shift in policy which would seek to solve disputes in the former
Soviet republics by internationalising them. The American officials
were reportedly exploring how bodies like the UN, CSCE and NATO
could become involved in mediation and possibly in peacekeeping
operations in the war zones. There were suggestions in the *Washington
Post* that financial aid to Russia could be used as leverage in situations
where it was suspected that Russian forces were instigating unrest.
However, such moments of optimism were soon confounded by events
on the ground. The CSCE agreement for Nagorno-Karabakh was
followed by a ruthless Armenian advance deep into Azerbaijan. In
Abkhazia, United Nations observers were powerless when the ceasefire was breached and the province fell to separatist forces. The rebel
victory in Abkhazia, accompanied by evidence of Russian support,
brought into sharp relief Moscow's strategic interest in the Caucasus
region.

It is also uncertain whether Turkey's efforts to promote itself as the
American and European vanguard will succeed. Azerbaijan, through

cultural links, has been identified as an important partner for Turkey and Iran. Armenia, although it has faced difficulties with Turkey, enjoys a degree of support in the United States. Only Georgia has been so bedevilled by conflict that it has been unable to formulate its own foreign policy goals.

Although the collapse of the Soviet Union and the initial lack of support for the CIS in the region led to a plethora of new common market and security groups, their survival is uncertain. Ideally, the Black Sea and Caspian Sea zones would complement rather than compete with each other. If the two groups began to function efficiently, they could serve as part of a trading system stretching across the Caucasus isthmus, and linking Europe to Central Asia. In the most optimistic vision, the Great Silk Road through the Caucasus would be revived. But the obstacles are formidable. If the two associations founder due to lack of funds or internal bickering, it is very unlikely that Western countries would actively seek out allies in the Caucasus for many years to come. Georgia, Armenia and Azerbaijan would have no alternative but to remain subservient to Moscow.

Notes

1. *Turkish Daily News*, 6 May 1992.
2. *Turkish Daily News*, 20 July 1992.
3. *Turkish Daily News*, 1 November 1992.
4. *Turkish Daily News*, 5 September 1992.
5. *Associated Press,* 17 January 1993.
6. *The Independent*, 8 May 1992.
7. Fuller, Elizabeth, 'Azerbaijan's Relations with Russia in the CIS'. Radio Free Europe/Radio Liberty Research Report, 30 October 1992.
8. *Moscow News*, 14–21 June 1992.
9. BBC Summary of World Broadcasts, 23 February 1993.
10. *Moscow News*, 26 April–3 May 1992.

4

Economy:
Trading in Chaos

For Russians, the word most commonly associated with Caucasian is 'mafia', in the economic as well as the underworld sense. During the Soviet era, people in the Caucasus were able to dress in, and fill their homes with, a style that owed much to a highly developed black market. When, at the beginning of the 1990s, the institutions linking the fifteen republics of the Soviet Union into a single economic whole fell apart, the Caucasian gangs were ready. They brought the products of a luxuriant climate north to the cavernous market halls of Russia and made a killing. The Caucasians, with their dark eyes and hair and their exuberance, became a visible symbol of Russian deprivation. There seemed to be no end to the price rises imposed by the foreigners from the south, and they appeared to control all the food supply lines.

But while observers have made much of this affinity for trade, seeing in it an innate grasp of capitalist principles, independence and moves to a market economy have created greater hardship in the Caucasus than in Russia. In all the former Soviet republics, the breakdown of the central planning mechanism left little to fall back on. The command system had deliberately encouraged the development of highly specialised economies so as to make the republics dependent on trade within the union. This, overwhelmingly, meant trade with Russia, preserving the colonial relationships that had existed since the Tsarist era. Trade between neighbouring countries had been overlooked in favour of agreements with Russia. In addition to the distortions of a colonial relationship, after decades of neglect the transport and industrial systems had collapsed. There was a drastic drop in production and in living standards. Despite high levels of education – the Georgians, followed by the Armenians, had the largest proportions of university graduates in the Soviet Union – there was an almost total lack of knowledge of market principles.

The Caucasus as a whole was more vulnerable to the changes than other regions because of its dependence on inter-republic trade, which contributed about 60 per cent of its net material production. With its uneven distribution of resources, it was poorly equipped for the task of moving towards a market economy at the same time as it struggled to create the financial institutions of statehood. In Armenia at first, and then later in Georgia and Azerbaijan, there were hesitant moves towards market reform. But although the republics had won political independence, their control over economic policy was limited. Because they shared a past and a currency – the rouble – the republics felt the reverberations of upheaval in Russia. Gradually people in the Caucasus began to reel under annual rates of inflation that had passed the three-digit mark.

As in the rest of the former Soviet Union, elaborate coping mechanisms emerged when pensions and other benefits of the inherited welfare system failed to keep pace with inflation. The extended family structures in all three societies helped to bear some of the burden. In Georgia, people relied on relatives in the countryside to be generous with their produce. Armenians also turned to their relatives – those who had emigrated, and who were able to find unofficial couriers willing to bring in hard currency. A fistful of dollars, gained through assiduous black-market trading, helped many Armenians through the cold winter under blockade and an annual rate of inflation believed to have exceeded 2,000 per cent. But again these mechanisms masked the fact that the effects of inflation were often worse in the Caucasus than elsewhere because of the political upheaval. Although wages in Russia lagged behind the rate of inflation, they increased more rapidly than those in the Caucasus. In February 1993, the average monthly wage in Georgia was 2,500 roubles against 12,000 in Russia. In Nagorno-Karabakh and war-torn parts of Georgia, the governments were unable to pay any wages at all.

There were moves in 1992 and 1993 to protect the Caucasus from inflation in Russia. Azerbaijan and later Georgia moved to introduce their own currencies to operate in tandem with the rouble, and Armenia also began to consider leaving the rouble zone in order to escape Russian inflation. But they found that their economies lacked the muscle to back the new currency; within weeks Georgia's coupon fell by 25 per cent against the sickly rouble. And when Russia withdrew all rouble notes in circulation in a drastic anti-inflation measure in July 1993, there were riots in Georgia and panic in Azerbaijan. Both countries decided to abandon the rouble for new national currencies, but Armenia declared that it would continue to accept the old roubles despite their withdrawal from circulation in Russia.

Notwithstanding the economic distortions it introduced, there were benefits to being part of the Soviet economic system. Azerbaijan, for example, had been a net recipient of transfer payments from the central government. When these vanished with the collapse of the union, so did the prospect of union-sponsored projects, mainly the construction of sports and cultural facilities. As a result, all three countries suffered declines in government revenues. In Azerbaijan, where official statistics are available, government revenues in the first half of 1992 were 8.2 billion roubles, and expenditure 9.6 billion. Presumably, the budget crises would be even greater in Georgia and Armenia. All three states imposed new taxes on business in an attempt to try to refill the state coffers.

Under the Soviet command system, each republic's planning unit had set import needs and export capabilities which were sent on to Gosplan USSR, the central planning authority. Gosplan then helped determine the volume of production and trade between republics. No Soviet republic was self-sufficient, and this was quite deliberate. The Soviet Union expressly developed in such a way that the component republics would be dependent on each other, and on Russia in particular. The non-Slavic republics had only a narrow range of industry, or were mainly agricultural. The artificial nature of trade relations extended to prices. No actual funds were exchanged between republics, and prices were set purely for accounting purposes. Gosplan, which had a monopoly on trading information, worked for a balance of imports and exports in every republic.

In 1991, after the system had disintegrated beyond repair, the individual states had to reconstruct their planning and trade data so that they could develop independently. Instead of dealing with just one central authority, they were forced into bilateral negotiations with as many as fourteen other newly independent states. In many cases, import and export volumes were set but prices left vague in anticipation of inflation. Georgia's decision after independence not to join the newly founded CIS left it at a disadvantage in the competitive market.

At first, the answer for the Caucasus seemed to lie in increasing hard currency earnings. After all, the region lies along the old Soviet borders and traditionally had been a crossroads for trade. Before independence, exports from the three republics were almost negligible; they also barely traded among themselves. Instead, they were locked into colonial-type trading relations with Russia. Armenia, for instance, sent only 3 per cent of its exports to destinations outside the former Soviet Union and Georgia 2 per cent, despite its fame as a trader nation. Azerbaijan fared slightly better, but it still sent 90 per cent of its exports – mainly refined oil and textiles – to Russia and Ukraine.

But despite all the evidence there was a widespread belief that almost anything could be sold abroad for hard currency. Azerbaijan had an obvious security in its oil, but there was a feeling that other resources could be lucrative too. For Georgia it was wine and champagne, despite reports by foreign entrepreneurs that disparaged their quality and the local bottling technology; for Armenia it was cognac. Another of the miracle cures was mineral water: nearly every region was convinced that their water could be sold abroad for immense profit. Even the leaders of South Ossetia, which was land-locked, lacking in modern bottling plants and under siege, believed in the waiting markets abroad. They would buy their independence with their mineral water.

These notions were soon laid to rest by the wars and blockades which paralysed economic life and absorbed an increasing share of the government's revenues. For months and even years, Armenia, Nagorno-Karabakh, Nakhichevan, Abkhazia, South Ossetia and Chechnya in Russia's north Caucasus have endured sieges as severe as Sarajevo. Although there are few reliable figures, Azerbaijan's former deputy defence minister, Leila Yunusova, estimated in December 1992 that defence spending was absorbing 60-70 per cent of the budget, which indicates the scale of the wastage. So long as war continues to ravage the Caucasus, there can be little hope of economic development.

The perennial conflicts have also diluted efforts to integrate the region into the world economy. All three republics were readily admitted to the International Monetary Fund and the European Bank for Reconstruction and Development (EBRD), an uneasy hybrid between development and merchant bank which was founded to revive the fortunes of the former East Bloc. Ostensibly, these memberships provided the institutional basis for the Caucasus to tap foreign aid. But the EBRD programmes for the Caucasus, which were drafted many months after independence, are relatively modest. Instead of development aid, the Caucasus has been a recipient of humanitarian assistance from the Red Cross, the United Nations, and many non-governmental organisations. Foreign investment has also been limited. Turkish business initiatives, while enthusiastically promoted by the government in Ankara, have failed to live up to the excitement generated immediately after independence.

Georgia: bitter fruit

The key to Georgia's past prosperity, and its future, lies in its climate and fertile agriculture. During the Soviet era, Georgia's exports to other republics of grapes, tea, citrus fruits, tobacco, mineral water and alcohol guaranteed an enviable standard of living. When there were food shortages in Russia, Georgia remained a land of plenty. The country's drinking bouts, of domestic champagne and raw, home-made red wine guzzled down by the jugful, became legendary. In these more sober times, many analysts believe that agriculture will emerge as the foundation for Georgian trade with Turkey and Iran. The country is perfectly placed to sell fruit and vegetables to its neigh-bours, which rely on food imports in certain arid regions.

Aside from agriculture, Georgian industry is well-developed in steel production, automobile assembly, textiles and food processing. It possesses mineral resources including coal and oil, and has small re-serves of gold and marble. At the turn of the century, the country was a leading producer of manganese. Georgia also has a potential source of revenue in tourism along the Black Sea coast, as well as its first skiing resort. In addition, there is room for developing hydro-electric potential, which was not exploited during the Soviet era because of artificially low energy prices.

In its first plans for Georgia, the EBRD took note of Georgia's hydro-electric resources. It expressed interest in expanding the Black Sea ports of Poti and possibly Batumi, which is the terminus of an oil pipeline from Baku and has a turn-of-the-century refinery. There have also been proposals for building bottling plants for mineral water, as well as for converting large machinery plants so that they can manu-facture the smaller agricultural equipment that has been needed since the *kolkhozes*, or collective farms, were privatised. But many projects remain at the proposal stage, delayed by Georgia's seemingly endless conflicts.

Georgia's economy was already in serious trouble by the late 1980s. The breakdown in Soviet trade created shortages of grain, meat, sugar and other staples for which Georgia had depended on imports. Its own agricultural production was slipping, and the protests and vio-lence which erupted in Tbilisi, Abkhazia and South Ossetia delivered a further shock. Less than a year after independence, national output had plummeted and inflation had risen to about 80 per cent a year, according to official data. Industrial output fell by about two-thirds from 1990 to 1992, and agricultural output by about one half. War in Abkhazia effectively imposed a Russian blockade on Georgia, starving its factories of fuel, spare parts and raw materials. Before 1990 unem-ployment had been unknown in Georgia, but according to incom-plete official data 36,000 people were out of work in May 1992 – more than ten times the number a year earlier.

When he first came to power, Georgia's first president, Zviad Gamsakhurdia, was opposed to 'shock therapy', and tried to protect

Georgia from the drastic price rises in Russia. Continued internal turmoil delayed the introduction of price reforms until March 1992, nearly a year after the rest of the former Soviet Union. Gamsakhurdia's successor, Eduard Shevardnadze, continued to try to cushion Georgians from the economic changes – his 1992 budget set aside 40 per cent of funds for welfare programmes. However, he moved quickly to break up the collective farms and to distribute housing stock in the cities to tenants. Before 1991, only 6 per cent of agricultural land had been privately owned, but within a few months in 1992 about half of all cultivated land in Georgia was distributed free of charge to farmers by elected village commissions. By the year's end virtually all houses and flats had been transferred to existing tenants. Rural housing had been mainly privately owned already. There was little progress on the sell-off of state enterprises, but by the end of 1992 most of the legislation enabling the introduction of private property was in place, including laws governing the sale of state assets.

But these efforts to overhaul the economy could not overcome the fact that Georgia's longest-running war, in Abkhazia, was jeopardising the country's future. In 1993, government officials said that the fighting in Abkhazia was costing 20 million roubles a day. It remained the largest brake on Georgia's development, and a stimulus for gun-running and other criminal activity that has also been draining the economy.

Armenia's energy crisis

Although the smallest republic in the former Soviet Union, Armenia had a well-developed manufacturing sector, specialising in light industry, electrical engineering and food processing. But while more industrialised than its two neighbours, Armenia is dependent on imports. Most of the land is unfit for farming, except for the Ararat valley where grapes, vegetables and flowers are grown. It has few mineral resources, and no coal, natural gas or oil whatsoever. Soviet Armenia imported 95 per cent of its energy requirements, mostly from Azerbaijan. This dependency has spelt its ruin following the outbreak of war over Nagorno-Karabakh.

Months before Azerbaijan imposed an energy and rail embargo on Armenia, the director of the Armenian Institute of Economics had predicted that it would take between twenty and twenty-five years for Armenia to achieve genuine economic independence. His gloomy forecast of June 1991 was based on an earlier catastrophe: the devastating December 1988 earthquake. This tragedy presaged a steadily worsening economic situation. Falling Soviet oil production had already forced a slowdown in Armenian industry; the Azeri energy blockade imposed in November 1991 brought the country to its knees. Gross national product fell by 43 per cent in 1992, according to official figures. The government estimated that Armenia was able to use only 30 per cent of its productive capacity. In 1993, the situation became so desperate that the government began to consider the re-opening of a nuclear power plant, closed after the earthquake amid fears of a Chernobyl-type accident. The Medzamor power station, about forty miles west of Yerevan, lies like much of Armenia along a major seismic fault. Before it was shut down, it accounted for about half the electricity produced in Armenia.

Doubts were cast on its safety well before the earthquake in a samizdat open letter to Mikhail Gorbachev in March 1986. The writers claimed that more than 150 serious malfunctions had occurred at the plant since it had come on line ten years before, and that on three separate occasions catastrophe had been narrowly prevented. In March 1987, the Armenian party first secretary, Karen Demirjian, admitted that 'the republic's workers are concerned about questions of ecology, nature conservation and the environment', and disclosed that construction of a second nuclear power station at Medzamor had been shelved.

By the beginning of 1993, the government had commissioned a French firm to undertake a feasibility study on re-opening Medzamor. As ecological groups gave voice to widespread safety fears, there were discussions on holding a referendum. The EBRD tried to put off the re-opening with a $60 million loan to complete a conventional power station at Hrastan, but this project would be unable to solve Armenia's short-term crisis. It also begs the question of funding for the safe decommissioning of Medzamor.

Despite such hardships, the Armenian leadership has persevered with reforms. Since 1990, it has demonstrated the greatest enthusiasm of any Caucasian republics for price and land reforms. By 1991, 80 per cent of agricultural land had been redistributed. About half the housing stock, mostly rural, was privately owned. The government was also canny enough to enact laws to allow diaspora Armenians to buy property.

There has been some foreign investment in Armenia, by Iran, diaspora Armenians and other entrepreneurs. In 1992, a branch of Benetton opened in central Yerevan, along with two clothes factories. However, the factories were forced to shut when they could no longer get supplies from Egypt. The lesson seemed to be that a liberal economic policy could not compensate for the losses and disruptions of war. Even if there were an end to the Nagorno-Karabakh conflict, Armenia would still be in an unenviable position. Communications and transport with neighbouring republics are poor. Its main route to the West is via Turkey, which closed its borders with Armenia indefinitely in March 1993, in protest at the war in Nagorno-Karabakh. Moreover, the rail line in eastern Turkey is of a different gauge from that in Armenia, which would require goods to be physically carried across the frontier.

Azerbaijan: captive wealth

The national emblem of Soviet Azerbaijan was an oil derrick surrounded by cotton flowers in bloom, and for many people Azerbaijan still means oil. It is the oldest oil- and gas-producing region in the world, famous in ancient times for the black sludge that bubbled up from the earth's surface. Tenth-century records refer to oil exports from what is now Baku and by the turn of the 20th century, the Baku oil fields supplied the majority of the world's requirements. They fuelled the Soviet military effort in the Second World War, when production reached 450,000 barrels per day. Later on, Azerbaijan was a pioneer in the making of machinery for the oil industry. Two-thirds of the equipment now in use in the former Soviet Union was produced in the republic.

After the war, however, large oil deposits were discovered in the Urals and in Siberia. Azerbaijan's output declined to one-half of its wartime peak. This was not because reserves were exhausted – offshore oil had been discovered in the Caspian Sea – but because of lack of investment. By 1990, Azerbaijan accounted for only 2 per cent of the former Soviet Union's oil production. In recent years, the annual output of crude oil had declined to between 11 and 13 million tons, and Azerbaijan began to import oil from Kazakhstan to be put through its under-utilised refineries. Its oil machinery could no longer compete in quality with the international market.

Azerbaijan's declining importance as an oil producer was reflected in employment and national income levels that lagged behind much of the Soviet Union. The republic had traditionally been a recipient of funds from the centre, relying on the payments for about a quarter of its gross domestic product (GDP). Although the economy continued to expand in the 1970s, wastefulness, inadequate investment, poor maintenance and outdated technology were taking their toll. From 1987 to 1990, Azerbaijan had a negative trading balance. The state of paralysis did not come to an end with independence; it was several months before an energy minister was appointed.

There is tremendous scope for developing Azerbaijan's energy industry. Its natural gas potential remains largely untapped, as do its offshore oil fields. Azerbaijan's known reserves total around 3 billion barrels, but experts believe they could be as high as 7 billion. However, all this must be weighed against the prohibitive costs of development. In addition to exploration, Azerbaijan needs to modernise drilling, improve refining capacity and protect itself from ecological damage if it is to succeed in drastically increasing oil production by the end of the decade.

After independence, Azerbaijan had a single state-owned oil company, called Azerineft, with two branches to oversee onshore and offshore development. Both refineries were also state-owned. The government's immediate preoccupation was with finding foreign partners for developing the three offshore oil fields – a project estimated to cost about $10 billion. The offshore fields, located along a geographical feature called the Aspheron Sill which lies between Azerbaijan and Turkmenistan, are as deep as the Gulf of Mexico or the North Sea. However, Azerbaijan itself lacks the technology for tapping the offshore reserves, so would need foreign capital. It also requires assistance in well-drilling and maintenance, secondary recovery and additional exploration if it is to reverse the decline in onshore production. The refining industry has also suffered because of ecological fears. Azerbaijan has had to refuse to refine oil from Kazakhstan, as it is high in sulphur. Outdated technology means that it is not getting maximum value from Azeri crude. The process of negotiating foreign partnerships has also been laborious. The first big deal negotiated by the Azeri state-owned oil company, Socar – with a consortium that included British Petroleum Co. PLC and its Norwegian venture partner Statoil, the US companies Amoco Corp, Pennzol, Unocal and McDermott and Turkey's TPAO – was to develop three offshore fields and was valued at about $1 billion. Smaller deals were negotiated with Turkish, Iranian, Saudi and even Omani companies.

Even with foreign collaboration, Azerbaijan faces another obstacle in transporting its oil to the marketplace. In early 1993, there was a tremendous amount of excitement about proposals to build a $1.4 billion pipeline to bring Azeri oil to western markets via Turkey's Mediterranean coast. The only existing line at the time of independence ran into Russia; otherwise Azeris were dependent on a collapsing rail network. The first route agreed on was to skirt Armenian territory and to proceed via Nakhichevan and Iran to Turkey, where it would link up with an existing Iraqi oil pipeline. The Iraqi pipeline had been out of action because of the Gulf War sanctions. Initially, it was hoped that Azerbaijan could export 25 million tonnes of oil a year this way. However, Western firms and the pipeline's bankers were uneasy at the prospect of the pipeline passing along the Araxes river through forty miles of Iranian territory, and threatened to withdraw funding from the project. The other routes envisaged had been rejected because they passed through Armenia.

Azerbaijan has another rich asset in the Caspian Sea: caviar. In August 1993, Azerbaijan and its neighbours along the Caspian Sea coast – Russia, Iran, Kazakhstan and Turkmenistan – agreed to set up a caviar cartel to arrest a two-year slide in prices. The decision to work together against the smugglers who had been flooding the markets with low-quality exports marked a real coup for Iran, which had been trying to promote economic co-operation in the region in which it has a proprietary interest. After the Soviet Union broke up, there was a caviar free-for-all and Russian trawlers off Daghestan ignored existing restrictions on over-fishing of sturgeon in a mad scramble for a share of the lucrative market. Azerbaijan, in turn, tried to stake its claim to a quarter of the entire Caspian catch on the grounds that its territory extended over a quarter of the coastline. The cartel agreement could regulate an industry shaken by industrial pollution from the Volga delta and the refineries of Baku, which has disrupted the sturgeons' migration routes.

Azerbaijan also has a relatively rich agricultural sector, which in Soviet times contributed about one-third of its GDP. The republic concentrated on cotton and tobacco, as well as fruit and vegetables. In 1990 one of its mainstays, grape production, was destroyed by Gorbachev's anti-alcohol campaign. Previously, Azerbaijan had produced about one-fifth of Soviet grapes. By the 1990s, strikes and other protests related to the Karabakh dispute were beginning to make their impact, cutting transportation links and curtailing productive activity.

In fact, while the hardships suffered by Armenia are well documented, Azerbaijan too has been held back by the war in Nagorno-Karabakh. The political focus on the war necessarily limited discussion about economics, and delayed many important decisions. While Armenia and even Georgia were beginning to implement reforms, Azerbaijan had still to enact the laws which would allow it to liberalise its economy.

Still, despite the upheaval during the early years of independence, there is certainly room for the three Caucasian states to improve their share of world trade and develop their economies. Although Azerbaijan currently appears to have the healthiest prospects, with British oil firms expressing interest in investment, Georgia and Armenia should not be overlooked. From Turkey, there is evidence of the millions of suitcase traders who visited last year to do business. Bigger gains could be made if this unrecorded trade were diverted to more normal channels.

However, all these flickers of hope are meaningless when seen against the darker realities of war. According to EBRD analysts, even Azerbaijan, which on the face of things has the brightest future, will experience four or five years of dislocation before the oil and gas sectors again become a major source of growth. And that is an optimistic prediction. It is based on the assumption that Baku will manage to end the Karabakh war, and win over foreign investors. Otherwise, the future is much bleaker.

5

Georgia: Disintegration of the 'Little Empire'

One of the enduring images of the first winter of Georgia's terrible freedom begins like this: a man, one leg amputated at the knee, is being interviewed on television after he has walked, on crutches, 300 kilometres from his village to the capital. There had been more snow than anyone could remember that year. Orange trees still in fruit were bent to the ground; the leaves of tea bushes turned brown. The road – running through Georgia to the Russian border – was empty but for pigs sniffing their way fearlessly down the middle. In western Georgia at least, there was no petrol, no heat, no hot water, no electricity and no bread. For the superstitious, and there were many, the freak weather was a fitting accompaniment to the civilian disturbances that were to rob Georgia of its hopes for independence.

The first of these had already erupted in January 1992, when the one-legged man arrived in the capital to appear on television. His language was as poor as his worn dark clothes and he could not explain the force that had propelled him onwards to Tbilisi. He gave up looking for the right words and instead began to chant as if in prayer, 'Zviadi, Zviadi'. He hopped up and down on his crutches until, transported, he let go and hovered in mid-air for a dangerous instant. But he found his balance, backflipped onto his palms and resumed his chanting, 'Zviadi'.

The scene lasted just a few seconds. But it was shown on television nearly every night, and many people in Tbilisi seemed to have seen it. It was a political barometer. Those who shared the travelling man's sympathy for Zviad Gamsakhurdia, Georgia's exiled first president, found the television clip unbearably sad. Those who despised Gamsakhurdia thought it hilarious. And that was what was so remarkable about the politics that emerged in post-Soviet Georgia: the huge gap in perception between the different camps, and the extremism. Virtually every Georgian had supported the independence struggle in the

81

late 1980s, but there was no accord on what it meant in terms of democratic practices, minority rights, or relations with Russia.

Twin forces have guided Georgia as it moved from a Soviet republic to independence: nationalism and personalism. Between them, the uncompromising loyalties to nation and leader have created the three civil conflicts that have blighted the early years of independence. These divisions have preoccupied Georgia's leaders to the exclusion of all else. Unless Georgia's internal wars are settled it is unlikely that any real attempts will be made to develop its economy or seek a positive role in the region. Instead Georgia will continue to look inward, consumed by its own divided loyalties. These fault lines are the war between the government and the rebels of western Georgia, and in turn between the majority community and the Abkhazians and Ossetians. The chauvinism with which Georgians have viewed the two minorities led the dissident Andrei Sakharov to proclaim famously in 1990 that the republic was 'a little empire'.

In this instance, the travelling man was professing his fanatical devotion to Zviad Gamsakhurdia, one of the fiercest champions of the Georgian nation. By the time the television film was made, Gamsakhurdia was already fading into exile after his disastrous eight months as Georgia's first elected president. Eduard Shevardnadze, the last Soviet foreign minister, was still in Moscow but had already assumed huge importance in the country's calculations.

Zviad Gamsakhurdia was rare among the leaders to emerge in the final days of the Soviet Union in that he had been a dissident for decades. Unlike in eastern Europe, where men like Lech Walesa and Vaclav Havel moved into positions of power, apparatchiks were dominant in almost all the post-Soviet republics. However, Gamsakhurdia's credentials as a campaigner for national rights in Georgia were unparalleled. His activities earned him the nickname of 'the Havel of the Caucasus' although the comparison was forgotten soon after he came to power. The limits of his commitment to democracy, as opposed to the national and church movements of which he was an important figure in the 1970s, swiftly became evident.

From the early days of Gamsakhurdia's rule, there were misgivings about his rampant chauvinism and his flamboyant disregard for the conventions of government. Finally, in September 1991, what began as a series of student demonstrations over inadequate grants careered out of control after Gamsakhurdia ordered a crackdown. Tengiz Sigua, who had been sacked as prime minister days before the August 1991 Soviet coup, set up a camp for opponents of the government outside Tbilisi. He was joined by Tengiz Kitovani, a boyhood friend of Gamsakhurdia who commanded the National Guard, and a growing

number of parliamentary deputies. Most had defected from Gamsakhurdia's Round Table coalition after despairing of improving the
situation from within. While the atmosphere deteriorated through the
autumn of 1991, Gamsakhurdia remained recalcitrant. The decisive
moment came in December when the leader of a powerful paramilitary faction, Dzhaba Ioseliani, escaped from prison. Ioseliani had been
jailed by Gamsakhurdia, as had dozens of his men, and he gave his
support to the disloyal pair, Sigua and Kitovani. The president and a
clutch of supporters moved into a bunker beneath the parliament and
armed themselves for a siege. The stand-off in the centre of Tbilisi,
punctuated by the use of mortars and sniper fire, lasted for a fortnight.
Then, during the final battle, Kitovani used a howitzer to flush
Gamsakhurdia out of the parliamentary bunker. Gamsakhurdia went
into exile on 6 January 1992, briefly in Armenia and then in Chechnya.

By then, more than 200 people had died and the square mile at the
heart of Tbilisi was left a smouldering wreck. Weeks after Gamsakhurdia
was ousted, knots of people would gather amid the rubble and broken
glass of Rustaveli Prospekt and weep for what had been the most
graceful avenue in the Caucasus. But although the three-man ruling
council of Sigua, Kitovani, and the paramilitary leader Ioseliani claimed
a victory for democracy in the bloody removal of Gamsakhurdia, there
was an atmosphere of fear in the capital. Unpredictable men in mis-
matched uniforms set up check-points along the city's main roads, and
there was a tank parked outside the telephone exchange day and night.

Nearly two months after Gamsakhurdia's flight, Eduard Shevardnadze
arrived from Moscow. Although he had publicly declared no interest
in the conflict bar the well-being of his fellow Georgians, Gamsakhurdia's followers were suspicious. Although a year earlier, when
Shevardnadze resigned as Soviet foreign minister, few Georgians would
have predicted that he could ever hope to become acceptable to his
countrymen, the returning Shevardnadze was hailed as a saviour. The
junta invited him to join their council, which he did before legitimis-
ing his rise to power by holding elections in October 1992.

It is impossible not to draw parallels between Shevardnadze's election as Speaker of the Georgian parliament in October 1992 and
Georgia's first (and as yet only) presidential poll eighteen months
previously. In retrospect, too, it is difficult to dismiss entirely the
suspicions of many Georgians during the early part of 1992 that
Shevardnadze's return was the finale of an elaborate Russian plot to
topple the hostile president of a strategic neighbouring country. In
October 1992, nearly eight months after his return to Georgia,
Shevardnadze was elected with 92 per cent of the vote in a turnout
that exceeded 70 per cent. He was the sole candidate, a throwback he

acknowledged. 'I am almost embarrassed by the result. It is like the old days, when I was first secretary of the Georgian communist party.'[1] Shevardnadze's was not the only familiar face in the new parliament: the bloc representing former communists won the most seats overall. This had not been the case in the presidential elections of the spring of 1991. In a turnout of 90 per cent, Gamsakhurdia had taken 87 per cent of the vote against an initial field of half a dozen candidates.

Both men in turn enjoyed huge popularity, and the followers of each were irreconcilable. Both were burdened by the public's unrealistic expectations of what any leader could accomplish. During the eighteen-month interval between the two polls, Georgia lumbered into wars against its minorities which in turn compromised relations with Russia, let loose two undisciplined military groups and ruinously damaged the economy. There was another change, too. The intervening months had seen the Georgian nation turn against itself.

The rebels of western Georgia

At first sight, Zugdidi is no different from the other towns of western Georgia. The usual white block of the former party headquarters overlooks the main highway. Beyond the square there is the jostle of crumbling family houses. These have been rebuilt over the years with balconies and additions to accommodate new generations. The houses and the citrus trees in the front gardens signal comfort as well as provinciality. In a country as obsessed by history as Georgia, Zugdidi boasts one claim to fame. A castle on its outskirts contains a copy of the death mask of Napoleon, brought to Georgia by Achille Murat. A nephew of Napoleon, he married a member of the local aristocracy, and later died by his own hand because of boredom. Or that's the story anyway. The death mask is still there, and the castle is now a museum.

Zugdidi has been the strongest centre of resistance to the Shevardnadze government in a region which has demonstrated almost fanatical loyalty to the fading memory of Gamsakhurdia. It acquired this position because of geography; the region borders the autonomous republic of the Abkhazian minority in the north-west where, in August 1992, tensions with the Georgian population exploded into open warfare. In rural areas, ties of blood and friendship figure strongly, and people in Zugdidi were predisposed to the same negative view of Abkhazians, and their secession campaign, as those Georgians actually living there. The Abkhazian demands antagonised local Georgians, and made them more receptive to the extreme nationalism of Zviad Gamsakhurdia.

During the first stage of the rebellion by western Georgia telecommunications and the railway line to Tbilisi were cut, and Zugdidi became isolated from events in the capital. Tbilisi was far enough away for western Georgians to feel out of touch; the distance also made the military junta nervous of sending in troops for fear of losing control of the capital. But more importantly, Zugdidi was the capital of Mingrelia. Unlike the Abkhazians or Ossetians, the Mingrelians are one of the component peoples of the Georgian nation, but they have always had an uneasy relationship with the authorities.

The principality of Mingrelia was the poorest of the small feudal regimes of Georgia. Nominally under Ottoman control from the 16th century, it was a neglected region with a population depleted by disease, poverty and the slave trade. Even the ruling Dadiani family had no permanent abode in a principality which included large areas of malarial swamp. The down-at-heel dynasty engaged in constant feuding with its neighbours, financed by dealings in the Ottoman slave trade. Throughout the 17th century, between 10,000 and 15,000 boys were exported each year from Mingrelia.[2] But while the aristocracy of Tbilisi greeted the approach of the Russian empire as a respite from Ottoman rule, the Dadianis kept Mingrelia apart. Although it was declared a protectorate of the Tsar in 1803, the Russians, like the Turks, were not much concerned about so backward an area. That changed in the 1850s after the Crimean War, when Mingrelian peasants fought on the side of the Turks. The principality was annexed in 1867.

The region's enduring poverty during the 19th century created a strong populist culture, with large pockets of support for the Narodnaya Volya peasants' movement. But despite its revolutionary potential, Soviet Georgia turned against the idea of a separate Mingrelian identity. Although the emergence of Mingrelian culture had been encouraged in the early years of the Soviet Union, an open campaign of repression began in the 1930s. Newspapers and books published in Mingrelian were banned by Stalin in 1937, and people were prohibited from declaring themselves as Mingrelian in their identity papers. In the ethnic hierarchy, the Mingrelians became the traditional butt of jokes by the Georgians of central Kartli and eastern Kakheti. Although the language, and a few crumbling books, survive in remote villages, there has been no obvious relaxation of the ban since perestroika.

The history of repression helps explain the Mingrelians' rather bewildering loyalty to Gamsakhurdia. For although Gamsakhurdia is by ancestry a Mingrelian, he has advocated a vision of Georgia as a unitary state. He has rarely mentioned, and never supported, a separate Mingrelian identity. His father, Konstantine, perhaps the best-loved writer in modern Georgia, was known and reprimanded for his

Georgian patriotism by the Soviet authorities. However, he refrained from defending the Mingrelian language in the Great Terror of 1936-37, concocted by a Georgian, Joseph Stalin, and executed by a Mingrelian, Lavrentii Beria. Gamsakhurdia *père* wrote always in conventional literary Georgian. Nevertheless, Mingrelians remain proud of the pair of them and Konstantine's home is preserved as a museum in Abasha, only a few miles east of Zugdidi. It could be that the Mingrelians were so inured to their secondary status that it was a triumph when even a closet Mingrelian like Gamsakhurdia came to power.

That brand of complicated loyalty is not without precedent in Mingrelia. During the mammoth drinking and feasting bouts that form a Georgian ritual, it is not uncommon in western Georgia for the *tamada*, or toastmaster, to dedicate a drink to Beria – at least towards the end of the evening. Stalin's henchman is today publicly admired almost nowhere, but he was, after all, a Mingrelian. The sneaking pride for Beria has some parallels in the support shown for Gamsakhurdia. Defying Tbilisi on Gamsakhurdia's behalf was an oblique way for Mingrelians to resist assimilation, and to express an identity that is still unrecognised.

The people of Zugdidi began protesting against Gamsakhurdia's overthrow within days of his fall. They were brave enough to continue when the three-man military council that had taken power fired on the unarmed demonstrators of Tbilisi. The rebels of Mingrelia were inspired by a rumour that Gamsakhurdia would return to set up a separate state in western Georgia and, even more improbably, Abkhazia. In the event, Gamsakhurdia merely left his first place of refuge in Armenia for a more permanent exile in Chechnya, an autonomous republic which had declared independence from Russia. The alliance between Gamsakhurdia and Chechnya's leader, Dzhokar Dudayev, seemed apt: both men enjoyed thumbing their noses at Moscow, both saw Russia as an enemy.

But while Gamsakhurdia and his entourage paced in front of the television sets in the red-brick state guest house, agonising over the news from Georgia, his return there was widely reported as fact. The Russian media even contained excerpts of a speech he had apparently made in Zugdidi. In the town itself, the confusion gave a second wind to the daily demonstrations in front of the white house. Men from the villages of Mingrelia began to drift into town, overly eager to join a battle for which they were woefully underarmed. Old men, huffing through snow drifts with First World War rifles, and young men so highly strung they smoked cigarettes with sticks of dynamite tucked under their arms, set up blockades of logs and burning tyres at the towns along the main road leading to Zugdidi. Crucial sections of railway track were blown up, halting all traffic between Russia and Tbilisi. Nobody went to work. But these defences were too flimsy for Dzhaba Ioseliani's paramilitary, known as the Mekhedrioni, or horsemen. Its better-armed and more experienced fighters, rather than the National Guard, became the main guarantor of the regime. With a half dozen tanks and a few hundred motley troops, the Mekhedrioni advanced along the main highway day by day. The actual battles were brief, and though casualties were few they created hysteria. When the Mekhedrioni took a town, they were treated not as Georgians but as foreign occupiers. Women would turn out in the streets to show their contempt, shrieking at the troops, grabbing their elbows, and hissing 'Shevardnadze, Moscow'. Moscow was the ultimate insult, an epithet reserved for traitors.

From exile in Chechnya, Gamsakhurdia made only sporadic efforts at national reconciliation. To the reporters who trooped to see him in exile, he denounced his overthrow as 'a criminal revolution', and Shevardnadze as ringleader of 'a great communist mafia'. Within a month of his flight, however, the sleek former president had become a forlorn character, his wrists flapping out of a grey suit that had grown too big. The conviction that had sustained him as a dissident was with him still, but it had become a liability. He was unbending in defeat, unwilling to compromise. His posture underscored his opponents' arguments that the only way to persuade Gamsakhurdia had been by force. When I asked him about the charges that he had become a dictator, Gamsakhurdia entertained no discussion. Instead, he went on the attack. 'You are a crazy person,' he said. 'Who told you to say such crazy things?'

Although the character of the resistance was forced to change, the sentiments behind the rebellion did not. The Mekhedrioni eventually subdued the rebels militarily, moving in troops as far west as the Russian border. Back in front of the mammoth colour television set in his office in Tbilisi, the victorious Mekhedrioni commander, Dzhaba Ioseliani, gloated. 'Zugdidi was a little fight, five minutes only.' His troops punished western Georgia as they withdrew. They burnt houses, took hostages among villagers and stole cars. Their revenge served only to convert open rebellion into terrorism. Shoot-outs, bomb blasts and kidnappings of government troops became a feature of the early months of Shevardnadze's rule.

For his supporters in Zugdidi, Gamsakhurdia's record in government was immaterial. But as president, he had created an atmosphere of dread by closing the writers' union and newspapers. He effectively restored television censorship by demanding exhaustive coverage of his activities. As opposition to his government increased, he began jailing his rivals on specious grounds. He introduced no significant reforms and was reluctant to move towards drafting a programme for a market-oriented economy, a goal which was supported by nearly all Georgians, because he was afraid price rises would make him unpopular. The biggest break with the past for the first and long-awaited post-communist government in Georgia was the introduction of legislation lowering the marriage age for girls to 15. This bizarre achievement sprang from the notion that the Georgian nation risked being outnumbered by fast-breeding minorities. It made the intellectuals of Tbilisi cringe in embarrassment. Although his failings as a democrat were debatable, given the strength and number of his opponents and their methods, Gamsakhurdia's incompetence as an administrator was undeniable. However, he had exercised such charm over his supporters that most remained convinced he was the country's sole legitimate ruler long after his flight. Almost every person I met in western Georgia, and several in Tbilisi although they expressed themselves less volubly, seemed convinced that, while some elements of Western-style democracy could be easily dispensed with, others were immutable. An elected leader, whatever his failings, could only be removed at the ballot box. They retained their belief that the charges that led to Gamsakhurdia's eventual removal were concocted: part of an elaborate plot between Moscow and revanchist communists in Tbilisi to install Shevardnadze as Georgia's leader.

After all, the reasoning went, Shevardnadze had been without a job since he resigned as Gorbachev's foreign minister in December 1990 (although he was re-appointed in the aftermath of the August 1991 coup). There was no place for him in Russian politics after the demise of the Soviet Union, but he could be counted on to be loyal and to look out for Moscow's interests. He would perhaps reconsider Gamsakhurdia's rejection of Georgian membership of the Commonwealth of Independent States. In Zugdidi and western Georgia, and other quieter bastions of support for Gamsakhurdia, Shevardnadze's accomplishments in the world arena did not rate. He was despised as a Russian stooge, and his resignation from the communist party in 1991 was treated with scepticism. It was thought that Shevardnadze's return could only mean that Moscow did not intend to let Georgia go free.

Communists and dissidents

Georgians had distinguished themselves during the Soviet era for their determination to maintain their national identity, a sentiment recog-

nised by the authorities in Moscow. Stalin and Beria, through a network of placemen, had controlled Georgian policy through Moscow.
After their deaths, Moscow was content to divest control to dependent
local party elites. During the lengthy tenure of Vasily Mzhavanadze as
first secretary (1953–71) the Georgian Communist Party consolidated
its control through family ties and a legendary underground economy.
There was a much higher membership of the party than in Russia or
the Baltics, and the party allowed for limited cultural expression. The
Georgian church was reconstituted in the war period, and Georgian
was the language of instruction in schools. The few open protests
staged before the advent of perestroika had a nationalist, rather than
anti-communist, focus.

In 1956, for example, more than twenty people were believed killed
when police broke up a demonstration by the banks of the Mtkvari
river in Tbilisi on the anniversary of Stalin's death. The protesters were
confused and angered by the denigration of the Georgian leader's
legacy after his death, mistaking it for a slur on their nation. 'The
generation of Georgians who grew up under Stalin lost the spirit of
anti-Bolshevism, although they preserved the traditional distaste for
the Russian presence.'[3] But there was a paradox in the liberty given
to Georgian culture, in that it did not extend to non-Georgian elements of the population. In contrast to the treatment of minorities in
other republics, however, it was fairly liberal. Abkhazians, for example,
had their own television station after 1978, a privilege denied the
more numerous Armenians of Nagorno-Karabakh. The historian
Ronald Grigor Suny explains how the control by local elites favoured
ethnic discrimination. In Georgia, for example, ethnic Georgians were
awarded more than 80 per cent of university places although they
made up only 70 per cent of the population. Armenians and Russians
had great difficulty in gaining admission. As Suny writes:

> In each union republic the titular nationality used its position to develop its
> own version of great power chauvinism, limiting where it was able the
> expression of its minorities. Georgia became a protected area of privilege for
> Georgians. They received the bulk of the rewards of the society, the leading
> positions in the state and the largest subsidies for cultural projects while
> Armenians, Abkhazians, Ossetians, Adzharians, Kurds, Jews and others were
> at a considerable disadvantage in the competition for the budgetary pie.[4]

In Georgia, ethnic favouritism was instrumental in the creation of
a large and influential intellectual class which thrived on the advantages given to the Georgian majority. In the 1990s, the powers of the
intelligentsia remained substantial and the class played a crucial role in
rejecting Gamsakhurdia and embracing Shevardnadze as his successor.

In dissident politics too, the focus was on the nation, and on the preservation of the Georgian Church and culture. Zviad Gamsakhurdia, though one of a handful of dissidents, was well connected to the Georgian political elite and intelligentsia because of the esteem in which his father, the writer Konstantine, was held. Although he was a member of human rights groups like Amnesty International and the Georgian Helsinki monitoring group, his samizdat journals, the *Golden Fleece* and *Georgian Herald*, were preoccupied with the collective rights of Georgians as a nation, rather than with individuals. In many of his ventures, he was joined by Merab Kostava, a dissident now universally revered in Georgia, who died in a car accident before Georgia became independent.

Along with poetry and banned texts, Gamsakhurdia published articles appealing for the preservation of religious monuments and consolidation of the status of the Georgian language. He was one of the earliest converts to the Georgian Orthodox Church in the 1960s. By the early 1970s, when the head of the Georgian Church was replaced with a more compliant patriarch, Gamsakhurdia helped to expose the links between the Church, the KGB, and the black market in antiquities. In 1975, he wrote to the regional Red Army commander to protest against the damage – including direct hits – done to a monastery and 8th-century cave frescoes that were in the middle of an artillery range. The commander rejected his entreaties to move the firing range to waste ground a few miles away: 'Unfortunately the ruins of the monastery are in the middle of our firing range and we do not intend to move this firing range.'[5]

Also that year, Gamsakhurdia accused prison authorities of torturing remand prisoners who were under investigation for financial crimes. The torture allegations, initially ignored, were confirmed later when two prisoners were tried in Tbilisi for beating to death a fellow inmate. They confessed to having been called in to more than 200 cases, and were said to have been paid by guards in drugs and vodka. At the time, Shevardnadze was first secretary of Georgia's Communist Party and ultimately responsible for the state of Georgia's prisons.

Three years later, Gamsakhurdia and Kostava were arrested. Gamsakhurdia was put on trial for anti-Soviet activities, specifically for distributing works by Sakharov and Solzhenitsyn. He was broken by the experience. He admitted guilt and expressed regret in a speech that so horrified his wife, Manana, that it provoked the following exchange:

'Zviad, come to your senses. Do you realise what you are doing'? He replied:

'It's you who don't understand what you are saying.'[6]

Gamsakhurdia was sentenced to three years in a prison camp and two years in exile, although his sentence was later reduced to the duration of his term of exile, which he served in Daghestan. Kostava, who was unrepentant, served out his entire sentence, and in faraway Siberia. Gamsakhurdia defended his posture, arguing that had he received the maximum sentence, it would have caused unrest in Georgia and destroyed all the good work he had done on behalf of the Church and the nation.

Shevardnadze, like Gamsakhurdia, came from a well-connected Georgian family, although one that derived its power from the political elite rather than the intelligentsia. He was born in 1928 in the southern Guria region. His elder brother Ippokrat was a powerful member of the central committee of the Georgian Communist Party, and had helped ease Shevardnadze's rise. Shevardnadze's wife Nanuli, however, came from a family which had been repressed during the Stalinist terror. Although trained as a teacher, Shevardnadze joined the civilian police. He rose in the ranks to become interior minister and then, after exposing the corruption of his predecessor Mzhavanadze as first secretary, was appointed to the highest post in the republic in 1972. Shevardnadze remained first secretary of the Georgian Communist Party until his summons to the Kremlin in 1985. It is his performance in this job, rather than in the high-profile position of Soviet foreign minister, which has lingered in the memory of Georgians.

Shevardnadze has written in his memoirs about his early realisation of the extent of corruption in the former Soviet Union, and the pain it caused him. Although raised as an ardent Stalinist – he wrote the usual verses about him as a schoolboy and feared the country would collapse with the dictator's death in 1953 – even while he was rising through the ranks of the party he had doubts about the totalitarian and greedy nature of Soviet society. It was through heart-to-heart discussions about these defects in the 1960s that he became friendly with another young idealist, Mikhail Gorbachev. During his first two years as Georgia's first secretary, Shevardnadze presided over an anti-corruption drive that resulted in the arrest of 25,000 people, among them twenty ministers and central committee members. But the anti-corruption drive also masked a parallel offensive – of which Gamsakhurdia was a victim – against dissident nationalism.

Shevardnadze paid his own token obeisances towards Georgian nationalism, but a remark he made as first secretary to the 26th party congress in Moscow has come back to haunt him as leader of an independent Georgia. 'Georgia is called the country of the sun. But for us the true sun rose not in the east but in the north, in Russia – the sun of Lenin's ideas.'[7] As first secretary, he acted to contain several nationalist protests. In 1978, tens of thousands of people demonstrated outside the Tbilisi Supreme Soviet to protest against proposed constitutional changes that would have diminished the status of Georgian in the republic by elevating that of Russian to an official language. The demonstrators refused to disperse until Shevardnadze appeared in public to promise that there would be no changes. There were nationalist protests in Abkhazia that same year. In 1981, Tbilisi University was made to reinstate a professor, Akaki Bakradze, who had been dismissed for his patriotic views. By 1983, when celebrations to mark the bicentenary of Georgia's absorption into the Tsarist Russian empire became a focus of nationalist protest, a new generation of dissidents, the heirs to Gamsakhurdia, had emerged.

Conspiracy or civil war?

Shevardnadze's past in Georgia lent itself to accusations by Gamsakhurdia and his supporters that his return was part of a grand Russian strategem to maintain control over its southern neighbour. The conspiracy theories that abounded in Zugdidi were typical of the climate in which Gamsakhurdia operated. The former dissident was unable to shake off his suspicions, and behind every critic he saw a KGB agent. But beneath Gamsakhurdia's hysteria, the case for suspecting Shevardnadze and Moscow of colluding in his downfall does seem plausible. He was certainly identified as an enemy long before Gamsakhurdia's political problems became terminal.

Another curious aspect of the Gamsakhurdia imbroglio was the unlikely association between the upright Shevardnadze and the convicted criminal Ioseliani. Gamsakhurdia's most formidable opponent had boasted of a friendship with Shevardnadze that stretched back decades, and had survived several lengthy jail terms. Although by the late 1980s Ioseliani was presenting himself as a playwright, he had been sentenced to jail terms totalling twenty-five years in the early 1970s for a series of robberies and for manslaughter. His Mekhedrioni force, which was proving an important prop to the Shevardnadze government, had been the first and most powerful of the armed formations to emerge in Georgia in the late 1980s. Interestingly, the Mekhedrioni were a product of the same fears and aspirations which had brought Gamsakhurdia to power. Founded ostensibly as a church and charity endeavour in the late 1980s, the Mekhedrioni made blatant use of traditional national symbols. Membership was virtually entirely Georgian and Orthodox; all wore St George medallions. Recruits were forced to swear loyalty oaths; traitors and informers were threatened with execution. The conspiratorial element was intensified by the likelihood of members having criminal records. Ioseliani was quite una-

bashed about his own criminal record, admitting to it freely in con-
versation. He tried to convince me that during the Soviet era, brushes
with the law – even involving blatant acts of violence or thievery –
reflected stifled initiative, rather than criminality. Not surprisingly, the
strongest Mekhedrioni chapter was in the border lands of eastern
Georgia. From the late 1980s, it had usurped the functions of the
police force to defend Georgians in areas where the Azerbaijani minority is concentrated.

At first, Gamsakhurdia tolerated the irregulars; they were older and
better educated than the inchoate National Guard, and proved useful
in fighting in South Ossetia. But he later became disturbed at the
extent of Mekhedrioni influence and in February 1991, he jailed
Ioseliani and a hundred of his followers. The Mekhedrioni were a
danger to Gamsakhurdia precisely because of the nationalist symbols
which Ioseliani had used to give his private army discipline and a sense
of purpose.

Despite the improbability of a friendship between Shevardnadze
and Ioseliani, the two came to an arrangement that served both well.
Shevardnadze needed a military force when he returned; Ioseliani
knew he would never be recognised as a legitimate political leader in
Georgia. Ioseliani seconded the formal invitation of the Democratic
Union, the successor of the Georgian Communist Party, to Shevardnadze to come to Georgia. Shevardnadze returned the favour, publicly
rebuking those who had criticised the idea of him running Georgia
in tandem with a former criminal. He told a reporter for *Moscow News*
soon after his return:

> Discussing the criminal records of certain people who are my partners now
> is offensive to me. One should not be reminded of sins committed in youth.
> On the contrary, I admire the people who had enough strength, will power
> and courage to overcome all and make a new start in life. I categorically
> disagree with those who keep reminding them of their past. Now they are
> great statesmen. ... Before returning to Georgia I resolved to forget old
> grudges and abstain from witch hunts.

There is little doubt that Russia, or indeed the West, preferred any
alternative to Gamsakhurdia, let alone a man of Shevardnadze's stature.
So long as Gamsakhurdia remained president, and determined to keep
Georgia out of the CIS, Georgia remained a pariah state. Its isolation
ended only with Shevardnadze's arrival as the friends he had made in
Europe welcomed the country back into the world community. Al-
though Georgia was still being run as a heavily militarised state,
Shevardnadze's reputation overcame doubts. The international organi-
sations which had expressed concern about human rights under
Gamsakhurdia fell silent.

Great things were also expected of Shevardnadze by the intelligentsia in Tbilisi. After a period of lawlessness generally and diminished
influence for the intellectuals in particular under Gamsakhurdia,
Shevardnadze appeared to offer stability and economic renewal. There
was a certain nostalgia for the stability of the Brezhnev era, when
Shevardnadze was the Georgian leader, and electricity, food and other
basic amenities were plentiful. His popularity in the West was a talis-
man for Georgians, who feel a powerful attraction to Western Europe
and the United States. Despite their geographical location and years
of isolation from the West under Soviet rule, Georgians feel resolutely
European. But their Western outlook, strengthened by the national
Church and a history of subjugation to the Muslim world beyond its
borders, sits uneasily with an attachment to Georgia's clannish and
patriarchal traditions and its former monarchy. Western aspirations
notwithstanding, during Shevardnadze's leadership as during Gamsakhurdia's, the intelligentsia was divided and uncertain about which
direction the government should take. There was broad support for
the principles of human rights, secret multi-party ballots and a market
economy, but no real understanding of what choices needed to be
made. The institutions for reform were powerless. The parliament had
failed to operate effectively under Gamsakhurdia, and the guardians of
public order had been supplanted by irregular forces. Georgia was
embroiled in domestic conflict and lacked the structures to implement
change. Shevardnadze was aware of the burden of the intelligentsia's
expectations:

> Everybody seems to be expecting favourable results now, but the reverse
> is happening. Mass robberies, murders and car thefts have become a regular
> feature. The impression is that the institutions responsible for public order
> are disorganised and demoralised.[8]

The intelligentsia had felt largely excluded from the Gamsakhurdia
government, and a parliament dominated by deputies they dismissed
as country bumpkins. A complicated balloting system combining
proportional representation and first-past-the-post had allowed relative unknowns from rural Georgia to enter parliament at the expense
of figures from the intelligentsia. The unworkable parliament which
resulted was also a product of the charged atmosphere that preceded
the vote, and the failure to form a united nationalist front.

Perestroika and elections

In January 1987, the central committee of the Communist Party of the
Soviet Union embarked on a policy of democratisation that for the

first time allowed national organisations to operate openly. Georgia's liberal intelligentsia set up the first such initiative in October 1987. The main aim of the Ilia Chavchavadze Society was to educate and otherwise prepare Georgians for eventual independence. The society recognised implicitly the impossibility of overthrowing existing structures. Its all-embracing slogan, 'Fatherland, language, and faith', illustrated the cultural rather than the separatist nature of its agenda. But its emergence was still perceived as a challenge to the Communist Party of Georgia, which, in response, set up its own official group, the Rustaveli Society.

The tenor of political debate changed in 1988, when two more radical groups appeared. Gamsakhurdia announced the foundation of the Society of Saint Ilia the Righteous, and Giorgi Chanturia, a young dissident, established the National Democratic Party. Where its precursors had concentrated on cultural and ecological issues, the National Democratic Party was explicitly separatist. Its slogan called for 'Georgia for the Georgians' and its charter stated that the NDP aimed to restore Georgian sovereignty through civil disobedience. Chanturia's parallel vision of an independent Georgia illustrated the dichotomy between the narrowly Christian and nationalistic aspects of Georgian tradition and the more liberal European tenets to which the campaigners for independence paid homage. Chanturia proposed a 'theodemocracy' for Georgia. The parliament would have a democratically elected lower house, with the holy synod of the Georgian Church forming the upper house.[9]

From the end of 1988 the rapidly changing alliances as parties formed and split, and the vitriolic and highly personal attacks exchanged between moderates and radicals, became a feature of Georgian public life. But the radicals began to gain the upper hand, capturing popular attention through a series of hunger strikes, public rallies and demonstrations. In November 1988, more than 200,000 people attended a rally on Rustaveli Prospekt in Tbilisi to protest against proposed amendments to the Soviet constitution which would have threatened Georgian sovereignty. The strength of the protest forced Moscow to modify its plans, and allowed the radicals to boast of the efficacy of their campaign. Even the pro-communist Rustaveli Society was forced to take account of the changing mood, electing the popular historian Akaki Bakradze as its chairman in March 1989.

The one event that did crystallise the reform process in Georgia was the brutal dispersal of a peaceful demonstration in Tbilisi on 9 April 1989. Soviet army troops armed with toxic gas and sharpened shovels moved in against a protest rally of 8,000 people. Nineteen people were killed, all but three of them women, and dozens were hurt. The day became a symbol of Georgia's martyrdom and its epic struggle against outside interference.

The demonstrations in Tbilisi, led by Chanturia and other radicals, were initially intended as a response to the demands for secession voiced by the Abkhazian minority. A month earlier, Georgian students in Sukhumi had launched a campaign against the rector of the university, who had signed a declaration calling for Abkhazian sovereignty. The students claimed that his action endangered the position of the Georgian language at the university. The communist authorities in Tbilisi had refused to allow a planned counter-demonstration. When the Georgian students withdrew from the town where the rally was to have been held, they were set upon by local Abkhazians and beaten up. But although support for the Georgians of Abkhazia was at the forefront, the theme of the Tbilisi protests had broadened to include demands for the restoration of Georgian sovereignty and secession from the Soviet Union.

At the time, the protests were among the most serious in the Soviet Union. From Moscow's point of view, the Abkhazian–Georgian tensions underlying the Tbilisi rallies were a sign of the danger of spreading ethnic conflict. A year earlier, demonstrations in Yerevan calling for the unification of Nagorno-Karabakh with Armenia had resulted in anti-Armenian pogroms in the Azerbaijani industrial city of Sumgait. Moldova and the Baltics had also seen demonstrations calling for independence. There was concern among the Tbilisi party leadership, too, that the situation was moving beyond its control. On 7 April, the Republican Party first secretary, Dzhumbar Patiashvili, sent a telegram to the Politburo in Moscow asking for permission to arrest opposition leaders and impose martial law. The politburo agreed the next day to send troops to Tbilisi. They moved in early on 9 April with devastating effect. Martial law was declared and leading activists, including Gamsakhurdia and Chanturia, were arrested.

The hardline approach was a terrible miscalculation. In the aftermath of the outrage felt in Georgia and abroad, the Kremlin tried to make amends by ordering Patiashvili and his prime minister to resign and sending Shevardnadze to Georgia. But the massacre had changed Georgian politics forever. 'Inevitably, it strengthened the hands of radicals who rejected any compromise with Soviet authorities and any goal short of total independence.'[10] The Georgian Communist Party was so tainted by the event that it was unable to resist the radical nationalist agenda. In May, the new first secretary, Givi Gumbaridze, allowed celebrations to mark the anniversary of the founding of the short-lived independent Georgian republic in 1918, and re-opened a number of churches. In the autumn of 1989, the Georgian parliament declared the supremacy of Georgian laws over Soviet legislation. In February 1990, Georgia was declared an annexed and occupied country, and in March the Communist Party's guaranteed right to a monopoly was removed from the constitution. With the reform process speeding out of control, the communist leadership was unable to resist pressure for multi-party parliamentary elections, made more acute by a rail blockade led by Gamsakhurdia. After several delays on the part of the communists, elections were held in October and a parliament selected according to a complicated system of proportional representation.

The elections were blighted by the same squabbling and disunity that had characterised the political scene around 9 April. There was a feverish amount of political activity after the massacre and scores of new parties were founded, although there were few real differences between them. Political labels were irrelevant beside the overpowering issue of Georgian independence. In part this was due to the close-knit structure of Georgian intellectual life, which allowed personal rivalries to transcend ideological debate. The loose alliance between Gamsakhurdia and Chanturia broke down and turned into an intense rivalry. Gamsakhurdia was able to build on his popularity through the sheer force of his personality. His support for the rights of Georgians living in Abkhazia and Ossetia also endeared him to a population fearful that the country was breaking apart in the upsurge of ethnic violence.

After a dirty campaign with attacks on the offices of rival parties, Gamsakhurdia's Round Table-Free Georgia coalition won 155 seats in the 250-seat assembly, against 64 for the communists, the next biggest grouping. The results were an affront to the intelligentsia. The party list system had hurt candidates from the Tbilisi elite, who were largely unknown outside the confines of the capital. They were unable to offer real competition to candidates who rode to victory on Gamsakhurdia's coat-tails. And so the house was dominated by inexperienced and unsophisticated deputies, politicians who had no support base of their own, but were dependent on Gamsakhurdia for their rise to power. Of course, not all of the Round Table deputies were from rural areas as Gamsakhurdia's opponents were to claim. Among Gamsakhurdia's supporters were several deputies with professional qualifications. But a myth was created that Gamsakhurdia and his deputies represented only the poor, badly educated and perhaps misguided people of rural areas.

The parliament of amateurs was ill-equipped to temper Gamsakhurdia's excesses. They put up little resistance when he proposed the jettisoning of local elections to make way for a system of appointed prefects in provincial towns who would report directly to him. There

was only feeble resistance when he asked parliament to vote him executive powers. The few members of the Tbilisi intelligentsia who had
been elected to parliament largely withdrew from active politics. Tamaz
Gamkrelidze, an Orientalist at Tbilisi University, acknowledges that he
and fellow deputies were ineffective in parliament. 'During that whole
time, the greater part of Georgia's intellectuals did not take part in
political life', he claimed somewhat disingenuously during a discussion
at his offices in a university tower block. Nominally a member of the
Popular Front, he did not attend the session which voted special powers
for Gamsakhurdia. The last parliamentary restraints on Gamsakhurdia
were removed after the attempted coup in Moscow in August 1991,
which he used as a pretext to ban the communist deputies.

The intelligentsia did reclaim its influence decisively after the October
1992 elections, which totally changed the face of the Georgian parliament. However, there were lasting implications growing from the
elite's early alienation from the Gamsakhurdia government. With
Shevardnadze's rule legitimised through election, there was little interest in Tbilisi circles in resolving the upheavals in Zugdidi and little sign
that the Gamsakhurdia fiasco had introduced tolerance into Georgian
politics. Among some intellectuals, there was a refusal even to acknowledge that anyone might have a legitimate reason for supporting
Gamsakhurdia. 'Georgia is divided, yes, but only between smart and
foolish people', said Akaki Bakradze, the professor who had been a
symbol of the national movement a decade earlier, when I asked him
what would become of the rebels of western Georgia. The unrest in
Mingrelia continued, but its political implications had receded into
the background.

Communist comeback: the October 1992 elections

Amid this climate of intolerance, in August 1992 Shevardnadze announced the date for parliamentary elections. Aside from the economic disruptions caused by the unrest in Mingrelia, the election
campaign coincided with the beginning of a far more serious armed
conflict in Abkhazia in the north-west. The early days of the campaign
were notable for the coyness with which Shevardnadze put forward his
own candidacy. He waited until the last day before the deadline for
registration to announce that he would run for the Peace bloc, which
was dominated by the former Georgian Communist Party. But this
public diffidence was at odds with the machinations behind the scenes
by the ruling council to facilitate Shevardnadze's participation in the
vote, and his candidacy for the chairmanship of parliament, which
would replace the post of president that had been created for

Gamsakhurdia. Six weeks before the 11 October ballot, the election commission changed the polling regulations to permit the election of a parliamentary chairman on the same day. The rules stipulated that the chairman must win one-third of the votes cast and must run as an independent candidate, a requirement that would have excluded Shevardnadze. But following appeals from several parties within the Peace bloc, Shevardnadze withdrew from the grouping and declared his candidacy for parliamentary chairman on 31 August 1992. He was 'compelled to agree' to their entreaties, Shevardnadze explained to reporters.

As in the 1990 elections, a plethora of parties took part in the 11 October poll. But of the forty-six parties participating, only three blocs were serious contenders. Among the rest, there were again few differences in ideology or style. All advocated a transition to a market economy and a Western-style democracy. In addition, they embraced the seemingly incompatible goals of defending human rights while preserving Georgia's territorial integrity against demands for sovereignty from the Abkhazian and Ossetian minorities. Although many of the parties were formed only in the weeks before the election, three had initially formed part of Zviad Gamsakhurdia's Round Table coalition. However, during the 1992 election, they joined with all the other parties in the universal acclaim accorded to Shevardnadze's candidacy for the post of parliamentary chairman. Not one of the parties was openly critical of the ruling council, although reservations were voiced privately, and there was no party representing the still loyal supporters of Gamsakhurdia.

The conduct of the polls was broadly supported by more than seventy representatives of international monitoring groups. Turnout was high except for parts of Mingrelia, and Abkhazia and South Ossetia which held a boycott. The results were a confirmation of Shevardnadze's popularity among Georgians: the Peace bloc of former communists emerged with the largest number of seats. However, it did not secure a majority and was forced into a coalition with the 11 October bloc, representing moderate nationalists, and the Unity bloc, dominated by the Tbilisi intelligentsia. In contrast to the results of the 1990 elections, when parliament was dominated by newcomers, the victors in 1992 included many familiar faces. Among the rehabilitated communists were the former first secretary Patiashvili, and Zhiuli Shartava, a Shevardnadze protégé from the industrial town of Rustavi. Chanturia took his seat in parliament for the first time, while the mainstays of the provisional ruling council, Sigua, Kitovani and Ioseliani, won new legitimacy by being elected as well. All three members of the council had run as independents.

Nationalism and minorities

Immediately after the elections, Shevardnadze announced the creation of an eight-man defence council with executive powers to deal with the threat to Georgia's territorial integrity posed by the war in Abkhazia. Despite the contempt with which the intelligentsia had come to view Gamsakhurdia, they had differed very little from him in their views on Georgia's minority communities. Although Gamsakhurdia's actions as president and the rhetoric he employed during the late 1980s had exacerbated ethnic tensions, he was rarely criticised for this by his fellow Georgians. However extreme Gamsakhurdia's intolerance of Abkhazian and Ossetian demands for secession, it reflected a large segment of Georgian opinion. For most of the intelligentsia, the demands of the minorities were beyond contemplation. From the earliest days of the national movement, political leaders had been insensitive to the fears of the minorities, and had made little effort to view these concerns as anything other than tactics by Moscow to forestall Georgian independence. In the late 1980s the campaign for laws to assure the dominance of the Georgian language caused fear among the Ossetians and Abkhazians, who generally prefer Russian. Other ideas in circulation before the 1990 elections included the proposal that proficiency in the Georgian language be a prerequisite for citizenship.

Although Shevardnadze had come to Georgia with a much more open mind towards a compromise between Georgians and Ossetian and Abkhazian demands for independence, he was forced to acknowledge the strength of national feeling. In his first days in power, the former statesman had risked outraging Georgian chauvinists by seeking peace talks with the Ossetian leadership. He went a step further, entering into an agreement to set up a joint Russian–Georgian–Ossetian peacekeeping force in South Ossetia, exposing himself to claims that he was selling out to Russia. Shevardnadze even began to explore ways of finding a solution to the plight of the Meskhetian Turks, previously a taboo subject, through discussions with Turkey. In the end, however, nationalist pressures proved too much for Shevardnadze. The chauvinism that had engulfed the perestroika era began to colour his own policies.

In contrast to Armenia or Azerbaijan, fears about Georgian security do not much involve neighbouring countries. It is within Georgia proper that boundaries and minorities became an issue. It was perhaps inevitable that an assertion of Georgian identity would prove a threat to the minorities on Georgian soil, and in turn an inspiration for minority national sentiments. Although the overwhelming majority of Georgians do live on their native territory, there are still large minority groups within Georgia, accounting for 30 per cent of the population. Of Georgia's 5.4 million inhabitants at the time of the 1989 Soviet census, 8 per cent were Armenian, 6 per cent ethnic Russian and 6 per cent Azerbaijani. Ossetians made up 3 per cent of the population and Abkhazians less than 2 per cent, although both peoples were given territories of their own within Georgia after the establishment of Soviet rule. The Abkhazians were given an autonomous republic, and the Ossetians the lesser status of a region.

Aside from the Ossetian and Abkhazian autonomous areas, there is a third autonomous republic of Adzharia in south-western Georgia of about 392,000 people. The Adzharians are ethnic Georgians, but Muslims, the descendants of those forcibly converted during Ottoman rule. In 1926, the last time the Adzharians were counted separately in a Soviet census, they made up 4 per cent of the Georgian population.

No other union republic outside Russia, Georgians complain, was forced to allot so much space to minorities when the Soviet borders were finalised in the 1920s. The Ossetians and Abkhazians between them occupy 18 per cent of Georgian territory. Both peoples have demanded to leave Georgia. The Abkhazians envisage an existence as an independent republic within the CIS, while the Ossetians would prefer to unite with North Ossetia and become part of Russia. Given that the demands of both minorities would affect Russian–Georgian boundaries, it is taken for granted in Georgia that the Ossetian and Abkhazian regions provide an opportunity to Moscow to meddle, and to keep Tbilisi unstable and divided.

The Armenian and Azerbaijani communities are concentrated in border areas – the Azerbaijanis in the south-east and the Armenians in the south – and since the late 1980s there has been tension with the local population. In the case of the Armenians, the sources of friction date back to Tsarist times when the community formed the bulk of the merchant class in Georgia, and dominated Tbilisi. Relations with Azerbaijan are complicated by the presence of ethnic Georgians on the Azeri side of the border, living on tracts of land prised off from Georgia by the Bolshevik leader Sergo Ordzhonikidze.

Of all the minorities laying claim to rights within Georgia, the Meskhetian Turks have attracted the least sympathy. In Stalinist terminology, the Meskhetians are a 'punished people'. Unlike other deported nations of the Caucasus, the tragedy of the Meskhetians has been prolonged by the refusal of the authorities to allow them to return to their place of origin. Most of the 200,000 Meskhetians today consider themselves Turkish, and Georgia has traditionally feared that allowing the returnees to settle on the border would encourage territorial claims from Ankara. The situation is particularly acute for the

11,000 Meskhetians who have not found permanent homes or jobs
since fleeing pogroms in the Fergana Valley of Uzbekistan in July 1989.
They have been living temporarily in the Krasnodar area, where they
have encountered hostility from local Russians. There is another refugee population of Meskhetians in Azerbaijan, consisting of families
who were resettled in Nagorno-Karabakh, from where they were forced
to flee once more.

No matter what government was in power, Georgia has consistently balked at readmitting the Meskhetians after they were rehabilitated in 1968. The 7,000 who returned then pitched tents in a park
in central Tbilisi before they won the right to trickle back to their
traditional border lands. Those who returned met so much harassment
and hostility that today only fifty-seven families remain in Georgia.

Abkhazians

The Abkhazian autonomous republic, on the Black Sea coast and
bordering Russia, was one of Georgia's resort areas. Its capital, Sukhumi,
had a charm that survived decades of neglect: whitewashed buildings
with colonial arches and a clear expanse of grassy lawn that overlooks
the sea. The republic itself occupies about half of Georgia's coast line,
and the port was useful to Georgia for the ferry links between Russia
and Turkey. The Abkhazian republic, which had its own parliamentary
assembly but was still subordinate to Georgia, was created in 1930 as
a homeland for a people who number only 93,000 today. In the 1920s
it had been a union territory, subordinate only to the authorities in
Moscow.

The Abkhazians were part of medieval Georgia and constituted a
separate principality when, like most of the Caucasus, the kingdom
was divided between Iran and Turkey. At one time Abkhazians were
included in the Georgian Orthodox Church, although they are now
mainly lapsed Muslims or pagans. There are different theories about
their origins. The one manufactured by Georgian historians is that of
a people living in the coastal areas from the first century, whose identity and language was obscured by invasions of north Caucasians.
According to the Georgian line of thought, present-day tensions between the two groups are unnatural and stem from Ottoman and later
Russian policies in the Caucasus. At its most extreme, the Georgian
argument holds that the Abkhazian identity is entirely a product of the
Soviet corruption of history, and was artificially reinforced to destabilise
and weaken the Caucasus. Of course, such explanations are totally
unacceptable to the Abkhazians. What is indisputable is that before the
war broke out in 1992 the Abkhaz numbered only 17 per cent of the

population of what they consider their ancestral lands. They formed a majority in only one district, Gudauta. The Abkhaz blame the reduction in their population on forced migration to Turkey. Unlike the Georgian monarchy, which was eager for an alliance with Russia against the Turks, Abkhazia fought Moscow's expansion until the middle of the 19th century. Its defeat led to exile and dispersion, the beginnings of what was to be a consistent policy of assimilation. The Russian Tsars settled Russian peasants in Abkhazia in the late 19th century when the emancipation of the serfs made land pressure unbearable inside Russia.

By 1926 ethnic Abkhazians accounted for a third of all residents in the republic. Their share of the population was further diluted when Greeks from the Black Sea Coast, Armenians, Russians and Mingrelians were forcibly relocated to the territory. The Abkhaz language also came under attack: Abkhaz language schools were abolished and a new script, based on the Georgian alphabet, was introduced. Family and place names were changed in a further effort to eliminate signs of an Abkhazian presence. Abkhazia suffered together with Georgia the Stalinist-era arrests and executions of its leading intellectuals and Bolsheviks. But there was a particular malice in the repression meted out to Abkhazians; behind every decree loomed the threat of cultural extinction. In 1941, more than a dozen Abkhazians were executed on trumped-up charges of having conspired to set up an independent state under Nazi sponsorship. According to Abkhazian historians, the plot was concocted to build a case for the planned deportation of the entire nation.[11]

The prospect of total cultural assimilation has naturally played a huge part in Abkhazian demands for secession. There is much support within the intelligentsia for measures to encourage diaspora Abkhazians to return from Turkey, Syria and other parts of the Middle East and to help rebuild the population. Their leader, the immaculately dressed Vladislav Aardzinba, has argued that their history of repression and exile excuses Abkhazians from certain requirements of Western-style democracy. He has dismissed criticism of the failure to hold a referendum on secession which, based on the territory's demographic balance, it would have almost certainly lost. Abkhazian radicals like Aardzinba believe they are justified in demanding total control over the territory despite their minority status – in fact *because* of their minority status.

Before their mass exodus in September 1992, Georgians made up 43 per cent of the population of Abkhazia, followed by significant numbers of Russians and Armenians as well as the vestiges of a Greek settlement. Tensions between the Abkhaz and the Georgians were brought to the surface in 1978, when the Abkhazians first voiced their desire to become an autonomous republic within Russia. Moscow responded by increasing economic aid and granting a number of cultural liberties to Abkhazia – including its own university – although the main demand was ignored. But not only did the concessions fail to abate Abkhazian demands, they also deepened Georgian concerns about discrimination at the hands of the Abkhazian minority. While the Abkhazians continued to press for more autonomy, there were counter-demonstrations by young Georgians who feared the preference shown to Russian and Abkhazian literature courses at the university at the expense of the Georgian curriculum.

The misgivings of Georgians grew after March 1989 when the Abkhazians renewed their demand that their republic be upgraded into a full-scale union republic in the Lykhny declaration, named after a town outside Sukhumi. As in 1978, the university campus became a battle ground. As the conflict intensified, Georgian professors left the campus to start their own branch college of Tbilisi university. Georgian anger about the independence declaration led to skirmishes throughout the summer of 1989.

Within the year, the impetus of the Abkhazian national movement had moved from the campus to parliament. But the response of the local Georgian community remained the same: all Abkhazian attempts at self-assertion were completely rejected and met by boycotts and walk-outs. A number of measures were introduced to strengthen the position of Abkhazians within the republic. For Georgians, one of the most worrying was the creation of an exclusively ethnic Abkhazian national guard. In August 1990, the separatist campaign culminated in a vote in the parliament at Sukhumi – during a session that was boycotted by Georgian deputies – to declare that Abkhazia had a right to seek full independence from Georgia. The vote was immediately annulled by the Georgian parliament in Tbilisi.

Ossetians

Meanwhile, on the other side of Georgia, another minority group had been watching the progress of events in Abkhazia with particular interest. The people of South Ossetia first began to express their national aspirations as a means of showing solidarity with the Abkhazians. In 1989, the Ademon Nykhas (Popular Shrine) group published an open letter, supporting the Abkhazian campaign against the opening of an exclusively Georgian branch of Sukhumi university. But the group went on to make demands on behalf of Ossetia – that it be upgraded to the status of an autonomous republic with a view to its eventual reunification with Ossetian territories within Russia.

The South Ossetian Autonomous Region is one of two homelands in the Caucasus region designated for the Ossetian people. During the 19th century, while much of the northern Caucasus was at war with Russia, Ossetia remained an ally. The territory was strategic, containing the sole mountain pass linking Russia to Georgia. When the Soviet borders were established in the 1920s, the Ossetian lands were divided between South Ossetia, within Georgia, and North Ossetia, within Russia.

The resurgence of interest in national histories that accompanied perestroika had a particular poignancy for the Ossetians. They are unrelated to any of the surrounding Caucasian nationalities, their language being distantly related to Persian. But their exact origins are obscure and this has helped Georgians to deny the Ossetian right to lands within Georgian borders.

Georgians call the region Shida Kartli, or Inner Georgia, and correct foreigners who persist in referring to it as South Ossetia. According to Georgian historians, Ossetians originated from the Russian side of the border and migrated across the Caucasus mountains only in the 17th century, when they were serfs on the Samachablu estate of Prince Matchabelli. Georgian animosity is no doubt influenced by the Ossetians' affinity for Russia. What is particularly galling for Georgians about the Ossetians, though, is the existence of a second autonomous republic across the border in Russia. In the same way that the identity and therefore the territorial claims of the Abkhazians are denied, the main school of Georgian history considers North Ossetia to be the true home of the whole minority.

But unlike the Abkhazians, Ossetians have demographics on their side. They form a two-thirds majority within South Ossetia, although before the outbreak of the war in late 1989 a significant number of Georgians lived in villages around the capital Tskhinvali. The capital itself was ethnically mixed, with high rates of intermarriage between Ossetians and Georgians as well as a sizeable Jewish population, Russians and Armenians. There were Ossetian communities in other parts of Georgia, in eastern Kakheti in particular, adding up to a total Ossetian population of 175,000 at the time of the 1989 census.

From 1989 onwards, each advance for Georgia's national movement revealed the growing rift between Georgia and the Abkhazians and Ossetians, including the pivotal and tragic demonstrations leading up to 9 April. At the end of that year, the strikes and protests in Tskhinvali bubbled over into violent clashes. Local Georgians complained of harassment and in January 1990 Soviet interior ministry troops were sent in to keep the peace. Both Abkhazians and Ossetians boycotted the parliamentary elections that took place in the autumn of 1990. Instead, the Ossetians used the occasion to declare themselves an independent democratic republic. And in a further rebuff to Georgian aspirations, the Abkhazians and Ossetians ignored a Georgian boycott and voted in the March 1991 referendum on Gorbachev's proposed union treaty. Fifty-two per cent of the population of Abkhazia voted; of this number 98 per cent supported the preservation of the Soviet Union. Both nations staged a boycott of their own during the 1991 presidential elections in Georgia to protest against regulations which disbarred locally based parties – the Abkhazian and Ossetian popular organisations.

Although the tensions between Ossetians and Georgians in the autonomous region had exploded into outright war before Gamsakhurdia's rise to power, he was instrumental in exacerbating the conflict. Under his chairmanship in December 1990, the Georgian parliament responded to an Ossetian declaration of sovereignty by abolishing Ossetia's autonomous status and jailing the relatively moderate Ossetian leader, Torez Kalambekov. Kitovani, the commander of the national guard, believed even more fervently than Gamsakhurdia that Georgia should remain a unitary state. He took a personal interest in the Georgian irregulars who had been fighting in South Ossetia for some months.

The effects of the war on the besieged Ossetian capital were horrific. Nearly every family lost at least one male and 100,000 people, Georgian and Ossetian, were made refugees. Many of the mixed marriages and friendships that had endured during peacetime gave way, although there were also cases of men exchanging ethnic loyalties to fight on the side of the community they had married into. The Ossetians have assembled a catalogue of torture inflicted on hostages, including photographs of Ossetian youths whose faces were burnt with blow torches.

Throughout much of 1991, the bombardment of Tskhinvali was so intense and the Georgian besiegers in such close proximity that for several months the Ossetians were unable to bury their dead. Because the cemetery lay in too dangerous an area, the playground of a local primary school was transformed into a graveyard, the graves of the war dead marked by black flags and photographs. For those who remained in Tskhinvali until the war quietened down in early 1992, there was no water or electricity and little food. If it had not been for the Soviet army helicopters, which were used to evacuate the wounded, many more people would have died of hunger and disease in a hospital that functioned without heating and medicines.

The Ossetians won a respite only in December 1991, when the Georgian irregulars became tied down in the power struggle in Tbilisi.

Within days of Gamsakhurdia's fall, the military council embarked on a series of initiatives aimed at securing a lasting ceasefire in the region. A delegation was sent to Tskhinvali to seek peace talks and Sigua, the council's acting prime minister, gave a press conference in which he repudiated the previous regime's policy towards South Ossetia. The council followed this up by freeing Kalambekov, who by then had spent a year in jail in Tbilisi.

Initially, the Georgian initiative met with distrust from the younger and more radical Ossetian leaders who had replaced Kalambekov. But their fears eased after several conciliatory gestures from the new Georgian government. Shevardnadze held direct talks with the Ossetian leadership and set up a human rights commission to investigate claims of atrocities carried out by Georgian irregulars. In June 1992, he and Yeltsin signed an agreement which led to the creation of a Russian–Georgian–Ossetian peacekeeping force in South Ossetia. The mediation proved successful and, after a few false starts, the fighting largely stopped. In the summer of 1992, refugees began to return to Tskhinvali.

Shevardnadze's war

In the light of Shevardnadze's conciliatory approach to the conflict in South Ossetia, his subsequent actions in Abkhazia initially proved incomprehensible. On 14 August 1992, Abkhazia was attacked from the east and from the sea in the west by Georgian troops. The soldiers were sent in ostensibly to hunt down supporters of Gamsakhurdia who had kidnapped government ministers. But in Abkhazia and elsewhere, this was seen as a convenient pretext because the perpetrators were Mingrelian – and hardly likely to have sought refuge with a hostile minority. The real purpose behind the invasion was not to crush the repositories of support for Gamsakhurdia, but to stifle the Abkhazian independence movement.

Days before the National Guard was sent in, the Abkhazian parliament had suspended its constitution. The parliamentary chairman, Vladislav Aardzinba, declared that the republic would henceforth be governed by a 1925 document that had designated the territory a sovereign state with ties to Georgia. While both communities swapped claims of harassment, he embarked on what would be seen by Georgia as an unacceptable provocation. He announced that he intended Abkhazia to enter into the Commonwealth of Independent States as a full member. The Georgian response came in an invasion launched with an attack on the parliament by Kitovani and his followers. Aardzinba and other Abkhazian leaders fled Sukhumi and set up a rebel headquarters in the provincial town of Gudauta.

The operation, which was led by Kitovani's Georgian National Guard, resulted in the longest and bloodiest of the wars which have afflicted independent Georgia. Estimates of the toll after a year of fighting climbed into the thousands; in the winter months there were reports of deaths from starvation in some of the towns under siege. At the outset, Shevardnadze expected an easy victory in Abkhazia. The Abkhazians were outnumbered, poorly armed and inexperienced fighters, while the Georgian troops had been tested in Ossetia and against the rebels in Mingrelia. But Georgian forces were soon bogged down in a bitter and protracted conflict that defied interventions from both Russia and the United Nations. After a final, short offensive by the Abkhazian fighters, the war culminated on 27 September 1993 in the fall of Sukhumi to Abkhazian separatist forces. It was a humiliation for Shevardnadze personally, and for Georgia a harbinger of the dismemberment of the country. Nearly 250,000 people, almost the entire Georgian population of Abkhazia, fled. Dozens of people perished during the trek through the frozen high passes of the mountains.

Georgia's unforseen defeat was almost entirely due to the reinforcements from Russia which fought on the side of the rebels. The first saviours of the Abkhazians were irregulars: Chechen and Kabardian volunteers from the north Caucasus. The military alliance was built on feelings of ethnic kinship with the peoples of the north Caucasus which the Abkhazians had made concrete through the founding of a Confederation of Mountain Peoples at Sukhumi in 1989. In March 1993, an Abkhazian leader stated that 380 men from the north Caucasus were fighting in the region. The participation of north Caucasians in the conflict in Abkhazia gave shape to Russian and Georgian fears of a conflagration that could spread throughout the region, destabilising southern Russia and the Black Sea coast.

Georgia's apprehensions increased when it became evident that the north Caucasians were not the only outsiders involved in the Abkhazian conflict. Georgian officials became convinced that forces from the former Soviet army base at Sukhumi were aiding the Abkhazians. There had been precedents for the involvement of ex-Soviet forces elsewhere in the Caucasus. The disintegration of the Red Army had left hundreds of thousands of servicemen without employment and housing; signing on as a mercenary provided a convenient alternative. In South Ossetia, ethnic Russians from the right-wing Russian National Legion had participated in the war. But there were indications in Abkhazia that Russian involvement meant more than a few renegade soldiers.

In December 1992, Georgia's parliament called on Russian troops to withdraw immediately in a statement that made clear Georgia's belief that Russia was not acting in a neighbourly fashion in Abkhazia, but was intent on defending its own interests as the regional great power. 'Russian troops deployed in Abkhazia have turned into one of the parties in the conflict and are pursuing the imperial policy of encroachment on the territorial integrity of Georgia alongside the separatists and reactionary circles of Russia', a statement from the parliament said. 'Russian–Georgian relations have clearly demonstrated of late that the aggressive factor is becoming more prominent in Russian policy, which threatens stability not only in the Caucasus, but also all over the world.'[12] Later that month, Georgia announced that it would shoot down Russian military planes flying over Abkhazia. A day later, it did so. It was one of the earliest illustrations of the ease with which the dispute over Abkhazia could wreck relations between Moscow and Tbilisi.

Aside from the immediate prospect of entering into a war by proxy with Russia, the conflict in Abkhazia forced Shevardnadze to take stock of his internal security situation. Instead of a standing army, Georgia had two badly disciplined militias, the Mekhedrioni and the National Guard. Both forces were dangerously subservient to the political ambitions of their commanders. Although Shevardnadze had managed to hold Kitovani and Ioseliani in check so far, the turmoil of the war presented dangerous opportunities. In the autumn of 1992 there was a series of raids on Russian ammunition depots, suspected to have been carried out by members of Kitovani's National Guard. The attacks revealed how little control Shevardnadze had over the paramilitaries despite the goodwill shown to him by ordinary Georgians, and how beholden he was to the two men who brought him to power.

The new Shevardnadze

There was evidence soon after the October 1992 election that Shevardnadze was no longer the man the West thought it knew. The war in Abkhazia was absorbing all of his energies, and sapping Georgia of its potential to introduce market reforms. The conflict had wiped out any possibility of rebuilding an economy laid waste by the first civilian conflict launched by Gamsakhurdia supporters. Factories were closed, starved of supplies because of severed transport links with Russia. The energy shortage was so acute in Tbilisi that trams and the Metro were shut down. Tensions with Moscow over Abkhazia had frozen any prospect of Georgia entering into a friendship treaty with Russia. As time went on, it appeared as if Shevardnadze was taking refuge from this economic devastation by adopting a radically more nationalist posture. He tried to broaden his appeal to Georgians by relying on the symbols that others such as Gamsakhurdia and even Ioseliani had used before him. In November 1992, Shevardnadze announced that he had become a Christian and had been baptised in the Georgian Orthodox church, as Giorgy. 'I have an icon in my office now, though there was a time when I had Stalin's portrait on the wall.'[13]

The conversion was followed by an uncompromising stand on Abkhazia. Throughout December 1992, Shevardnadze warned that time was running out for the secessionists. It was a posture seemingly at variance with his earlier image while Soviet foreign minister as a statesman and conciliator. Now he was forced to present two images to two separate constituencies: the nationalist at home, and the reasonable reformer abroad. 'People are tired of this war. It must be stopped as quickly as possible', he told the local radio station in Tbilisi. 'I have reached the painful conclusion that Georgia has to settle its problems alone.'[14] Shevardnadze appeared to abandon all hope for negotiating a peaceful end to the conflict. 'Everything that was possible to do for a peaceful settlement of the conflict was done. Ethnically, politically, we fulfilled our duty.'[15]

For Shevardnadze, the conflict in Abkhazia proved to be the breaking point. He had returned to Georgia with a formidable reputation, but he had proved unable to reconcile all of the divisions which blighted Georgia's future. Shevardnadze's success in mediating an end to the Ossetian war was overshadowed by his failure to resolve Georgia's dispute with the Abkhazian minority. Dangerous in its own right, the war in Abkhazia also carried with it the seeds of a far more serious threat to Georgia's territorial integrity. Although Shevardnadze had initially been viewed favourably in Moscow, Georgia's interests in Abkhazia proved to be incompatible with Russia's. As the war continued, Russian–Georgian relations deteriorated, and with them hopes for rebuilding Georgia's economy.

In July 1993, as the first anniversary of the outbreak of the war approached, Abkhazian forces launched an offensive to take Sukhumi. For a few days, the fate of the town was held in balance amid real fears that Sukhumi's defences would crumble. Shevardnadze, forecasting disaster, flew to the battlefields to urge the Georgians on – narrowly escaping injury in the process. In the end, the Abkhazians were unsuccessful, and were forced to draw back. The Sukhumi campaign was followed by a flurry of peacemaking attempts and on 27 July by an agreement between Georgian and Abkhazian representatives. The ceasefire accord, which was brokered by Russia, required the phased withdrawal of all troops from the war zone, and a gradual demilitarisation. It allowed for the return of Aardzinba and the other Abkhazian leaders to power and promised unspecified changes to Georgia's constitution, redefining the relationship with Abkhazia. For the first time in the former Soviet Union, it was to involve participation by UN peacekeepers once a ceasefire was secure.

Remarkably, the ceasefire held for several weeks although each side accused the other of violations and there were minor skirmishes. On 14 August, a year to the day since the Georgian invasion, government troops began to move back eastwards from Sukhumi. On the other side of the line, Abkhazian forces moved from positions near the Gumista river. The Chechen and other north Caucasian fighters handed in their arms and crossed back into Russia. The withdrawal was slow, and punctuated by Abkhazian accusations of a deliberate Georgian delay. Shevardnadze in turn issued alarmist statements about the situation, and urged the UN to send more observers to back up the eighty or so already en route.

The prospect of a total withdrawal from Abkhazia and Aardzinba's return to the parliament from which he had originally preached secession, were seen in Tbilisi as a capitulation. The Georgian parliament refused to vote on the peace package, forcing Shevardnadze to take the decision alone. It represented a personal snub to Shevardnadze, and one he could ill afford. His personal popularity was ebbing because of the economic situation, and two incidents earlier in the year had revealed the extent of opposition to him from within his own government. In January, Shevardnadze had had to deny widespread rumours that he had suffered a mild heart attack. A fortnight later, an article by Giorgi Chanturia accused Kitovani of plotting a coup that had been called off at the last minute. Together, the incidents were seen as a sign of Shevardnadze's weakness.

In May, Shevardnadze tried to reassert his authority by sacking Kitovani, and easing Ioseliani out of power when the military council was disbanded. In seeking to impress his authority on the military and polish his nationalist credentials at a stroke, Shevardnadze chose as defence minister a 26-year-old national guardsman. Giorgi Karkarashvili had won notoriety by publicly advocating the use of genocide to end the war in Abkhazia. If 100,000 had to die for a Georgian victory, then so be it, he declared. Kitovani did not readily accept his removal; he remained lurking in the wings, offering his services to the war effort should Georgia's fortunes not improve. In July 1993, Shevardnadze accepted assistance from the Central Intelligence Agency in setting up a security network. The next month, Fred Woodruff, a US diplomat identified later by American newspapers and officials as a CIA agent, was shot dead outside Tbilisi while travelling in a car with Shevardnadze's security chief. American officials hastened to describe the incident as a chance killing, an explanation which failed to satisfy widespread curiosity.

It was the desperation of his own and the country's position that pushed Shevardnadze into a treaty from which Georgia gained nothing after months of war. In the following days, he embarked on a series of changes that appeared to reflect his hope that the peace agreement for Abkhazia would prove some kind of turning point. On 20 August, Shevardnadze appointed a new prime minister, an industrialist from the rebel stronghold of Zugdidi, Otar Patsatsia. Observers saw the move as an attempt to placate Gamsakhurdia's supporters. But the departure of the previous prime minister, Tengiz Sigua, also signalled a final break with the troika which had brought Shevardnadze to power, the two military men, Ioseliani and Kitovani, having been dispatched earlier. Three days after the appointment of Patsatsia, Shevardnadze met Yeltsin in Moscow and expressed confidence that Russia and Georgia would be able to sign a co-operation treaty in September.

But Shevardnadze's efforts to put his imprimatur on Georgia could not of themselves guarantee his political survival or his country's recovery. On 14 September, Shevardnadze tried to press home his campaign of change by asking parliament to disband for three months and approve a two-month state of emergency to allow him to crack down hard on a resurgence by Gamsakhurdia loyalists in the west, and on the criminal gangs that plagued Tbilisi. Parliament balked at ceding such sweeping powers, and Shevardnadze got their agreement only by walking out of the uproarious session and threatening to resign. Two days later, disaster struck.

With the bulk of the Georgian troops withdrawn from Abkhazia, the separatists launched a new and merciless offensive. Shevardnadze flew to Sukhumi to try to raise the morale of the defenders. But the Abkhazians pushed on, pinning down the Georgians in hand-to-hand fighting. In the closing days of battle, they tightened their siege of the town, shooting down planes sent to evacuate civilians, and forcing Shevardnadze into an ignominious retreat. Sukhumi fell on 27 September, a catastrophe the Georgian leader blamed squarely on the Russian defence minister, Pavel Grachev, who had refused to come to his aid. He repeated his charges that the Russian military was aiding the Abkhazian leadership at Gudauta. 'The evil empire is still thriving, still sowing seeds of death', he wrote in a letter to the United Nations Secretary-General Boutros Boutros Ghali. 'Who stands behind this clique, who finances it, provides for and supervises it?'

Although Shevardnadze returned to Tbilisi, vowing that Sukhumi would again belong to Georgia 'if not in this generation, then in the next', he behaved even more like a hunted man. With the Mingrelian uprising revitalised by the return of Zviad Gamsakhurdia (ostensibly to commit his forces to the defence of Sukhumi), defeat seemed to be closing in around him. On 8 October, he shamefacedly announced that Georgia would join the Commonwealth of Independent States, arguing that there was no future for the country so long as it remained alienated from Russia.

It was a last-ditch attempt at salvation. The nationalist imperative had betrayed the world statesman. With the departure of Abkhazia a reality, and the loss of Mingrelia a real possibility, Shevardnadze's and Georgia's own futures had never seemed so insecure. The institutions that were disregarded by Gamsakhurdia had not revived under his successor. The real power in the country was not vested in the parliament, bureaucracy, or courts, but in the paramilitary groups before whom Shevardnadze was newly vulnerable after the catastrophic defeat in Abkhazia. Focusing on the threat to Georgian territory embodied in the Abkhazian secession campaign had seemed a useful distraction for the country's ills. Unfortunately, it led to a war from which Shevardnadze was unable to extricate himself. And it wounded Georgia so deeply that it was forced to embrace the power that had brought about its downfall.

Notes

1. Reuters, 13 October 1992.

2. Allen, W.E.D. (1932), *A History of the Georgian People from the Beginning down to the Russian Conquest in the Nineteenth Century*, Paul, London, p. 282.

3. Alexeyeva, Lyudmilla (1985), *Soviet Dissent: Contemporary Movements for National, Regional and Human Rights*, Wesleyan University Press, p. 106.

4. Suny, Ronald Grigor (1989), *The Making of the Georgian Nation*, I.B. Tauris, London, p. 290.

5. Amnesty International (1975), *Chronicle of Current Events, Journal of the Human Rights Movement in the USSR*, London, No. 38, December.

6. Amnesty International (1978), *Chronicle of Current Events, Journal of the Human Rights Movement in the USSR*, London, No. 50, November.

7. Nahaylo, Bohdan and Swoboda, Viktor (1990), *Soviet Disunion: A History of the Nationalities Problem in the USSR*, Hamish Hamilton, London, p. 189.

8. *Moscow News*, March 1992.

9. Aves, Jonathan (1991), 'Paths to Independence in Georgia, 1987-1990', unpublished paper, School of Slavonic and Eastern European Studies, London, p. 13.

10. Ibid., p. 28.

11. Lakoba, S.Z., 'On the political problems of Abkhazia', *Central Asia and Caucasus Chronicle*, March 1990.

6

Azerbaijan:
Still Not Free

It was just about midnight when one of the sleekest and most senior advisers to the Azerbaijani president, Ayaz Mutalibov, arrived at the flat in Baku where foreign journalists were congregating. He wore jeans, carried a bottle of gin and was evidently on a mission of great urgency. He had worked side by side with Mutalibov for months, but now he was anxious to be heard denouncing him. Mutalibov, the official said, was a traitor. He had sold the country to the communist forces of Moscow, and could never be trusted or forgiven. The adviser's outburst followed a day of changes. It was March 1992, Mutalibov was in danger of being overthrown, and his associates were looking out to save themselves. This one did not know who would eventually emerge from the current power struggle, but he strongly suspected it would be best to switch sides.

Once he had established his nationalist credentials with the foreign press and the drinks began to take hold, the official relaxed enough to name the man he really wanted to take over: Heydar Aliyev. It was a strange choice. Aliyev was in political purdah. Once the most powerful Muslim in the Soviet Union, he had been sacked in disgrace by Gorbachev in 1987, and was licking his wounds in his native region of Nakhichevan, an enclave on the Iranian and Turkish borders entirely cut off from Azerbaijan by Armenia. There, he had become chairman of parliament. Now approaching 70, he didn't look like a winner. But the adviser was insistent. 'Heydar Aliyev, honestly, he's the only man for the job.' He argued that Aliyev would be a good leader because, unlike Mutalibov, he wasn't a communist apparatchik. One of the journalists spluttered into his drink. Aliyev, a protégé of Brezhnev, former chief of the Azeri KGB, first secretary of the republican Communist Party, deputy Soviet premier and third man in the Soviet Politburo, and not an apparatchik? No, the bureaucrat repeated, Aliyev had changed. How did he know? He knew. Sure enough, fifteen months later he was proved right. Heydar Aliyev, once condemned to obscurity, had emerged as the most trusted politician in Azerbaijan. Ordinary men and women saw him as a saviour during a time of crisis, and he became the country's leader.

Of all the upheavals that have shaken the Caucasus during the first two years of independence, Azerbaijan experienced the most bewildering political shifts: electing a communist apparatchik before disposing of him in a coup, and then a dissident nationalist, before plumping for an old-style Brezhnevite in Aliyev. While the rise and fall of both Ayaz Mutalibov, the first president, and Abulfaz Elchibey, the second, were bound up with the government's conduct of the war against Armenia over Nagorno-Karabakh, the shifts reveal Azerbaijan's attenuated transition towards multi-party politics. Observers believed at the time that Mutalibov's overthrow represented a bloodless revolution, the final casting off of the old colonial relationship with Russia. A year later, they saw Moscow's hand in Elchibey's removal, and the beginnings of a new separatist movement in southern Azerbaijan, evidence of its desire to keep the oil-rich country unstable and within its orbit.

Struggle to break away

Like Georgians, for whom the crushing of a protest in Tbilisi on 9 April 1989 became a turning point in moves towards independence, there is for Azeris a single instance of Soviet brutality that crystallised years of petty oppression. For Azerbaijan, the moment of realisation was in Baku in January 1990. For Armenians, the date is inextricably associated with the rampages against Armenian homes and shops that drove them out of the city for good. The Azerbaijani interpretation focuses on what came after: the entry into Baku of Soviet interior ministry troops, and the suppression of the main threat to communist authority, the Azerbaijani Popular Front. To this day, many Azerbaijanis believe that the pogroms against the Armenians were the result of KGB provocations, a bloody sideshow intended to destroy any centres of opposition to the communist government.

The Popular Front was founded in July 1989, in part to pressurise the communist authorities to resist more forcefully Armenian claims on Nagorno-Karabakh. The group, loosely knit and relying on existing regional and clan loyalties, grew massively popular. It regularly commanded crowds of hundreds of thousands in Baku, filling Lenin Square, the vast space that yawned between the two Intourist hotels in the centre of the city. In the summer and autumn of 1989, the Front organised a series of strikes leading to an economic embargo against the enclave and Armenia. Until that point, the Azeri government, like its counterpart in Georgia, had made little attempt to accommodate emerging unofficial groups. The blockade, and the ensuing tension, forced it to recognise the Popular Front and to enter into negotiations with its leader, the former political prisoner Abulfaz Elchibey. Elchibey called off the blockade in return for the granting of official recognition for his movement.

As in Armenia, the Karabakh agitation turned into a wider struggle for power. From questions of territory, the Popular Front embraced concerns like ecological damage, lack of democracy, free speech and independence. By the end of the year, the Azerbaijani Communist Party had lost much of its authority, and it looked as if it would be defeated in the multi-party elections scheduled for March 1990. Then on 11 January 1990, members of the Popular Front occupied the police station in the town of Lenkoran, a city on the Caspian Sea close to the Iranian border, to protest at the government's handling of Nagorno-Karabakh. Two days later, hundreds of thousands of people attended a front rally in Baku where speakers called for the resignation of the republic's first secretary, Abdul Rahman Vezirov, and for a referendum on Azerbaijan's secession from the Soviet Union. Some of the people at the rally then joined in horrific attacks on the few thousand Armenians remaining in Baku (there had been more than 200,000 when the Karabakh dispute began in 1988) although the violence was allegedly led by Azeri refugees who had been forcibly expelled from Armenia and Karabakh two years earlier. On 18 January, the Azerbaijani Popular Front declared that it had taken power in Azerbaijan.

The next night, the Soviet army moved into Baku and 160 Azerbaijanis were believed killed in the wave of repression that followed. Martial law was declared, Popular Front leaders arrested, and the elections postponed. The timing of the deployment of the Soviet troops remains controversial to this day. Armenians detected a degree of malice in their late arrival, seeing it as a deliberate ploy to ensure that they were 'taught a lesson' for the boldness of their demands for Karabakh. For their part, it continues to rankle with Azerbaijanis that their democracy movement was crushed on the pretext of protecting the Armenian minority. The appalling attacks on Armenians had ceased by 14 January, days before the troops actually arrived. For the Azeris the tragedy was compounded by the fact that their aspirations for independence were linked indelibly to the inhuman actions, tarnishing their cause and their national identity in the eyes of the world. Soon after the crackdown, the discredited first secretary, Vezirov, was replaced by Ayaz Mutalibov. He was a technocrat rather than a career politician. An oil engineer and a jazz enthusiast, he was seen as a capable administrator. There were changes too in the opposition ranks. Some more moderate elements of the Popular Front were hived off to form the Azerbaijani Social Democratic Group.

When elections eventually were held in September, martial law was still in force and the atmosphere in Azerbaijan was extremely tense. The Azerbaijani Communist Party secured an overwhelming majority, and the Popular Front and its offshoots were limited to forty of the 350 seats in the house, and those mainly in Baku. The democrats alleged that there had been widespread fraud, and even Mutalibov himself conceded to reporters later that there had been irregularities. So despite evidence of the popularity of the democracy activists in the massive street protests months earlier, they were denied representation in parliament and kept away from any real power.

As first secretary, Mutalibov was conservative in the extreme. He gave no quarter to those who wanted Azerbaijan to move towards independence. Instead, he sought to mollify the more chauvinistic strands of Azeri popular opinion by making large tracts of northern Azerbaijan 'Armenian-free', deporting entire villages and towns. During the August 1991 putsch against Mikhail Gorbachev he was in Iran, where he was quoted by Western news agencies as welcoming the coup as 'the natural consequence of the policies that have brought chaos into the Soviet Union over the past few years'. The statement made him one of the only republican leaders openly to support the Moscow emergency committee. In an attempt to restore the initiative after the coup failed, Mutalibov called an emergency session of the parliament at which he announced his resignation from the Communist Party. The next day, on 30 August 1991, Azerbaijan declared independence. It was an empty gesture. By that point, it was becoming clear that the Soviet Union was on the verge of collapse and that the conservative forces with which Mutalibov had aligned himself were in eclipse.

After he was elected president in the single-candidate polls of 8 September, Mutalibov struggled to acquire some nationalist credentials – but without much conviction. Soon after his installation, he was forced by a series of boycotts and endless arguments to expand representation for the Popular Front by creating a fifty-member national council, split between parliamentary deputies and the opposition. It began to supplant the role of the existing parliament, serving as the main chamber for debate between the government and the opposition. Under pressure from the Popular Front, Mutalibov moved – albeit slowly and reluctantly – to create an Azerbaijani armed forces in the autumn of 1991. However, he enraged the Popular Front at the end of the year by committing Azerbaijan to the Commonwealth of Independent States despite a unanimous 'no' vote in the National Council.

The unfinished revolution

In late 1991 and January 1992, Azerbaijan transformed the conflict in Karabakh from guerrilla raids to all-out war by launching an intense bombardment of the Armenian capital of Stepanakert. But the Azeri forces were unprepared for a counter-attack in late February and fled before the troops advancing on the town of Agdam, their military headquarters six miles outside the enclave. Along the way, the Armenians overran the village of Khojali and as evidence emerged that they had committed massacres against civilians, a mighty wave of anger built up in Baku. The entire city seemed convulsed by rage. Elderly women approached me on the street, pulling newspapers out of their shopping bags and stabbing shaking fingers at the headlines. They were consumed by grief and anger and desperate to explain the extent of their loss.

At first, Mutalibov and the interior ministry downplayed reports of atrocities in a badly judged attempt at concealment. But the mood of public anger steadily grew, venting itself in demonstrations of tens of thousands in the heart of the city, and in calls for Mutalibov's resignation. On 6 March, while war widows raged and wept before the huge crowds of demonstrators and while baying mobs surrounded the parliament, Mutalibov was forced to step down, making way for an interim leader, Yakub Mamedov. The old communist parliament was dissolved and all of its power transferred to the national council pending fresh parliamentary and presidential elections.

Two days later, I went to visit Elchibey, at the offices of his Popular Front, on the shaded square where a monument recalls the twenty-six Baku Commissars, the mainly Armenian Bolshevik martyrs of the revolution. After the furious demonstrations demanding Mutalibov's resignation, the city was relatively calm. People still bristled at mention of Khojali, but there was a remarkable lack of curiosity over who would now lead the country. Elchibey, thin and frail but suffused with nervous energy, sat at his desk reading a copy of the Turkish paper, *Hurriyet*. For him, the debacle in Karabakh was of lesser import than the opportunity Mutalibov's departure presented for reworking an essentially colonial relationship with Russia. 'The most important question is how the democratic movement in Azerbaijan is progressing and the situation in the Caucasus. That has got to be the main question. Karabakh, South Ossetia and Abkhazia are internal arguments,'

Elchibey said. 'We haven't got our own government. We are a colony of Russia. Mutalibov resigned because he was the worst example of someone who was completely in the hands of Russia. He was frightened of them.'

Despite Mutalibov's flight to Moscow, little changed in the government. Yakub Mamedov, the interim president, disappointed the expectation among the Popular Front and other democratic groups that they would be included in the new government by refusing to appoint them to ministerial portfolios. Meanwhile, the Armenians capitalised on success after success, capturing Shusha, the last major Azeri-held town in Karabakh in May. In the panic that followed, Mutalibov attempted to lead a constitutional coup and cancel the elections. Within forty-eight hours, he was forced to flee once more after Popular Front members seized the television centre and the parliament building. Isa Gambarov, a Popular Front leader, was made acting president.

The elections took place as scheduled on 7 June, but again amid extreme tension. Demonstrations were banned, and one popular leader, the National Independence Party president Ittebar Mamedov, withdrew from the ballot in protest. Another potential rival to Elchibey, Heydar Aliyev, was barred from the contest by an age barrier, setting the upper limit for candidates at 65. As in Georgia and Armenia, there was little to distinguish the candidates save their approach to minority rights. All advocated Azerbaijan's withdrawal from the CIS and the necessity of market reforms; all considered Karabakh to be the most pressing problem, but while some candidates favoured a military solution, Elchibey argued for settling the conflict through negotiation. Elchibey emerged with 59 per cent of the vote, doing well in areas bordering Karabakh as well as in Baku and Sumgait. His nearest rival, scientist Nizami Suleymanov of the Democratic Union of the Intelligentsia of Azerbaijan, polled 20 per cent. Interim president Yakub Mamedov, representing the old communist-style bureaucracy, came in third. Voter turnout was reported at 74 per cent.

Elchibey's greatest asset as president was his reputation for integrity, which has assumed almost legendary proportions. It was acquired during the Brezhnev era, when he was one of the few Amnesty International prisoners of conscience in Azerbaijan. Born in 1938 in the border region of Nakhichevan, which has produced a disproportionate share of Azeri leaders, he studied Arabic at university and worked for a short time as an interpreter in Cairo. During the election campaign, he told journalists that he had returned from Egypt without any money, forcing his wife and two children to move in with relatives. 'I thought it immoral to make money in a poor country. So I gave everything I earned to poor people in Cairo', he told *Moscow News*. In 1975, he was dismissed from his teaching job at Baku State University and jailed for anti-Soviet slander. Following his release in 1977, Elchibey worked in the manuscripts section of the Azerbaijani Academy of Sciences. He was jailed again in 1990, in the aftermath of the crackdown on democracy protesters. The experience was said to have deeply scarred him psychologically and to have caused his gaunt, almost tubercular, appearance.

But despite his outstanding personal qualities, Elchibey had absolutely no experience of government. Aside from his stated commitment to democracy, he had a powerful affinity for all things Turkish and an idealistic notion of the brotherhood of Turkic peoples. He also harboured a romantic yearning for the unification of the two Azerbaijans – the former Soviet republic and the Iranian region centred on Tabriz. Elchibey saw Azerbaijan as the product of the cross-fertilisation of Turkish and Iranian culture. His vision was an antidote to the confusion seventy years of communism had created about national identity. It is only within the last century that Azerbaijanis have seen themselves as a nation, creating a vulnerability that Armenians have exploited with devastating effect in their arguments about historic claims to Karabakh. Azeri identity remains fragile, and has been cosseted in recent years by elaborate reconstructions of architectural monuments in some areas of Baku. While Elchibey gloried in this rich native culture, he accorded little importance to religion, dismissing the fears of Western observers of an Iranian-style Islamic revolution. But while such ideals were necessary during the struggle for democracy, they were difficult to reconcile with the requirements of administration. Elchibey's idealism, and the inspiration he took from Turkic sources, also made the former communists in the republic extremely nervous. They continued to look towards Russia for direction.

Elchibey's original government reflected these facts, exhibiting a degree of continuity with the old regime, but ushering in a member of the Popular Front's radical right. He named Rahim Gaziev, who had been a defence minister under Mutalibov, as prime minister and defence minister, and handed the critical internal affairs ministry to Iskander Hamidov, who had links with the fascist Grey Wolves of Turkey. Other portfolios were shared out among members of the Popular Front, the Social Democrats and other allies. It was not a happy combination. There was resistance to moves towards a market economy from former communists and the directors of state enterprises. On one occasion, Elchibey had to step in to veto a bill that would have made a mockery of attempts to expand trade by imposing crippling taxes on profit. Gradually Elchibey tried to expand his control over the government by edging out representatives from the old regime – but that left him without any experienced personnel and made the government vulnerable to errors. On the war front, meanwhile, Hamidov was unashamedly stoking anti-Armenian feeling by issuing blood-curdling threats. He told reporters in December 1992 that Azerbaijan would fire nuclear missiles on Karabakh should the Armenians 'fail to come to their senses'.[1] Despite his sabre-rattling, Azerbaijani forces were unable to turn around a series of defeats, even though a call-up of youths had been ordered in September, and new defence ministers appointed.

In Nakhichevan, meanwhile, Heydar Aliyev lay in wait. Since his elevation to parliamentary chairman in the wake of the August 1991 coup, he had deliberately cultivated a power base in his home republic following his public humiliation by Gorbachev. As first secretary of the Azerbaijan Communist Party from 1969 to 1982, Aliyev, like his contemporary in Georgia, Eduard Shevardnadze, had acquired a reputation as an anti-corruption campaigner. He enjoyed Brezhnev's patronage, and induced him to visit the republic on three occasions. In 1982, Yuri Andropov made him deputy premier and a full member of the Politburo. His fall started soon after Gorbachev took control in the spring of 1985, and questions began to be raised about the true nature of his tenure as the Republican Party first secretary in Azerbaijan. Aliyev was put in charge of transport but was soon attacked for his inefficiency. A year later, despite rising criticism from Gorbachev of leaders who had permitted themselves to become objects of adulation, Aliyev had a bronze bust of himself installed in Nakhichevan. He dropped from public view in May 1987 amid unconfirmed reports that he had suffered a serious heart attack, and was retired on a pension on the grounds of ill health in the autumn. However, Soviet newspapers said he had been sacked for gross corruption. A leading anti-mafia campaigner, Arkady Vaksberg, told reporters that Aliyev had hounded officials who sought to reveal corruption when he was Azerbaijani party chief and in one case had had an investigator executed on trumped-up charges. He was also accused of having faked his service record in order to avoid being sent to the front in the Second World War. Aliyev consistently denied the charges.

He resurfaced in January 1990, when he appeared at a Moscow rally to denounce Gorbachev for ordering troops into Baku, and resigned from the Communist Party. Aliyev then made a heroic return to Baku as an anti-communist Azerbaijani nationalist. Regarded as suspect by the communist apparatus he once controlled in Baku, Aliyev set up camp in Nakhichevan. There, he used his clan links to rebuild his popularity, drawing on old acquaintances to increase the territory's importance and, subsequently, his own. He was elected to the territory's parliament in September 1990. A year later, as parliamentary chairman, he did not bother to wait for the collapse of the union before he abolished the old Soviet holidays and presided over the introduction of the Latin alphabet to replace the Cyrillic script. He was in regular contact with Iran and Turkey, enjoying increasing freedom of action from the authorities in Baku. He opened the borders to both neighbours, signed treaties of co-operation and won promises of foreign aid. Iran in particular was pleased at Aliyev's overtures, feeling excluded from positions of influence in Baku because of Elchibey's unabashed preference for Turkey. Although Aliyev's relations with Elchibey were cool from the start, he did not come into direct conflict with the government in Baku until Popular Front forces tried to rein him in. On 24 October 1992, local Popular Front activists tried to seize control of government buildings and stage a coup in Nakhichevan, but they were forced to retreat. Understandably, Aliyev's relations with Elchibey deteriorated sharply after that. One month later, Aliyev founded his own political party called the New Azerbaijan Party, which committed itself to a market economy but, even more interestingly, to guaranteeing the rights of the Russian, Lezgin, Talysh, Kurdish and other minorities, who were growing fearful of the fiery rhetoric of leaders like Hamidov. Aliyev, on the other hand, promised stability, and a return to the relative prosperity of the 1970s.

It was a prospect that seemed increasingly alluring as the Elchibey government struggled to cope with rampant inflation and the new evil of unemployment. Its failings, military and economic, soon became glaringly obvious, and Elchibey's personal probity could not compensate for a government still infected by the clannishness and corruption of past regimes. The government became increasingly repressive, moving against newspapers and other sources of criticism. By the beginning of 1993, Aliyev, and a man half his age, the army commander Suret Husseinov, were emerging as centres of opposition to the government. In January, the Itar-Tass news agency carried an interview with Aliyev where he boasted that he was 'full of strength and energy, and ready to give all my strength to lead my people out of the disastrous situation in which they find themselves'. The offer of an experienced hand at the helm became more appealing in April after fresh humiliations in the war, this time the capture of territory lying outside Karabakh. Later that month, there were large protests in Gyandzha following the appointment of Panakh Husseinov as prime minister. Husseinov, a youngish history graduate who had been a founder of the Popular Front, was to have been given considerable independence to try to speed the country towards a market economy. The rallies were presided over by Aliyev's new-found ally, Suret

Husseinov. The protesters called for the prime minister – and the entire government – to be sacked.

Stability – at a price

Although discontent with the Elchibey government had been rising for some time, once the crucial moment arrived it took just two weeks to get rid of him. It began with a confrontation in Gyandzha, Azerbaijan's second city, between the authorities and rebel troops led by Suret Husseinov. Husseinov had been a member of the Popular Front and the commander of the Azeri army's second corps. He won national acclaim in 1992 in Karabakh, where his division scored substantial victories over the Armenians in the Agdere (or Mardakert, to the Armenians) region. In a war fought without the benefit of a unified national command, he had won the loyalty of his men by his ability to keep them well-fed and shod. The manager of a textile factory, he had amassed a great deal of wealth and was revered in his hometown of Gyandzha, where local people called him 'our president'. But he encountered later defeats and in February was dismissed over his unilateral decision to withdraw from the Kelbadzhar area south-west of the enclave, allowing it to be overrun by Armenian forces. Husseinov's sacking was part of a wider re-organisation of the Azeri army which saw the dismissal of Rahim Gaziev, who was defence minister as well as his personal patron. With Gaziev's removal, Husseinov had little hopes of a reprieve and, enraged by his treatment, retreated with his troops to Gyandzha, about 190 miles west of Baku.

According to Ali Karimov, who held the pivotal post of cabinet secretary in the Elchibey government, Husseinov was ordered five times to return to the front line in between his flight in February and the start of his rebellion on 4 June. But he defied these orders, building a force of up to 1,000 men. Many of Husseinov's soldiers were ethnic Russians, mercenaries who had chosen to defect from the large Russian army base at Gyandzha, Karimov said. Husseinov also arranged to buy weapons stocks from the Russian troops who were supposed to have been entirely withdrawn from Gyandzha by 25 May. The stand-off between the Elchibey administration and the rebel troops came to a head when the then defence minister, Dadash Rzayev, ordered government troops into Gyandzha. Somewhat ingenuously, Elchibey officials maintain that they were not anticipating violence. Troops were sent in only as a form of 'psychological pressure', according to Karimov.

The government forces proceeded to try to disarm the rebels, provoking a five-hour gun-battle in which at least seventy people were

killed before the government forces withdrew. The rebels also kidnapped four senior officials sent to engage them in negotiations for the
surrender of the seized weapons: the prosecutor general, a first deputy
security minister, a deputy interior minister and a top army commander. President Elchibey went on national television to apologise
to families of the victims, accusing the rebels of using civilians as
human shields. Husseinov replied that the government was responsible
for the bloodshed and that all of its members should quit, including
Elchibey. He also expressed support for Heydar Aliyev, and urged that
he return to power.

Two days after the initial clash, on Sunday 6 June, the stand-off
erupted into violence again, with ten people killed. Husseinov said he
was setting up a military tribunal to try the men seized on 4 June.
'These men led the operation. They must therefore be punished', he
declared at a news conference. Meanwhile, Aliyev had arrived in Baku
from Nakhichevan at the invitation of Elchibey, who had hoped that
his presence would calm the situation. He began to act as a go-between
for the government and the rebel camps in an attempt to defuse the
situation. But despite his public attempts at conciliation, in private
Aliyev began to wage a campaign against the dwindling authority of
the government. While Elchibey worked feverishly to calm the situation, Aliyev met foreign diplomats and international oil executives,
promoting an image of himself as the saviour of the country. However,
he was careful. He made no direct attempt to remove Elchibey himself, mindful of the flight of foreign oil industry personnel and the
statements of support from the United States and other countries for
the 'government of the democratically elected president'.

Seeking an escape from the confrontation, Elchibey secured the
resignation of his unpopular though relatively new prime minister,
Panakh Husseinov. The job was offered to Aliyev in the hope that this
would placate him and dilute the force of Suret Husseinov's demand
for the resignation of the entire government. Aliyev refused the prime
ministership which, as in other former republics, was restricted largely
to economic matters. On 11 June, parliament offered an amnesty to
the leader of the rebel citadel in Gyandzha and his followers, saying
no one would be punished. There were further efforts to appease
Husseinov and Aliyev. On 13 June, the parliamentary chairman, Isa
Gambarov, resigned. That cleared the way for the more important post
to be offered to Aliyev. Two days later, the parliament chose him as its
chairman. Though Aliyev referred repeatedly to Elchibey as his 'host',
it was clear that he had now seized control of the government. He told
parliament immediately after his election that he would seek to end
the war with Armenia as soon as possible, but demanded that Armenia

return all of the seized Azeri territory. He appealed to Husseinov to end his revolt, and gave his word that he would not be punished.

Initially at least, Husseinov appeared unimpressed by Aliyev's elevation and promises. His troops continued to drift towards the capital, drawing within fifty miles of Baku. There was heavy fighting at a few towns along the way, and government troops dug fortifications at one point along the Gyandzha–Baku road, but mostly the rebels just melted into the towns and villages unopposed. At each stop along the route, the Popular Front mayors were sacked and former communists installed in their place. Elsewhere, Armenian forces were taking advantage of the disarray in Azerbaijan to plot their offensive against Agdam, the crucial staging post of the war about six miles east of Karabakh.

On 18 June, when the troops were about ten miles from Baku, Elchibey fled to Nakhichevan, and his hometown of Ordubad. He portrayed his flight as an act of self-sacrifice, saying he wanted to avoid any further bloodshed. However, army commanders had told him that they would not oppose Husseinov's advance. Although he had left Baku, Elchibey clearly had every hope that he could negotiate a solution to the crisis. He did not resign, ensuring that whoever tried to supplant him would find it difficult to legitimise their actions, and continued to claim that he was the legally elected president. 'Only the people can remove me from power by means of a referendum,' he told reporters. There seemed initially to be some concurrence from watching countries. Turkey, the EC and the US all indicated that they would continue to regard Elchibey as the country's legitimate ruler, although Aliyev immediately declared that he was in charge. But already an element of suspicion had emerged in the unfolding of events. In a statement distributed to the Turkish press only days after his flight, Elchibey accused foreign interests of backing Husseinov's revolt, and suggested that they were pursuing a larger prize than the presidency of Azerbaijan. 'The aim of the rebels is to bring the former communists to power. Against this, our aim is to pursue the ideal of an independent Azerbaijan at the cost of our lives.' Although the fugitive president declined to name the foreign interest groups, it was evident that he believed Russia to be seeking his overthrow.

Three days after Elchibey's departure, Husseinov's men reached the outskirts of Baku. After all the panic and excitement of the previous fortnight, it was a bit of a non-event. Bands of men drifted off from the main force towards kebab shops on the edge of town; others, village lads, were simply mesmerised by the sight of the big city and drifted off to sight-see. In some parts of Baku, the rebels were greeted with kisses or cheers, but by and large their arrival was met with indifference. Although there were reports of gunfire, there was no organised resistance. While the parliament continued to meet in emergency session, and appealed to Elchibey to resign or return, the rebels waited. Husseinov remained in Gyandzha.

On 22 June, he stated directly for the first time that he wanted Aliyev to step aside so that he could assume the post of president. 'A power vacuum has been created and the reality of today's situation does not allow the chairman of parliament to take responsibility on himself', he told a press conference. 'So I am obliged to take all responsibilities and powers on myself.' There was no direct reply from Aliyev but on 25 June, that vacuum was filled when the national council voted by a large majority to strip Elchibey of his duties. The vote strengthened Aliyev's claim to be acting head of state. He received further help from an unexpected quarter with news of another military defeat in Karabakh. The loss on 28 June of Agdere, effectively the last Azeri settlement in Karabakh, had a sobering effect on Husseinov's ambitions. The new urgency of the situation demanded unity and two days later Husseinov formally renounced his presidential ambitions and took on the post of prime minister.

As an inducement the job had been tailor-made to his demands for more power, embracing the defence, interior and security ministries as well as economics. The first act of the new regime was to announce a nationwide call-up of all Azeri males over the age of 18, and to attempt to unify the armed forces. In a significant display of the new government's loyalties, Rahim Gaziev, who had been sacked as defence minister by Elchibey, was returned to the post. A new state secretary, a woman, was imported from Moscow. But Husseinov's momentary capitulation in no way signalled a permanent cessation of the rivalry between him and Aliyev. On the very day of Husseinov's accession, a reporter asked Aliyev who was now in charge in Azerbaijan. Aliyev roared back: 'You have to know that I have not transferred all my powers to Suret Husseinov.'

The calm reception given to the rebels was indicative of the deep depression that had hung over the country for the last three years. Since the brutal repression of the Popular Front in January 1990, many ordinary Azeris had grown more fearful and more cynical about the political process. The insurgents also struck a chord of sympathy among those who were unimpressed by Elchibey's performance and the record of his Popular Front leadership. Under Aliyev, some measures of stability returned. Despite lingering support for Elchibey from Turkey and other countries, negotiations with foreign companies for development of the offshore oil fields resumed. But Azerbaijan's performance in Karabakh was disastrous.

Moreover, it became evident that the government was resorting to repression to stifle opponents. Protests against the new regime were inevitably put down with the use of armed troops. Popular Front activists whispered among themselves of a 'political terror' after several Saturday demonstrations in support of Elchibey were broken up by force, with mass arrests and beatings and the harassment of journalists. Diplomats in Baku reported signs of a return to press censorship with the unexplained disappearance of the Popular Front newspaper. State-run television ceased carrying statements about Elchibey and resorted to broadcasting Soviet-era documentaries on Aliyev, describing him as a 'builder of modern Azerbaijan'. The offices of the Popular Front and other groups were ransacked and in July a number of Popular Front leaders, including Isa Gambarov and Panakh Husseinov, were detained on charges of organising coups and armed revolts. Aliyev retained control of Baku through such strong-arm measures, but pockets of the country, particularly in the west, remained loyal to Elchibey.

But the biggest threat to Aliyev came from within. It was clear even during the negotiations on a proposed power share that Husseinov harboured greater ambitions than the prime ministership. Although he and Aliyev had had a common purpose in removing Elchibey, their personal interests soon collided. The first signs of rivalry between Aliyev and Husseinov were seen in the upheaval that heralded the elder statesman's return to power. The challenge was couched as a secessionist movement in the south-west, launched at the beginning of June by the Talysh minority.

The Talysh are an Iranian people concentrated around Lenkoran and Astara on the Caspian Sea coast, speaking an Iranian rather than a Turkic language. Although they were counted at 21,000 in the 1989 census, this is thought to reflect a campaign of assimilation from the Soviet era, and their true numbers are believed to be ten times that. In June 1993, while the rebellion in Gyandzha was under way, a former Popular Front leader and a colonel in the Azerbaijani army, Ali Akram Hummatov, declared a separate republic of Talysh-Mugansk in Lenkoran port and seven other districts and set up border posts with Azerbaijan. Like Husseinov, Hummatov had been a favourite of the Mutalibov-era defence minister, Rahim Gaziev. And like Husseinov initially, he demanded as the price of ending his rebellion the resignation of the Azeri leader – in this case Aliyev – and the return to power of Mutalibov. The government claimed to have crushed the rebellion in August 1993, but though the Talysh uprising appeared short-lived it illustrated the fragile cords holding Azerbaijan together, and the ease with which the country could be carved up in the power struggles both among former communists and between former communists and democrats.

From the events of January 1990 onwards, Azerbaijanis viewed with great suspicion Moscow's intentions towards the region. For many observers, Russia's colonial interests did not vanish with the collapse of the Soviet Union – they simply went underground. According to this way of thinking, securing control of Azerbaijan continues to be a tenet of Russian foreign policy. The state's oil wealth and its proximity to Turkey – a perennial object of Russian mistrust – make it a coveted possession. Supporters of Elchibey, in exile in Nakhichevan, believe that both Husseinov and Aliyev are representatives of forces in Russia anxious to retain control over Azerbaijan. Though such intricate designs are impossible to prove, suspicion of Russian involvement in Azerbaijan's internal struggles is widespread. Moscow newspapers were matter-of-fact about the prospect of Russian involvement in the Gyandzha mutiny. At the time of the rebellion, the Russian forces were already supposed to have been withdrawn from Gyandzha. Although the clandestine movement of arms and supporters from the Russian armed forces to rebel groups has become normal in the Caucasus, Elchibey's supporters claim that the uprising was carefully timed to block a number of events on the horizon that would have guaranteed Azerbaijan's stability and, consequently, its independence from the Soviet Union. When the rebellion erupted, parliament was close to passing a new law that would have democratised the chamber. Mediators from the Conference on Security and Co-operation were close to securing the agreement of all parties to the conflict in Karabakh to a peace proposal that would have seen the withdrawal of Armenian troops from the Kelbadzhar region. At the end of June, Elchibey had been scheduled to visit London to sign a multi-million-pound agreement for offshore oil exploration with a five-member consortium that included British Petroleum. The deal, the biggest yet for Azerbaijan, was viewed as an important signal to foreign investors that the time was ripe to have confidence in the government in Baku.

Conspiracy theorists have also scented the hand of Iran in the upheavals of the summer of 1993. Aliyev, because of the contacts established in Nakhichevan, is said to have important allies in Tehran who preferred to see him in power rather than Elchibey. But while such theories remain unproven – no matter how realistic they seem – the coups and instability which have plagued independent Azerbaijan are an illustration of its halting and incomplete moves towards democratic politics.

As Aliyev acted to strengthen his position, public life in Azerbaijan began to slide back in time towards the era when he ruled as first secretary. With newspaper censorship restored, television strait-jacketed and photographs of the leader omnipresent, Aliyev declared a referendum to legitimise his rule in the eyes of foreign countries, and silence those who argued that Elchibey still maintained popular support. The vote on 29 August took place as an estimated 200,000 refugees fled before advancing Armenian troops to the Iranian border. The latest catastrophic defeat in Karabakh put Aliyev's claims of stability in sharp relief and he walked away with 97 per cent support in a turnout of 92 per cent on a question that asked whether people still had confidence in Elchibey.

As Azeri nationalists feared, Aliyev also began to move the country back into the Russian orbit. On 24 September Azerbaijan applied to rejoin the Commonwealth of Independent States, an about-turn that most Azeris believed was essential to prevent their country's dismemberment. On 3 October, still reeling from the shock of defeat in Karabakh, the beaten country gave Aliyev a final seal of approval in presidential elections. With an opposition boycott cutting the estimated turnout to less than half the electorate, Aliyev took 98.8 per cent of the vote. One of his two rivals had promised to make every Azeri a millionaire and to open a bank account for every child. It was an even more dramatic victory than that a year earlier of Eduard Shevardnadze, a republican Communist Party chief of similar vintage.

Although independent Georgia and Azerbaijan appeared to have embarked on similar trajectories, there were marked differences in the overthrow of the two elected leaders, the dissidents Zviad Gamsakhurdia and Elchibey. While the overthrow of Gamsakhurdia was more violent, it also came on the heels of widespread dissatisfaction with his government. There were weeks of protests against autocratic rule before force was used against Gamsakhurdia. In Azerbaijan, the removal of Elchibey was much more of an orchestrated affair. There was little pretence that the mutiny was being carried out on behalf of a stifled democratic movement. Instead, Husseinov cynically used the government's failed attempts to crush his rebellion to justify his grab for power. The result of the actions of Husseinov and Aliyev also do not augur well for Azerbaijan's stability.

Although, like Shevardnadze, Aliyev was immediately beset by civilian strife in the Talysh separatist campaign, he has not faced open conflict between former communists and democrats. Within the Georgian polity, all politicians have been forced to renounce their connections with the former Soviet government in order to achieve credibility. In Azerbaijan, despite Aliyev's posturing, there have been no serious efforts to establish nationalist or democratic credentials. The war in Karabakh continues to consume all Azerbaijan's national aspirations. Because of the failure of the war against the Armenians of Karabakh, the present government in Baku has been able to make palatable the fact that it is binding Azerbaijan ever closer to Russia and to the past.

Notes

1. Fuller, Elizabeth (1993), 'Transcaucasia: Ethnic strife threatens democratisation', *Radio Free Europe/Radio Liberty Research Report*, Vol. 2, No. 1.

7

Armenia: the Politics
of Exile

Yerevan. 8.45 a.m. I sit in the growing light by my hotel window. The lights, heat, and probably water too snapped off at eight, just as the beeps were coming through on the BBC time signal. How can people live like this, climbing nine flights of stairs by the aid of a cigarette lighter, as I did last night, groping down the hallway to find the right door. There is a steady indoor chill although it is relatively warm outside. Still, things are better than they were. Hakop told me that while I was away, Turkmenistan cut off the gas supplies altogether and he showed me the little white candle contraption which he had used to make tea in the dark. Like a fondue set. I don't know where people get their food from. There was nothing open last night.

In the Caucasus, one quickly accepts extraordinary conditions as normal. With the breakdown of civil society so widespread and total, it is difficult to imagine a time when violence and disruption were not a part of life. Even in Armenia, where the scale of human suffering under an Azerbaijani economic embargo has been so high, it is possible to forget that it has not always been so. After a short time away, it becomes difficult to conjure up the misery of the blockade which has been in place since November 1991.

I wrote the entry above in my notebook at the beginning of 1992, when the ring of steel around landlocked Armenia was tightening. Intended to put leverage on Yerevan to withhold support for the secessionist campaign in Nagorno-Karabakh, the blockade created an energy crisis that brought industry to a halt. Previously, Armenia had depended on imports for virtually all of its oil and gas, and all but 16 per cent had come from Azerbaijan. Even this portion was transported via Azerbaijan so that when Baku shut off its own taps, it was also able to halt supplies from Kazakhstan and Russia.

The blockade stripped Yerevan of all the comforts of the 20th century. The capital of more than a million people was forced to cope with no heat, no hot water, and rotating power cuts for twelve hours at a time. The city was as still and quiet as a cemetery. Mutilated tree trunks – the branches had been hacked down for firewood – served as its gravestones. Only in the new 'commercial shops', tiny tucked-away dens where tinned foods jostled with winter boots and perfume, were there any signs of economic life, and prices were prohibitive. It was no use fleeing from the cold indoors. The misery followed you in. The solid stone buildings trapped the freezing air inside on the sunniest and mildest of winter days. And so it continued for two long winters until, at the end of 1992, Armenia's President Levon Ter-Petrosian declared his country a disaster zone.

Endurance has been the Armenian legacy. In 1918, when the ancient nation got its first independent state, the country was known as the 'land of stalking death'. Famine, contagion and exposure scythed through the population, nearly half of whom were refugees, claiming 200,000 lives within a year. In vain, Armenian community newspapers in the United States appealed for pioneers to build up the land, and in late 1920 a desperate government in Yerevan inaugurated the Help Armenia Committee. A few months later, the country ceased to exist, and was swallowed whole by the emerging Soviet Union. Life in present-day Armenia is nowhere near as precarious, but it is certainly bleak. As during the first republic, many local Armenians have looked for help from their community abroad.

Though Soviet rule brought great economic improvements to Armenia – the smallest of all the former republics – the Azeri blockade has ensured that it is now undoubtedly the poorest. It has practically no natural resources. But while Georgia and Azerbaijan discarded their elected leaders, Zviad Gamsakhurdia and Abulfaz Elchibey, and descended into disorder soon after independence, Armenia remained stable and Ter-Petrosian, its elected leader, survived in office. Its stability remains all the more remarkable given the depths of the country's economic crisis, and the weight of nationalist opinion arrayed against the relatively moderate Ter-Petrosian.

The country has hidden strengths in the dispersal of the Armenian people, and in its ethnic make-up. Armenia has traditionally been the most homogenous republic of the entire Soviet Union, with at least 93 per cent of its population ethnically Armenian. The tiny Russian, Azeri and Kurdish minorities were never in a position to challenge Armenian supremacy as the Ossetians and Abkhazians did in Georgia, or as the Armenians themselves did in Azerbaijan over Nagorno-Karabakh. In Georgia, as in Azerbaijan, the autonomous status granted to minorities became the sources of division, a misfortune that Armenia was able to avoid. Since 1989, Armenia has become even more

ethnically 'pure' following the forced exodus of virtually the entire
Azerbaijani population, and the migration of Russians seeking better
economic conditions.

This combination of internal cohesion and external dispersal has
created a bond of ethnic solidarity that extends far beyond the country's borders. There are more Armenians living outside the republic
than within its boundaries. More than a million Armenians live in
other parts of the former Soviet Union, notably Russia, and Georgia
where they are concentrated in the border region. But there are also
sizeable Armenian communities in Central Asia. Even though Armenia is now independent, there is little likelihood that a great infolding
of the nation will reverse this outward trend because there is no viable
industry and little arable land. Instead, a secondary migration from the
Caucasus is under way with Armenians from war-riven Abkhazia and
volatile Chechnya leaving for the safety of southern Russian towns
like Stavropol and Krasnodar.

A community of exiles

The Armenians have always been a far more mobile population than
the Georgians or Azerbaijanis. Silk merchants, who were intermedi-
aries between the courts of the Russian tsars and the Persian shahs in
the 17th century, expanded their own mercantile empires as far away
as Calcutta and Rangoon. But the diaspora, known in Armenian as
the *espiurk*, is made up overwhelmingly of refugees. Most diaspora
families trace their roots to Western Armenia; what became known as
Soviet Armenia is in Eastern Armenia. The appellation is important,
denoting different dialects and customs, but more importantly different empires. The experiences accumulated by Armenians living under
different regimes on either side of their divided historic homeland
have left their imprint. By the close of the 19th century, the people
of Western Armenia, the far larger and more populous region, were
suffering extreme poverty and discrimination under Ottoman Turkish
rule. The persecution mounted in the 1890s, culminating in the 1915
genocide during which 1.5 million Armenians are thought to have
died. The Armenians of the Caucasus, though bridling at the restrictions of Tsarist rule, were at least assured of their physical security.

Today there are few traces of the Armenian presence in eastern
Anatolia – Armenians accuse the Turkish authorities of having wilfully
destroyed their villages and churches – but the region continues to
exert a powerful hold on the national consciousness. Over the years,
the diaspora has become the repository of memories of Turkish persecution, and nostalgia for the lost lands of Anatolia. In all three cen-

tres of the *espiurk* – North America, the Middle East and Europe – the Armenians have struggled for cultural survival. They have campaigned for greater recognition of their suffering at the hands of the Turks, and for the Ankara government to acknowledge the crimes of the past. Even after the children of the refugees joined the ranks of the middle-class professions, Armenians were assiduous in preserving their language and heritage. Charitable institutions founded to care for the destitute of Turkey at the beginning of the century evolved with the times and moved into fundraising for schools, churches and scholarships in places as far-flung as Argentina and Cyprus. Armenian diaspora communities have also been the guardians of pluralist political activity. While non-communist parties were suppressed in the motherland, they endured abroad, forming an unbroken link with the groupings that emerged in the Caucasus during the last century. In the US, party affiliation was largely a matter of habit, but in Lebanon, where before the civil war Armenians had comprised 6 per cent of the population and were guaranteed seats in parliament, the parties were influential.

In Baku, the Armenian diaspora is seen as a mighty force, a pressure group and a source of funds. Azeri politicians have attributed America's refusal to send aid to Azerbaijan pending a resolution of the war in Nagorno-Karabakh to the success of Armenian lobbyists in Washington. In response, Azerbaijan has tried to strengthen ties with its own dispersed community. There are fifteen million Azeris in Iran, where they are well integrated into the population, and about two million more in Turkey. The government-sponsored Azerbaijani Society for Cultural Relations with Countrymen Abroad has been allocated an elegant turn-of-the-century mansion in Baku. Staff sit in high-ceilinged pink rooms and beneath gilt chandeliers seeking donations from Azeri brethren abroad.

Although the diaspora has lent Armenia a certain stability, expectations over how much material support Yerevan can count on from the émigré community have been cruelly inflated. Because of the diaspora's focus on restitution for the genocide and because the majority of the diaspora has its roots in Turkey, the Caucasian territory was not able to compete against the powerful nostalgia for the lost lands. The politics of the Cold War and the unfamiliarity of Eastern Armenia to Western Armenians further reduced its significance as a symbol of national identity.

Even after the diaspora became involved in independent Armenia, there was a hidden sting. While there is no ethnic fault line in Armenia, exile politics have been integral to the dangerous and destabilising rift between the elected president, Ter-Petrosian, and hardline nationalists who oppose any compromise with Turkey. Although the immediate issue of contention between nationalists and moderates has been Karabakh, the divisions it has exposed between moderate and nationalist Armenians have been played out in the diaspora for more than a hundred years.

The first Armenian political parties to emerge in the Caucasus over a hundred years ago were all concerned with the situation in Turkey, and the disaster that befell Armenia in 1915 continues to motivate them. The Dashnaktsutiun, or Armenian Revolutionary Federation, was founded in 1890 at Tbilisi with a strongly nationalist and socialist orientation. The party formed the government of the Armenian republic from 1918 to 1920, when it was forced to observe the humiliating signing over of the formerly Armenian territories of Kars and Ardahan to Turkey. The recovery of these lands remain on the Dashnak agenda. Although it became fiercely anti-Bolshevik it nonetheless ran on Bolshevik lines, taking decisions in secret and presenting them to a rubber-stamp parliament. After Soviet rule was consolidated in Armenia in 1922, the Dashnaks were harshly repressed, and party leaders driven out or deported to punishment camps in Siberia. In exile, the party has been characterised by its fiercely anti-Soviet stance which has at times led fringe elements into surprising alliances – with Francoist forces in Spain and with the Nazis during the Second World War. After the war was over, the Dashnaks were staunchly pro-American, eager converts to Cold War ideology. Members took part in the propaganda broadcasts of Radio Liberty and Voice of America. But despite such practical alliances, officially the Dashnaktsutiun remained a socialist party. Following independence, the Dashnaks have been seeking ways of accommodating their professed socialism to an electorate grown deeply suspicious of the ideology.

The Dashnaks' main rival for the loyalty of the broader Armenian community was the Ramkavar Azatkan Kusaktsutiun. Created in October 1921 by the merger of two earlier liberal parties, the Ramkavar group represented the intelligentsia, although it was disparaged by more radical opponents as the mouthpiece of wealthy Armenians. It met irregularly and was mainly a pressure group. Unlike the Dashnaks, who were uncompromisingly pro-American, the Ramkavars maintained contacts with Soviet Armenia. Like the Armenian merchants of old, the Ramkavars believed in Russian protection, seeing it as a necessary bulwark against the Turks. They remained grateful to the Tsarist armies for rescuing Armenians from the massacres of 1915–16, and to the Bolsheviks for taking over the first republic and thwarting a Turkish invasion. Not having shared the Dashnaks' fate at the hands of the Bolsheviks, they were less categorical about dealings with the Soviet Union.

Although for younger generations of Armenians, membership in either the Ramkavars or Dashnaks was based on tradition rather than ideology, competition between the two groupings was intense. The division was maintained in all aspects of cultural life, leading to rival philanthropic groups, community organisations and occasionally inter-Armenian violence. Even national symbols like holidays and the tricolour flag from the short-lived republic were hotly contested. While the Dashnaks marked the anniversary of the Armenian declaration of independence in May 1918 as the national day, the Ramkavars marked 29 November, the anniversary of Armenia's deliverance from Turkish troops at the hands of the Red Army in 1920. While liberal Armenians patronised the Armenian General Benevolent Union (AGBU), founded in Cairo in 1906, the Dashnaks gave to the Armenian Relief Society which was founded in 1911. The two parties also carved out geographical spheres of influence. Ramkavars dominated in America during the first half of the century and Dashnaks in the Middle East. In Iran, Dashnaks had a virtual monopoly on party affiliation and held all the seats reserved for Armenians in the Lebanese parliament.

The rivalry between Ramkavar and Dashnak also poisoned the relationship between the two branches of the Armenian Apostolic Church: Echmiadzin, near Yerevan in Soviet Armenia, and Cilicia, near Beirut. While there are substantial numbers of Armenian Catholics and Protestants, the indigenous Church had served as a unifying national symbol since the 19th century. It had split in the fifteenth century but there was rarely conflict between the two sees until after the establishment of communist rule. During the Cold War, many diaspora Armenians were uncomfortable with the fact that the ultimate authority of their Church resided inside the Soviet Union. They suspected the church hierarchy of being a hostage of the communist regime. This suspicion was not unfounded; the Soviet attitude towards the Church was at times nakedly hostile. In 1938, the Echmiadzin Catholicos was swept up in the waves of purges that announced Stalin's Great Terror, and killed. The leadership of the Church later was left vacant for long periods. In the 1970s, Zviad Gamsakhurdia and others in Georgia came to dissident politics after formal religious conversions. But the Armenian national Church never became a focus of dissident activity. Dashnaks abroad tried to capitalise on suspicions that it had been compromised to further their own Cold War politics. The result was a number of unseemly squabbles that reduced the stature of the Church in the eyes of many Armenians abroad, and, not incidentally, increased the power of the political parties.

The Soviet authorities tried to deepen the conflict between the two camps, tolerating or even cultivating Ramkavar loyalists, while isolating Dashnaks. Armenian patriotism was encouraged, and there were efforts to promote the Soviet republic as a genuine national homeland although such gestures were undermined by subsequent events. In 1946, all diaspora Armenians were invited to return to the Soviet republic to help rebuild the motherland after the devastation of two world wars. Incentives such as half-price housing and the waiving of customs duties were thrown in. But it was the moral argument, coupled with the instability of the countries in which they were living, which carried most weight. Both diaspora blocs supported the programme, with the AGBU organising special collection funds, although Dashnaks themselves were barred unless they renounced the party.

Eventually about 110,000 Armenians took up the offer, mainly from Greece, Lebanon, Syria, Iran and Palestine. Many of them were members of communist parties in their native countries. Among them was the infant Levon Ter-Petrosian. His father was a member of the politburo of the Syrian Communist Party, and had headed the local underground in Aleppo during the war. The newcomers represented 9 per cent of the population, and their arrival caused serious disruptions. There was real resentment from local Armenians of the sweeteners offered to the returnees at a time of severe housing shortages and economic difficulties. A year after the great migration, there was another wave of purges organised from Moscow, and many of the newcomers were accused of harbouring Dashnak sentiments and deported to Siberia. After Stalin died in 1953, many of the disillusioned newcomers seized on the chance to return home. There was another, better-planned attempt to gather in the diaspora in 1961, but only 26,000 Armenians responded. Most were from Cyprus, Iran and Lebanon.

By the 1970s, the upheavals of the Middle East and the momentary relaxation of Soviet immigration controls had set in motion a new wave of Armenian migration which transformed America into the centre of the diaspora. With the pressure of new arrivals – about 100,000 from the Soviet Union and 120,000 from Lebanon – the Armenian community outgrew its traditional base in the Boston–New York area. The new arrivals moved westwards, to California, in such large numbers that Los Angeles came to be referred to jokingly as Los Armenos. There was an additional exodus of Armenians from Iran after the 1979 revolution, but many settled on the east coast rather than in California. In all, the three waves of immigration increased the size of the US community to 600,000, with 300,000 Armenians in California alone. Among them is the former state governor, the Republican George

Deukmejian. The population shift increased the standing of the Dashnaks in America as the refugees from Lebanon took up politics in their new homes.

New times, old memories

The rise in Arab and Palestinian nationalism which made the 1970s such a volatile time struck a chord in a new generation of Armenians. In the West, the campaign to force Turkey to acknowledge the atrocities of 1915 gathered new momentum, with frequest protests outside Turkish embassies. The Armenian Assembly of America was founded in Washington in 1975 to lobby senators and congressmen on the question. The assembly was supported by the Ramkavars and non-party Armenians, but not by Dashnaks although it was meant to be a non-party grouping. In Lebanon the more radical factions went underground, forming in 1975 the terrorist cells of the Armenian Secret Army for the Liberation of Armenia (ASALA) as well as the Justice Commandos of the Armenian Genocide. For the next seven years, ASALA waged war against Turkish officials abroad, and was linked to the assassination of twenty-one diplomats and a similar number of other Turkish government officials.

Within Soviet Armenia small dissident nationalist groups had begun to emerge even earlier. As in Georgia, some focused on cultural concerns, protesting at the spread of the Russian language, but the Armenian dissidents embraced wider concerns like the demand for Turkey to stop denying the genocide. The first known nationalist groups surfaced at Yerevan State University: the Union of Patriots in 1956 and the Union of Armenian Youth in 1963. In 1967, thirty-two students were expelled for anti-Soviet activity. By then, national feeling was more widespread. On 24 April 1965, while government and church officials gathered at the Yerevan opera house to commemorate the fiftieth anniversary of the genocide, a crowd of 100,000 congregated outside demanding the return of lands seized by Turkey, and the transfer of Nagorno-Karabakh from Azeri to Armenian administration. The demonstration was broken up by the militia, and many of the student leaders were jailed. At around the same time, Ter-Petrosian, then studying medieval Armenian manuscripts, spent ten days in jail. He was also involved in a semi-official campaign to erect a memorial for victims of the genocide.

Another dissident nationalist party, the National Unification Party (NUP), emerged at the same time, and among its early leaders was Paruir Hairikian. After his arrest in 1969 at the age of 20, he spent much of the next seventeen years in jail. In 1988, during the Karabakh

agitation, he would be stripped of his citizenship and expelled to
Ethiopia. In 1977, the NUP issued a charter calling for a national state
to be established on the territory of historic Armenia following a
referendum. It called for both Karabakh and Nakhichevan to be included in the proposed republic. The samizdat declaration was the first
to link the issue of Karabakh with Armenian independence. Several
founders of the NUP were also part of the republic's Helsinki Watch
group, which was monitoring compliance with the Helsinki accords.
But in early 1978, the authorities cracked down hard on the NUP,
essentially crushing it with the arrest of its main leaders. In a further
attempt to discredit the dissidents, they were linked to a series of
explosions on the Moscow Metro the previous year. In January 1979,
an NUP activist and two others were executed after having being
convicted of setting the bombs.

But despite the corresponding development of national movements
within and outside Armenia, events took place largely in isolation.
While the Soviet Union had encouraged cultural exchanges with the
diaspora to promote Soviet Armenia as a national homeland, these
contacts were carefully controlled. Armenians in the Middle East sent
their children to study at Yerevan State University, but Armenians in
the West had a more tenuous connection with the republic. They were
equally interested in their Armenian heritage; one of the main tasks
of the AGBU was to raise money for Armenian schools, and there are
two dozen in California alone. But Soviet Armenia did not serve as
a focal point. Some of the isolation was a product of the Soviet regime
which barred known Dashnaks from contact with visiting artists or
intellectuals.

However, the distance was psychological as well. Armenians in the
diaspora were bound up with the anti-Soviet outpourings of the Cold
War and the antipathy towards Turkey. Overwhelmingly, the diaspora
Armenian agenda was devoted to gaining recognition for the genocide. Beyond the visiting dance troupes, the closely shepherded tour
groups, and the small year-abroad programme at the university, there
was a yawning gap. Even politically active American-Armenians have
admitted that they were unaware of the Karabakh question until it
intruded on the consciousness of the entire world in 1988. Only then
did Armenians really begin to take notice of events inside the republic.

Moving towards independence

As in Azerbaijan, the struggle over Karabakh took precedence over
other topics of perestroika. The question of attaching the Azeri-ad-
ministered region to Armenia merged with the traditionally Armenian

issue of nationhood and survival, old discontents about corruption and environmental destruction and the new debates on democracy that had been made possible by Mikhail Gorbachev's perestroika. While the first demands for unification between Karabakh and Armenia were voiced by activists in the territory, the beginning of the conflict generally is traced to the week of protests in Yerevan that began on 20 February 1988. A group of prominent intellectuals, many with family ties to Karabakh, began co-ordinating the actions of the demonstrators. It came to be known as the Karabakh committee, and one of its members was the Orientalist, Levon Ter-Petrosian. In the diaspora, meanwhile, the violence at Sumgait in February 1988, in which at least thirty-two Armenians were killed and hundreds injured by Azerbaijanis, had rekindled old memories of Turkish persecution. For many Armenians abroad the Karabakh issue appeared inseparable from the age-old question of survival, rather than being seen as the catalyst for independence and democratisation that it was proving on the ground.

Although the Karabakh campaign won the attention of Armenians in the diaspora, it was a natural disaster that provided the spur for closer ties with the republic. That was the earthquake on 7 December 1988. About 25,000 people are believed to have died in that catastrophe, and hundreds of thousands made homeless. Two cities, Leninakan (since renamed Goumri) and Spitak, disappeared as blocks of flats came crashing down on top of their inhabitants. Northern Armenia, the epicentre of the earthquake, had been the destination for refugees from Azerbaijan, and they were left destitute and without shelter for a second time. President Gorbachev cut short a visit to the West and flew to the earthquake zone. But rather than offer comfort to grieving survivors, he found himself the focus of their rage over Karabakh.

In the outpouring of sympathy around the world that followed the disaster, the Armenian diaspora community stepped in to help raise the funds that would be needed for a drastic reconstruction programme. It was the first time that the diaspora was allowed to contribute financially to Soviet Armenia. Previous offers of aid had always been rebuffed on the grounds that the Soviet Union could provide for its own people, but the scale of the disaster removed such inhibitions. The diaspora was generous, raising more than $15 million from private donors, including $1.5 million from a single individual. Other projects included the flying in of twenty planeloads of relief, a cold-storage unit in the disaster zone and a special plastic surgery unit in Yerevan. The tragedy provided the opportunity for Armenian organisations to locate to Yerevan for the first time. The Armenian Assembly lobby group opened a branch office, as did the AGBU and specialised relief agencies. But the emergency situation could not bridge the gulf between liberals and nationalists, Ramkavars and Dashnaks. The factions had their own fund-raising efforts and relief programmes so that Aid Armenia, a specific appeal started after the earthquake, had little Dashnak involvement.

Meanwhile, the Armenian authorities had become alarmed at the scale of the anger directed at Mikhail Gorbachev during his dramatic visit. While the world was still preoccupied with rescue work in the earthquake zone, there was a crackdown on the Karabakh movement and all eleven members of the steering committee were jailed. The strategy backfired. Ordinary people in Armenia had greeted Gorbachev's reforms with genuine enthusiasm, and most believed that the Karabakh campaign was in the spirit of perestroika. There was a conviction that if the Armenians provided evidence of their historic claims to Karabakh, and of the Karabakhis' desire for self-determination, then Moscow would award them the territory. Moscow's refusal to countenance border changes and the pervasive corruption of the then Armenian communist party chief, Karen Demirjian, had worn down their faith in the existing system. And the detention of the Karabakh committee members destroyed it utterly. For the next six months, the central fact of Armenian political life was the detention of the Karabakh committee, which set off further protests. By the time the last of the committee members was released in May 1989, they effectively had been deified. For Ter-Petrosian, the prison term proved a salvation in another respect. While inside, he was diagnosed with cancer, and on his release flown to France for surgery. 'If Gorbachev hadn't imprisoned me, I wouldn't have lived longer than six months', he told reporters after becoming president. Later in 1989, the Karabakh committee and the other small groups it had spawned joined together under the name of the Armenian National Movement (ANM), or Hayots Hamazgayin Sharjum.

Amid disenchantment with the failure of perestroika to resolve the issue of Karabakh in their favour, and exhaustion from their efforts to recover from the earthquake, Armenians held their first multi-party elections in May 1990. There was less than a 50 per cent turnout, partly because of a growing sense of futility but also because of confusion over what the various informal groups stood for. Even the Communist Party now favoured greater autonomy. Observing how its counterpart in Georgia had become utterly alienated from the people, it sensed that outright opposition to emerging nationalism would finish it off completely. The only contention between the groups was whether Armenia should strive for autonomy within the Soviet Union, for complete independence, or – as the more radical factions wanted – independence and recovery of lands lost to Turkey. Ter-Petrosian's

Armenian National Movement was then perceived as favouring autonomy rather than secession.

After three rounds of voting, no party emerged with a clear majority, and the parliament that emerged represented a bewildering array of factions. Seventy-three per cent of the deputies were members of the Communist Party, but some had been elected on behalf of the Armenian National Movement, making it the largest party in parliament. Paruir Hairikian, the dissident from the 1970s, was elected from exile in California. After a fortnight of procedural wrangling, on 4 August 1990 Ter-Petrosian was elected chairman of the Supreme Soviet with 140 votes, nearly double the number won by his rival, the Armenian Communist Party chief Vladimir Movsisian. His elevation, and the choice of a prime minister, Vazgen Manukian, from his own Armenian National Movement effectively wrested control of the parliament from the Communist Party.

On 23 August 1990, less than three weeks after the formation of the first non-communist government, parliament adopted a declaration signalling Armenia's intention to begin moving towards independence. The resolution declared 'the beginning of the process of establishing independent statehood'. Bound up in the resolution was the historic fear of Turkey. The declaration called for the creation of Armenian armed forces to safeguard its border with Turkey, and for Ankara to recognise the crimes committed against the Armenians by the Ottoman empire. It pledged the determination of the new Armenian leadership to gain international recognition of the 1915 genocide, and declared invalid the Soviet treaty establishing the borders with Turkey on the grounds that Armenia was now a sovereign country. Although the parliament held back from openly demanding recovery of the lands ceded to Ankara, the declaration included a section setting out Armenia's claim on Karabakh. It also called for the setting up of internal troops and a police force subordinated to parliament, a national currency and a national bank. It reaffirmed Armenia's right to pursue its own independent foreign policy, and guaranteed freedom of speech and freedom of the press. The declaration was also significant in its moderation. While more radical groups espoused the idea of immediate secession, Ter-Petrosian envisaged a gradual severing of ties over five years before forming a new relationship with Russia along the lines of the European Community. He argued that Armenia needed to retain some leverage with Russia because of economic necessity and for the sake of its own protection and the fate of Nagorno-Karabakh. However, his own prime minister, Manukian, argued for swifter progress. In a phrase that has often been repeated, he urged parliament: 'It's time to jump off the train.'

After the independence process was set in motion, Ter-Petrosian came into conflict with more nationalistic forces. One of his first acts was to impose a state of emergency and night curfew and to ban nationalist paramilitary groups after an Armenian National Movement deputy and activist were killed in a shoot-out at the party headquarters. The Armenian government had already been under pressure from Gorbachev to disband unofficial paramilitary groups. Formed to protect Armenians in Karabakh, the paramilitaries had become engaged in fighting in Yerevan, and in attacks on Soviet installations to seize weapons and fuel. By some estimates there were as many as 100,000 men under arms. Two earlier incidents had amplified Moscow's fears about these unofficial formations. In April, the irregulars had launched attacks on the Armenian Supreme Soviet and KGB buildings in Yerevan, engaging a month later in direct clashes with Soviet troops in which twenty-three people died. While the Armenian authorities had at times turned a blind eye to the Armenian National Army – the organisation involved in the attack on the ANM building – Ter-Petrosian's own tolerance had expired, and he called on interior ministry troops to hunt down the paramilitaries. 'The people's patience has run out', he said in a national radio broadcast on 29 August 1990. 'They can no longer bear the adventurism of these armed detachments which endanger both the security of our citizens and the formation of our statehood.'

Ter-Petrosian managed to keep the paramilitaries in check, and the republic began to embrace multi-party parliamentary politics. The old parties of the diaspora, no longer considered hostile and unacceptable, were invited to return. At a stroke, Armenia had a far more sophisticated party system than either Azerbaijan or Georgia, where parties were fractious groups dominated by a single powerful personality. Although still unfamiliar to indigenous Armenians, the diaspora parties gained in popular support. The Dashnak party, which had had its headquarters in Athens under the leadership of Khrayr Marukhian, relocated to Yerevan officially in August 1990 although there had been secret cells in operation from 1988. The party commanded the loyalty of ten members of parliament. Like the Ramkavars, it began to build up local support with its own party newspaper. Hairikian returned from exile in November 1990. Both the Dashnaks and Hairikian seized on the Karabakh issue, adopting a much more militant stance than that of Ter-Petrosian on the degree of support that Armenia should be extending towards its brethren there. Like the Dashnaks, Hairikian's own party, the Union for Self-Determination, went beyond support for Karabakh, calling for the recovery of Nakhichevan and the territories lost to Turkey. Hairikian's followers were openly confrontational. They occupied Communist Party-owned buildings in Yerevan, disrupted the meetings of rival groups, and vandalised statues. The revival of old-style nationalist politics, and the tactics adopted by Hairikian in particular, met with some resentment from local Armenians and great concern from the authorities. In February 1991, parliament introduced a law banning parties whose headquarters lay outside Armenia. It also banned receipt of funding from abroad.

Meanwhile, moves towards independence were going ahead. In February 1991, parliament agreed on the procedure for the holding of a referendum on independence, while deciding to boycott the all-Soviet referendum for a new union treaty scheduled for the following month. On 21 September 1991, in compliance with the procedures laid down in the Soviet law on secession, the Armenian referendum duly went ahead. Ninety-five per cent of the electorate voted to withdraw from the Soviet Union. But it seemed an empty exercise. In the aftermath of the failed coup against Mikhail Gorbachev in August 1991, virtually all the other republics had declared independence, making the Armenian vote something of an anachronism. On 23 September, when Armenia formally declared itself independent, it was the only republic to do so entirely on the basis prescribed in the Soviet constitution, an indication yet again of the debt of gratitude Armenians feel for Russian protection. Three weeks later, on 16 October 1991, Ter-Petrosian became the country's first directly elected leader, capturing 83 per cent of the vote. Eventually, his government incorporated ten of the eleven members of the original Karabakh committee as cabinet ministers, heads of parliamentary committees, and even mayor of Yerevan.

Ter-Petrosian demonstrated a great deal of enthusiasm for tapping the skills and goodwill of the diaspora Armenians. He included foreign-born Armenians in his cabinet, and welcomed them as advisers. Despite this official sanction for diaspora participation, only a few hundred Armenians moved to the republic from the diaspora, but they were highly skilled and extremely dedicated. Most were in their twenties and thirties, university-educated, well-paid professionals willing to live off their savings and in difficult conditions for a time to help get the republic on its feet. Many of the diaspora returnees chose not to collect their salaries – in any case their wages, paid in roubles, would have been derisory compared to the amounts they could command at home.

One of the hothouses for talented volunteers from the diaspora was the Armenian Assembly, which served as an unofficial foreign ministry co-ordinating visits from Congressmen and other Western politicians. It was an early port of call for Western journalists, with a young and pleasant staff eager to dole out contact numbers and advice, and to allow the use of their reliable telephones. In this alone, the Assembly office in Yerevan probably proved its value as a good PR move. The man who set it up, the large and moustachioed Californian, Raffi Hovannisian, eventually became the country's first foreign minister in 1991 at the age of 32. The fast-talking son of the prominent historian Richard Hovannisian, he had devoted several years to diaspora politics in the Armenian Assembly in Washington, and on aid projects in Yerevan. Other lobbyists from the Armenian Assembly, mainly young third-generation Armenian-Americans, took up posts in the foreign ministry and even in the president's office. Sepouh Tashjian, the energy minister faced with the monumental task of relieving the country's energy crisis, was an older man and Jerusalem-born, though he had worked for a southern California electricity company after emigrating to America.

Outside of the government, one of the first concrete expressions of diaspora goodwill was made in September 1991 when the American University of Armenia opened in Yerevan with a hundred students. A branch of the University of California, set up by three American professors from the state university system, the Yerevan campus was intended to train Armenians for the free market. It offered just three programmes, all in English, in business and computers and seismic engineering. The university, which received an initial $1.2 million from the AGBU, also sponsored a databank which was supposed to help foreigners seeking Armenian business partners. Unfortunately, Armenia's energy crisis and the continuing war with Azerbaijan discouraged even ethnic Armenians from investing in the country. Indeed, the most striking fact about the university is how transitory its American staff were. Some members of staff commuted from their jobs in California.

If, as sometimes seems convenient, one compares the Armenian diaspora to the support Jews have extended to Israel, then the Armenian contact has been much more fleeting. In part, this is because there is no ideological basis for diaspora support as there is with Zionism. While the Jewish state has been able to count on institutionalised financial support and the long-term commitment of immigration, diaspora support for Armenia has been much more individualistic and, like the founding of the university and earthquake relief, geared towards specific projects. However, some Armenians have argued that this new fluid pattern suits the present era. 'I don't think we should think in terms of the 19th-century concept of where you live. The world is your whole environment. The whole concept of immigration and settlement is changing', Stepan Karamardian, dean of business management at the university, told me. Himself a Syrian-born immigrant to the US, Karamardian had spent several months shuttling between the West Coast and Armenia to set up the university.

The first cracks

Despite this involvement, most Armenians would emphasise that financial support from the diaspora does not even begin to approach the level of spending on schools and other institutions in the diaspora. Armenia has had to rely on the generosity of individuals in donating their skills and funds; there has been no systematic campaign to rescue Armenia from economic disaster. For their part the diaspora Armenians interested in investing in the republic have been bewildered by the intervening bureaucracy, and the unfamiliarity of local officials with Western business practices. In February 1993, Armenian officials admitted to reporters that they felt they had been let down by their brethren abroad, and that the diaspora was too preoccupied with power struggles between Dashnaks and Ramkavars. 'I think the help from the diaspora so far has been miserly', David Vardanyan, head of the foreign affairs committee, said. 'The diaspora is not united ... I do not think we have sufficiently fertile soil for co-operation with the diaspora.'[1]

Within the first six months of independence, the government of Ter-Petrosian began to encounter rising tension between the moderate policies he had adopted and nationalistic forces. While he took the realist's approach to Turkey, recognising that landlocked Armenia needed an outlet to the sea and to the West, his opponents were against any rapprochement before Ankara recognised the genocide. Ter-Petrosian was also more hesitant to be seen openly supporting the fighters in Karabakh for fear of alienating Turkey and Russia. Almost invariably, Armenians with their roots in the diaspora, nurtured on the idea that Turkey represented the ultimate threat to their survival, found themselves on the side of the opposition, favouring a harder line against Ankara. The divisions over Armenia's support for Karabakh intensified in late 1991 after the Dashnaks were elected to power in the Armenian-dominated territory. The elections solidified the connection between radical elements in the territory and their supporters in Armenia. It gave the Dashnaks in Yerevan added leverage against Ter-Petrosian, allowing them to cast doubts on his patriotic commitment to the struggle in Karabakh. The new parliament in Stepanakert immediately voted for independence and in the following months, Ter-Petrosian came under increasing pressure to recognise its declaration. It was a step he was loath to take, for it would set Armenia outside the general consensus that the demise of the Soviet Union should not lead to any redrawing of internal boundaries.

Ter-Petrosian's reluctance to recognise Karabakh became the main fault-line with the opposition. It deepened in March 1992 when the Armenian president re-affirmed that his government had no territorial claims against Azerbaijan over Karabakh, effectively positing Yerevan as a concerned party, but not one directly involved in the dispute. Throughout the spring, the opposition parties hammered home their demand for Ter-Petrosian to reverse this decision, or resign. They created a clamour in parliament and in the streets, calling out demonstrations that took place, almost invariably, outside the opera house. In June 1992, seven of the more radical opposition parties in parliament – including the Dashnaks and the Union for Self-Determination – combined forces in a coalition called the National Alliance to help advance their campaign over Karabakh.

One month later, this uneasy state of affairs between government and opposition exploded into scandal, and a welter of accusations and counter-accusations about KGB connections and betrayals. As a result, Khrayr Marukhian, the Dashnak leader from Greece who had initiated the charges that Ter-Petrosian had served as a KGB informer while a student, was expelled from the country and put on a plane for Paris. He was accused of collaborating with the KGB and of trying to destabilise the situation in the country. Marukhian's departure led to a momentary accord between the National Alliance and the government, and a compromise in August under which parliament passed an ANM resolution expressing support for the rights of the Armenian population of Nagorno-Karabakh.

For the next year, the pressure on the authorities to do more for the people of Karabakh remained constant and forceful. Almost every month brought a new blow for the Ter-Petrosian government, and its popularity went into deep decline. The dire economic situation, largely a result of the blockade and the war, also stoked discontent. In October 1992, Ter-Petrosian lost his youthful and high-profile foreign minister.

Raffi Hovannisian had for months found himself at odds with the president's moderate stand on Karabakh, with his reluctance to alienate potential supporters in the US, and with his evident eagerness to establish relations with Turkey. Hovannisian had long disagreed with Ter-Petrosian on the degree of accommodation to be made with Turkey over recognition of the genocide, and over Ankara's involvement in Nagorno-Karabakh. But their quarrel came to a head after a speech by Hovannisian at the Council of Europe meeting in Istanbul in September 1992. Not only did Hovannisian broach the delicate topic of the 1915 bloodshed, but he strongly criticised Turkey for rebuffing Armenian attempts to normalise relations. He openly accused Ankara of becoming involved in the war.

'Turkish military advisors and officers are in Azerbaijan', he told the meeting. 'Reports abound that arms have flowed to Azerbaijan through Turkey and Turkey has played a less than constructive role in the CSCE-sponsored talks on Nagorno-Karabakh.' Hovannisian went on:

> Turkish obstacles to Armenian participation in European institutions are indeed ironic. According to many, Turkey, despite its being a senior member of the Council [of Europe], has yet to meaningfully demonstrate its commitment to European values. ... Despite the fact that some suggest Turkey be a model for the new states in Central Asia, Turkey cannot yet claim to be a model of European values and cultural identity.[2]

The Dashnaks viewed the departure of Hovannisian with dismay.

During the winter months of 1992–93, the Azerbaijani blockade meant that sheer survival was the main issue, and the public seemed to be wearying of politics. Although virtually everyone was adamant that Karabakh should belong to Armenians, the regular weekly demonstrations in support of the territory dwindled to crowds of just a few thousand. The difficulties of life under blockade had ground down the population, and support for Ter-Petrosian was ebbing away. Then, on 2 February 1993, Ter-Petrosian dismissed his prime minister, Khosrov Harutunian, who had publicly criticised the draft budget, and accused him of failing to design a coherent economic strategy. The radical nationalist Hairikian took advantage of this breach in the government benches to call a new series of protests. He again demanded Ter-Petrosian's resignation, but this time over the energy crisis, food shortages and runaway inflation. It was his most successful campaign ever: 100,000 people turned out on 5 February to demand that the government go. The demonstration was endorsed by 120 deputies in the 185-seat house, an indication of how tenuous Ter-Petrosian's position was becoming. But Hairikian stepped back from the brink, telling reporters: 'The adventure of overthrowing the authorities is alien to us.'

Ter-Petrosian tried to recapture some of his lost popularity by including members of the National Alliance in his cabinet, but they turned him down. One week after the huge demonstration he announced a new cabinet, with the 34-year-old Grant Bagratian as prime minister. Bagratian, an advocate of radical economic reform, was well-regarded in the West for his enthusiasm for the free market. The divide between the more radical nationalists in Armenia and moderates like Ter-Petrosian showed no signs of abating after the government was installed. Ter-Petrosian's Armenian National Movement clung to the levers of government even while increasing numbers of parliamentary deputies drifted towards the opposition. By February 1993, as the Hairikian demonstration showed, more deputies opposed the government than supported it. The following July, Ter-Petrosian was again forced to sack one of his own, the defence minister Vazgen Manukian. Although a long-time ally, Manukian had become a focus for nationalist opposition in the government as well as the armed forces, and had tried to scupper internationally sponsored peace agreements for Karabakh. There has been only one small reversal of this trend of declining support for the government. That arrived through the revival of the Social Democratic or Hunchak (Bell) party, a relic from the Tsarist past. The party was founded in 1887 in Geneva by Armenian political exiles who were under the influence of the Russian philosopher, Aleksandr Herzen, and his celebrated journal, *Kolokol*, which means 'bell' in Russian. In May 1993, the party announced its support for the government of Ter-Petrosian.

The strength of nationalist opinion has limited Ter-Petrosian's manoeuvrability. Despite his desire to retain the goodwill of the United States and other Western supporters by endorsing efforts to end the war in Karabakh, he cannot be too pliable for fear of angering his more nationalist opponents. In June 1993, for example, on the day the government agreed to a peace plan sponsored by the Conference on Security and Co-operation in Europe, the Dashnaks showed their contempt by burning a Turkish flag. The rounds of demonstrations deepened the atmosphere of instability and hopelessness that shrouds Yerevan. And as the government stumbled through ever-worsening states of economic collapse, it became uncertain how long it would be able to maintain order. As a harbinger of the lawlessness that has afflicted its two neighbours, two former communist officials, including the former Armenian KGB chief, were shot dead by unknown assassins in the summer of 1993.

Although it would be far-fetched indeed to pin Ter-Petrosian's dilemma entirely on the influence of the diaspora, the struggle played out between the government in Yerevan and its opponents is of a piece with the pattern of events in the diaspora for the last century. Pluralist politics survived outside the Soviet realm, bequeathing to present-day Armenia a degree of political sophistication that, together with its ethnic cohesion, has enabled it to avoid the upheavals that have plagued Georgia and Azerbaijan. But diaspora politics also institutionalised a horror of Turkey and a distrust of Moscow that have precluded a realistic vision of the country's position, and created obstacles in the search for peace. Policy towards Turkey, and by proxy Azerbaijan in the war over Nagorno-Karabakh, has been the constant dividing line in Armenian politics. In present-day Armenia, hardline nationalist opinion threatens to deny Yerevan the possibility of coming to some sort of accord with Turkey that would end its geographic isolation, and enable it to begin to build some kind of economic future. While the divide does not yet risk plunging the country into the same chaos that has befallen Georgia and Azerbaijan, it could ensure that Armenia remains the disaster zone Ter-Petrosian deemed it after just one year of independence. Although the diaspora has been generous, it is too fractured, and its pattern of giving too individualistic, to pull the country out of its economic morass.

Notes

1. Reuter, 11 February 1993.
2. Hovannisian, Raffi, 10 September 1992; text of a speech to the Council of Europe meeting, Istanbul.

8

The Black Garden: the War in Nagorno-Karabakh

The warlords of Nagorno-Karabakh know that their victories are meaningless if they are holding empty towns and villages, and so they try to stop civilians from fleeing. People still leave. Their terror finds a way around the militias' threats and the disappearance of motorised transport. They negotiate dirt roads or steep hills by foot or by donkey; some women lay their babies in prams crammed with bread or jars of pickles. At times, amid the paranoia that breeds as easily in Karabakh as its famous sheep, it seems that the warlords are determined to make sure journalists stay too. That way they would not write their nasty propaganda. But it was really only the prevailing chaos and petrol shortages that kept journalists standing by for days to get out.

It was on one such day of waiting in early March 1992 that a village man volunteered to show me a 7th-century Armenian church nestled in the hills. The alternative was several more hours at Kholotak, the desperately poor village where the Armenian helicopters would touch down briefly in the perilous shuttle between Yerevan and Karabakh. There was nothing at Kholotak – just a field churned into liquid mud by the throngs of people. The ill and wounded waited in the open air. With no direct communications between Yerevan and the base, it was impossible to guarantee that the sick would be evacuated. We turned our backs on Kholotak and started walking, slipping on the mud and wet ground until the ruins came into view still some distance away. It felt strangely peaceful. Below was the Azerbaijani village of Khojali, where all was absolutely still. On the horizon, there were smudges of smoke, and we could hear the faint rumble of tanks engaged in battle. Days before, Khojali had fallen. The Armenians had driven me around its outskirts through a valley of tower blocks that seemed out of place in such a remote area. But they had been guarded about their victory. That evening when we returned from our walk I turned on the radio and found out why.

In Azerbaijan, evidence had emerged of a massacre of men, women and children who had fled Khojali ahead of the Armenians and had tried to walk to safety on the eastern edge of the enclave. Some managed to reach their haven at Agdam, the Azerbaijani military headquarters, but many, many more were mowed down by snipers as they crossed an exposed valley. To this day, it remains uncertain how many civilians were killed in the valleys outside Khojali on 25–27 February 1992. Amid the grief-stricken and wild allegations, some Azerbaijanis put the toll as high as 2,000. At first the foreign press were reluctant to believe that such an atrocity had taken place; the Azerbaijani authorities had falsified reports in the past. But then eyewitness accounts confirmed the worst fears. According to forensic scientists, the bodies of 184 people were identified, including fifty-one women and thirteen children. Many more were believed to have been buried without being included in the toll because of the haste required by Muslim rites. Thirty-three of the bodies recovered had been scalped, had body parts removed or had been otherwise mutilated, according to reports which were later confirmed by Helsinki Watch. I switched off the radio and turned to the villager who had so kindly shown me the ruins of the church. 'I can't say I am sorry', he said.

Hatred and distrust swirl about the hills of Karabakh and the two cities which are obsessed with the war, Yerevan and Baku. While the conflict has grown ever more hi-tech thanks to weapons looted from former Soviet forces, it has revived concepts that seem unfamiliar to our era: betrayal, revenge, Christendom, honour. In an area of natural beauty, it has created a people kind enough to show a stranger the local sights while being utterly indifferent to the fate of a neighbour. This lack of concern for the fate of civilians on the opposing side is displayed by Azerbaijanis as well as Armenians. In Yerevan, a few intellectuals have tried to understand the conflict and to find forgiveness. In Baku, where it is keenly felt that the war has been lost, the Karabakh question is all-consuming. There is no room for generosity towards the other side; instead the government is flayed for its military ineptitude. I lost count of all the atrocity stories I heard in Yerevan and Baku. Some were so blood-curdling that I could only hope they were not true. The only reason for mentioning atrocities committed by Armenians here is that they have at times been forgotten in all the confusion and lies that have grown up around the conflict. Azerbaijani forces have also been condemned by international human rights monitors, most notoriously for the indiscriminate shelling of Stepanakert with multi-rocket launchers from December 1991 to February 1992.

The war in Nagorno-Karabakh is the oldest conflict in the former Soviet Union. It was also the first territorial dispute to give birth to genuine nationalist movements. From its beginnings in 1988, it has been a dispute of extremes. What began as a protest at discrimination against Armenians descended rapidly into violence with little attempt at mediation in between. On 20 February, the local assembly of Nagorno-Karabakh, which was dominated by Armenians as the majority population, adopted a resolution calling for the transfer of the region from Azerbaijani to Armenian administration. Within a week, the debate about the enclave's future had spread beyond its borders. Sumgait, an ugly, soul-destroying industrial town in Azerbaijan, reacted wildly to the declaration, and armed mobs turned on the Armenian minority.

The pogrom rekindled memories of persecution branded on the Armenian collective consciousness. It has been a feature of the dispute that the Armenians, although they have had the upper hand militarily, remain convinced that they face annihilation in Karabakh. The imprint of suffering left by the Ottoman slaughter of 1915 has given each stage of the conflict an added dimension. Armenians regularly refer to the Azerbaijanis as Turks or Tatars, an identity interchangeable with their tormentors from the past. Armenian militants in the United States have also borrowed the Jewish slogan against anti-semitism, 'Never again', which relies on echoes from the Nazi holocaust. As Lyudmilla Harutunian, a Yerevan sociologist and one-time deputy in the republican Supreme Soviet, put it: 'We have forgotten the noble pages of our history and we have created an image of Armenians as victims and it is a very deep image.' This embedded image of suffering at the hands of a far more powerful Turkic enemy has often been cited as a factor in the incredible resilience the Armenians have shown against a country twice its size and infinitely better off economically. The blurring of lines between Azeri and Turk also plays on the European prejudice against Muslims. So when a prominent Karabakhi, the former foreign minister Levon Melik-Shakhnazarian, speculates on the fortunes of the war he says: 'I think that in this case civilisation will win.'

The events of the two years following the Sumgait pogrom could serve as a testament to Soviet inertia. While the authorities dithered, the situation in Karabakh and on the borders between Armenia and Azerbaijan became more and more violent. Hundreds of thousands of Armenians and Azerbaijanis, who had for generations lived outside their own republic, lost their homes in a forced population transfer. Others fled because they anticipated violence. In 1990 Mikhail Gorbachev, originally sympathetic to the Armenian Karabakhis, shifted towards the Azerbaijani position. The fall of communism and the Soviet Union at the end of 1991 turned the relatively minor but ugly skirmishes in the enclave into an open and fierce war involving two sovereign states. In November 1991, Azerbaijan imposed an embargo which starved Armenia of energy supplies. Weeks later, the Karabakhi Armenians declared outright independence, and threw themselves into an offensive that by June 1992 gave them effective control of all the main towns in the enclave. At the five-year mark, the war had claimed 10,000 lives, according to some reports, and created hundreds of thousands of refugees. On the Azeri side, United Nations High Commissioner for Refugees officials estimated in the autumn of 1993 that nearly one million Azeris had been displaced from Karabakh and its environs, and that Armenians occupied more than 20 per cent of Azeri territory.

As the deadliest of the post-Soviet conflicts, Nagorno-Karabakh has been the subject of the most peace initiatives. Kazakhstan and Russia have both tried to mediate despite Moscow's obvious fears of a continued commitment of troops so far afield. So have foreign countries and international organisations, in a tacit admission of the gravity of the situation. Following Russia's failure to act as a regional policeman, exhaustive efforts have been made by the Conference on Security and Co-operation in Europe, which in 1991 formed an eleven-member committee on Karabakh.

In theory the war illustrates the tension between the principles of self-determination and the inviolability of frontiers – both enshrined in the CSCE charter. Armenians argue that the enclave was unfairly handed to Azerbaijan in 1923, an injustice that was compounded during the Soviet era by a deliberate campaign to increase the number of Azeri settlers while encouraging the Armenians to leave. They say their people, who form a majority in the enclave despite Azeri efforts at population management, have a right to choose their own destiny. If Karabakh stays in Azerbaijan, the Armenians argue, they face extinction: either by stealth through Azeri settlements, or by outright persecution and pogroms. The Azerbaijanis maintain that the loss of Karabakh would be an insupportable blow to its survival as an independent state. It would lead to a return to the colonial type of dependence on Russia that Azerbaijan endured for nearly 200 years. Any grievances the Armenians have about ethnic prejudice, they reply, can now be rectified within the confines of the newly democratic state. Whatever the justification, the eventual outcome of the conflict will influence the course of other territorial disputes in the former Soviet Union. Like Bosnia, it has tested the international community's commitment to peace.

In Karabakh itself the arguments are framed in simpler terms. Sometimes religion intrudes when Armenians raise the spectre of a Christian nation's last stand against a Muslim foe. Some Armenians believe that the West would automatically be sympathetic to a Christian nation, but the majority of Armenians and Azerbaijanis are emphatic that Karabakh is not a dispute over faith. The Armenian president, Levon Ter-Petrosian, has also explicitly rejected the idea of any religious factor in the conflict. Mostly, then, the debate over Karabakh is reduced to one question: that of who has lived there the longest. Even that is not as simple as it appears. Armenians certainly formed a majority in the enclave before the outbreak of the war, with the 1979 census giving them about 75 per cent of the population of 189,000. But the ethnic composition of the enclave has been in flux at least since Russia gained control of Karabakh in the early 19th century. The boundaries of the territory have also changed over the decades, shrinking during the Soviet period.

In retrospect, Armenia's capture of Khojali a few days before my visit was a turning point. The Azeri village had prevented Armenian helicopters landing at Stepanakert airport, diverting arms and food deliveries to distant Kholatak. Its fall helped to lighten the despair that had descended on Stepanakert with the Azeri siege, and the merciless pounding of the Grad rocket launchers. It created the momentum for a chain of victories which inevitably undermined the authority of the government in Baku. Within days of the loss of Khojali, Azerbaijan's President Ayaz Mutalibov was forced out of office. Local militia commanders were also sacked, a decision which was ultimately to cripple the Azeri forces. From Khojali onwards, every Azerbaijani defeat was followed by personnel changes in the army, undermining an already demoralised and disorganised force, and adding to political upheaval.

Khojali was crucial in the bigger picture too, jeopardising the propaganda advantage the Armenians had enjoyed since the Karabakh campaign began. The massacre revealed Yerevan's inability to control the militants. More importantly, it showed the Armenians themselves committing crimes which had become associated with Ottoman Turks. For the first time, Western diplomats began to entertain serious doubts about the Armenian conduct of the war. News of the massacre was slow to filter out – Mutalibov was anxious to conceal the scale of the disaster – but when the true story did emerge, it was front-page news in the *New York Times* and the *Washington Post*, both opinion formers in the country that is the most valued ally of Armenia.

Azerbaijan and Armenia each claim Nagorno-Karabakh as the cradle of their cultures. The Azeris say that the enclave has been a storehouse for their identity, nurturing their finest musicians and poets and the composer of their national anthem. Armenians see Karabakh as a symbol of survival despite great suffering. According to their historians, it has remained an area of Armenian settlement despite centuries of destruction and dispersal. They point to a distinctive Karabakhi dialect as evidence. This history of endurance explains why Armenians in Yerevan shared so deeply in their brethren's campaign against discrimination. Many Armenian homes have picture books showing the ancient churches and monasteries of Karabakh. Karabakhis themselves are proud to point out the *khatchkars*, or distinctive crosses, that litter the hillsides. But though the Armenian claims to a long history in Karabakh are convincing, they deliberately obscure a parallel Muslim presence, which explains the Azerbaijanis' passionate, though often poorly articulated, attachment. The Azerbaijanis have their own historical claim to the region which has often been overlooked. There is no universally accepted version.

As early as the 4th century BC, Armenians claim, the mountainous region was part of a great Armenian kingdom, a province known as Artsakh. But from the end of the 4th century onwards, Karabakh was always aligned to kingdoms in the east; that is in Azerbaijan. The overlords of the province changed frequently in the upheavals that have been endemic to the Caucasus, although Karabakh itself was preserved as a discrete entity. It passed from Christian rule under Caucasian Albania (there is no relation to the Balkan state), to Arab, Mongol, Turkic and finally Safavid Persian control. This diversity is reflected in the name: a combination of Turkish and Persian, meaning 'black garden'. The name (*kara*, meaning 'black' in Turkish and *bagh*, meaning 'garden' in Persian) comes from the enclave's rich dark alluvial soil. Nagorno, a Russian word added later, simply means mountainous.

The Armenians lived among a mixed Muslim population of Azeris, and nomadic and Kurdish tribes. By the 14th century, a local Armenian leadership had emerged, which enjoyed considerable autonomy from its Safavid Persian overlords. The five ruling houses, headed by *meliks* or clan chieftains, survived until the middle of the 18th century when they were destroyed by internal feuding. In their place, the region came under the sway of a single semi-independent Muslim ruler who made the capital of his khanate in the fortress of Shusha.

In 1813, the Treaty of Gulistan between a victorious Russia and a much-weakened Persia ceded Karabakh to the Tsar. Initially, the Russians left the existing Muslim rulers alone, but they later encouraged Armenians to settle in the Tsar's dominions. The reasons for this are not entirely clear, but it is known that the Armenians had appealed to Russia decades earlier to absorb them under its protective Christian rule. It may be that their loyalty was being rewarded, or that they were being used to counter the influence of Muslims, whom the Russians saw as unreliable. Whatever the reason, from 1828 there was a mass migration of Armenians from Persian-held territories to Russia, and a movement in the opposite direction by Muslims.

About 57,000 Armenians are believed to have migrated to Karabakh and Yerevan province after 1828, while about 35,000 Muslims – Kurds, Lezgins and various nomadic tribes as well as Azeris – out of a population of 117,000 left the area. The Russo-Turkish wars of 1855-56 and 1877–78 encouraged a further exchange, with Armenians leaving the Ottoman empire, and Muslims departing for Turkish-held territory. But the biggest migration happened immediately after 1828, when Persia ceded Yerevan province to Russia in the Treaty of Turkmenchai. Some scholars, quoting reports prepared by Russian military officials in 1823, have put the Armenian share of Karabakh's population as low as 8.4 per cent, with Muslims making up 91 per cent.[1] Even in 1832, after considerable migration had taken place, it is generally accepted that Muslims were a majority in Karabakh. An official Russian survey of that year recorded that Muslims made up 64.8 per cent of the region and Armenians 34.8 per cent.[2] However, by the end of the century when the first Russian census was carried out, Armenians had achieved a majority. They made up 53.3 per cent of the population, and Muslims 45.3 per cent. The percentages were nearly as drastic in Yerevan province, where Armenians made up only 20 per cent of the population in the 1820s and Muslims (that is, Lezgins, Kurds and other small groups as well as Azeris) made up 80 per cent.

Under Russian rule, Shusha became the most important town for Armenians after Baku and Tbilisi. By the turn of the century, it had become a cosmopolitan town, luring British and German oil magnates away from Baku with its delightfully cool summers, and providing a haven for foreign missionaries. It had several theatres and printing presses, as well as churches. But despite this flowering of Armenian culture, in administrative terms Karabakh was considered part of the Russian province of Elizavetpol (Gyandzha), where Muslims formed a clear majority. In 1905, inflamed by disturbances in Baku following the first Russian revolution, the tensions between the two communities exploded and Shusha was gripped by several days of rioting.

The town was the scene of more horrific violence in the last days of the First World War when Karabakh, like much of the Caucasus, was hotly disputed by Ottoman, British and local forces. In October 1918, invading Turkish forces and local Azerbaijanis turned against Armenian residents. Ethnic clashes in Karabakh continued after the Ottoman defeat and withdrawal, preoccupying the British forces who had moved in to replace them. The British re-affirmed Azerbaijani jurisdiction over Karabakh by appointing a Muslim governor at Shusha.

At first, local Armenians refused to accept the decision. But in the face of mounting pressure, on 28 February 1920 the Armenian elders of Shusha reluctantly agreed to recognise Azerbaijan's authority. They were opposed by local partisans who had joined forces with fighting units from Armenia proper.

But in any case, the question was becoming academic. On 4 April, Azeri forces entered Shusha to put down an Armenian rising. They sacked the town, burning hundreds of houses and beheading a number of prominent leaders. Three weeks later, with the Azeri forces still tied down in Karabakh, the Red Army was at the gates of Baku. It was clear that Karabakh's future would not be decided locally. As for Shusha, it had already ceased to exist as it was. In another of the population shifts that have characterised the Karabakh dispute, there was an Armenian exodus from Shusha to Khankende, just a few miles away. Shusha was transformed from an Armenian cultural centre into an Azerbaijani outpost, with only a few Armenian families remaining.

Soviet Karabakh

It took the Bolsheviks three years to decide whether to attach Karabakh to Armenia or to Azerbaijan, so deep was the controversy it aroused. And neither side was satisfied with the result. Azerbaijanis later claimed that they had been outnumbered by ethnic Armenians, Russians and Georgians on all the decision-making forums, while Armenians felt they had been cheated out of what had once been promised them.

At first, Karabakh was given to Armenia, a gift announced by the Azeri communist leader Nariman Narimanov to a newly Bolshevised brother state. The decision was made public by Stalin, who was then commissioner of nationalities, on 2 December 1920, but later repudiated by Narimanov. The Kavburo, or Caucasian section of the Russian Communist Party, then intervened, sending one Armenian and one Azerbaijani to Karabakh and Baku to advise on what should be done. Initially, the Kavburo supported the original plan. At a meeting in Tbilisi in July 1921 at which Stalin was present, it voted to include Karabakh in Armenia and then ratify the decision by a referendum. But a day later on 5 July, under protest from Narimanov, the Kavburo retreated. It did not bend entirely to Narimanov's demand that the enclave remain an integral part of Azerbaijan. Instead, the Kavburo adopted a motion to leave Nagorno-Karabakh within Azerbaijan while granting it a large measure of regional autonomy.

The Kavburo justified its decision on the grounds of the ancient economic links between Karabakh and the Azerbaijani lowlands to the east, and claimed it would promote Muslim and Armenian harmony.

But the timing of the decision coincided with a period of co-operation between the new Soviet and Kemalist governments. Armenian writers have viewed the granting of Karabakh to Azerbaijan and the ceding of Kars to Turkey as elements of a greater regional strategy. Armenian lands were sacrificed so as to consolidate Soviet–Turkish relations. For the next year, there was friction between Baku and local Armenians over how much autonomy Karabakh should enjoy. It was not until 7 July 1923 that the Baku authorities published the decree establishing the Autonomous Region of Nagorno-Karabakh inside the then Trans-Caucasian republic. The boundaries were contentious, omitting the northern districts of Shaumian (formerly Gulistan) and the western areas of Lachin and Kelbadzhar, which Armenians had considered an inalienable part of Karabakh. On 1 August, Khankende replaced Shusha as the capital of Karabakh. It was renamed Stepanakert, after Stepan Shaumian, the Armenian hero of the doomed Baku commune.

The difficulties the Bolsheviks encountered in deciding the fate of Karabakh applied to other regions too. Zangezur and Nakhichevan were the two main disputed areas, but there were dozens of contentious little pockets along the Armenian–Azerbaijani frontier. As with Karabakh, Narimanov initially favoured giving Zangezur, which lies to the south-west of Karabakh, and Nakhichevan, a territory along the Iranian–Turkish border, to Armenia. Eventually, Armenia won control of Zangezur and Azerbaijan was given Nakhichevan, although it lies entirely within Armenian territory. Nakhichevan was an area of Armenian settlement, but its population became almost exclusively Azeri. It was declared an autonomous republic attached to Azerbaijan in 1924, a designation of higher status than the one accorded to Nagorno-Karabakh. In 1923, another autonomous district to the south-west of Karabakh around Lachin and Kelbadzhar was set aside for the Kurds. However, Red Kurdistan was abolished in 1929, and most of its inhabitants were forcibly deported to Central Asia. In different ways, all of these areas have impinged upon the modern-day Karabakh dispute.

With hindsight, the distribution of territory appears to have been intended to amplify disputes rather than avoid them. The antipathy between Armenians and Azerbaijanis was well known: it had been a feature of the 1917 revolution and civil war in the Caucasus. Creating enclaves for the rival communities seems a sure-fire way of allowing resentments to fester. It also ensured, and this was probably the intent of Stalin, that the domestic situation in both Armenia and Azerbaijan would remain too volatile to contemplate serious challenges to the authority of the Soviet Union.

Throughout the period of Soviet rule, the Armenians of Karabakh felt that they were being deprived of the relative cultural freedoms enjoyed by other peoples of the Caucasus. Unlike the autonomous republic of Abkhazia, which had its own television station and university from the 1970s, there were few cultural outlets for Armenians in Karabakh. They were isolated from their kin in Armenia and, because secondary schooling was available only in Russian or Azeri, many Armenians lost their own language. In economic terms, the enclave was a neglected area, comparing unfavourably with conditions in Armenia. While Azerbaijanis have argued that Karabakh was no poorer than other mountain regions, Armenians were convinced that the authorities were disinclined to develop a region in which they were a minority. The net effect was that Armenians who wished to go on to higher education, or to professional jobs, migrated. The exodus created whole communities of well-educated Karabakhi émigrés in Moscow, Baku and Yerevan which ultimately contributed to the vigorous outside support for the unification campaign.

By the 1960s, the Armenians of Karabakh had begun to express their resentment at these injustices. In 1963, a petition from 2,500 Karabakhis was presented to Khrushchev, denouncing Azeri chauvinism and an economic policy that was designed to force Armenians to leave. It complained that 'in 40 years, not a single kilometre of road has been built to link the villages to the regional centre',[3] and that nothing had been done to promote agriculture. The petition concluded by calling for Karabakh to be attached either to Armenia or to Russia. Khrushchev ignored it, and later that year there were violent clashes in Stepanakert, leaving eighteen dead. In 1965, the issue seized the agenda in Yerevan, where protesters at an unofficial demonstration to mark the fiftieth anniversary of the genocide began calling for Karabakh to be joined to Armenia. In Stepanakert, meetings were held at factories and schools, and pro-unification petitions were circulated. So even in the time of stagnation during Brezhnev's rule, the question of Karabakh's future refused to disappear. It was as keenly felt in Armenia as in the enclave itself. Mikhail Gorbachev's perestroika merely let the campaign come out into the open.

The Karabakh debate surfaced in isolated and sporadic incidents throughout the autumn of 1987. In Baku, there had been growing indignation among local Armenian academics at the publication of a Ph.D dissertation which they believed exaggerated the Azeri influence in the region. In Yerevan, a series of small demonstrations to air the important issues of perestroika had raised the topic of Karabakh. It became the object of a petition campaign which gathered 80,000 signatures. In the enclave, a number of small local assemblies had begun to consider motions for incorporation into Armenia. In London, Abel

Aganbegyan, an Armenian who was Gorbachev's economic adviser, spoke of the sense of injustice felt over the division. And in Moscow and elsewhere, liberal intellectuals became aware of the Armenian cause.

These isolated stirrings began to coalesce into a mass movement on 21 February 1988, the day after the Karabakh Soviet voted 110 to 17 for the transfer of the territory to Armenia. In Yerevan a number of pro-democracy activists formed a Karabakh committee, while in the streets hundreds of thousands of people joined demonstrations calling for unification. Other issues were raised at the rally outside Yerevan's Opera House – official recognition of a genocide memorial day, pollution, corruption, democratisation – but the focus was on Karabakh. The demonstrators were remarkable for their faith in perestroika's ability to resolve the conflict. After being frustrated in their demands by the Armenian party chief, Karen Demirjian, who ruled out any change to the status of Karabakh, the marchers carried posters of Gorbachev. Nevertheless, the authorities in Moscow were alarmed at the size of the demonstrations. That week, the first peace-keeping forces were dispatched to Stepanakert; they were to remain there until early 1992. On 27 February, one of the members of the Karabakh committee, Zori Balayan, travelled to Moscow to meet Gorbachev. Balayan agreed to a one-month moratorium on the demonstrations in return for Gorbachev's pledge to bring a 'renaissance' to Karabakh.

But that evening, violence broke out in the Azerbaijani industrial town of Sumgait, following the deaths of two Azeris during skirmishes in Stepanakert. Thirty-two people were reportedly killed in the anti-Armenian pogroms. That figure is an artificial one, however; the real toll is generally believed to have been far higher. Although for much of that spring Armenians and Azerbaijanis pursued the dispute by parliamentary means, any real hope of dialogue had been brutally rubbed out by the events in Sumgait. The pogroms and the unshake-able belief that the authorities were not interested in punishing the killers had destroyed the trust the Armenian activists had placed in Gorbachev's perestroika. Their suspicions appeared to have been con-firmed on 23 March, when the USSR Supreme Soviet made it clear that Karabakh's incorporation into Armenia was unacceptable.

The relevant assemblies continued to adopt rival and conflicting resolutions. On 13 June, the Azerbaijani Soviet rejected Karabakh's declaration of 20 February, while on 15 June the Armenian Soviet reaffirmed its support for the same motion. On 28 June, Gorbachev intervened again, by ruling out any possibility of frontiers being modi-fied. Undeterred, on 12 July the Karabakh assembly voted to secede

– the first such vote ever in the Soviet Union. In the meantime, the Armenian Communist Party was seeking an accommodation with the Karabakh Committee, which had become increasingly popular.

But while the political leadership remained deadlocked over Karabakh, they were being overtaken by events. In November, there was a wholesale expulsion of Azerbaijanis from Armenia, and of Armenians from Baku, Kirovobad (Gyandzha) and other towns. In the space of a month, 180,000 Armenians left Azerbaijan, and 160,000 Azeris left Armenia, uprooting communities which had existed for years.

Finally, on 12 January 1989, the USSR Supreme Soviet decided to explore ways of giving Karabakh more autonomy. The region would remain formally part of Azerbaijan, but would be administered directly by an official appointed in Moscow, Arkady Volsky. The Azerbaijani Communist Party had not even been consulted. But although the decision was initially seen as a victory for the Armenians, their triumph was short-lived. Within three months, they were complaining that the initiative was a failure. Funds intended for economic development were held up in Baku, giving the lie to claims of greater autonomy. Clashes between rival militias went on unabated. A discouraged Moscow handed control of the enclave back to Azerbaijan in November 1989.

While the Armenians complained that their movement had had little effect in Karabakh, it brought radical changes to Armenia and Azerbaijan. The issue belatedly introduced perestroika to both republics. Moscow was forced to replace discredited and long-serving party leaders who were glaringly out of step with its new ethos. In Azerbaijan, Moscow's direct intervention in Karabakh had been seen as highhanded. It strengthened the case of pro-democracy activists, who organised six months of strikes and protests. In July 1989, a broadbased pro-democracy movement emerged in the shape of the Azerbaijan Popular Front. Aside from urging greater control over affairs in Azerbaijan, it took a militantly nationalist stance on Karabakh, spearheading a boycott of Armenia and a railway blockade of the enclave.

In Armenia, meanwhile, the Karabakh campaign was gaining momentum. The detention of all eleven members of the Committee had enhanced its popularity. As in Azerbaijan, the issue of Karabakh became inextricably linked to demands for greater democracy. So closely associated did the issue of Karabakh become identified with perestroika in Armenia that on 9 January 1990, the Armenian Supreme Soviet was forced into discussing the preparation of a budget for the enclave. In Baku, retribution was swift. On 12 January, armed gangs began attacking Armenian neighbourhoods. Dozens of people were killed, and hundreds wounded or forced out of their homes. A state of emergency was declared and some 11,000 Soviet troops were sent in to restore order. While they were too late to rescue the Armenians, they put down with great brutality a series of Popular Front protests, further alienating Azerbaijanis from Moscow. By the time that calm was restored, the only remaining Armenian communities in Azerbaijan were those of Nagorno-Karabakh and two regions lying directly to the north. Only the very old, or those tied to Azerbaijan through mixed marriages, remained behind.

Dark dawn of independence: the war intensifies

As the prospects of Soviet collapse became more real following the August 1991 putsch, the struggle over Nagorno-Karabakh intensified on both the political and military fronts. Contrary to the harmonious picture painted by the authorities in Baku, Armenians and Azerbaijanis had rarely lived happily together. Most villages belonged entirely to one community or the other. As for the towns, the Armenians occupied professional niches in Karabakh as in Azerbaijan, while the Azeris were primarily agricultural workers. There had never been much intermarriage. But the dispute made the divisions between the two peoples unbridgeable. The few Armenian families remaining in Shusha packed their belongings – an opportunity that was denied some of their brethren. In what was considered the ultimate betrayal, Soviet troops co-operated with Azerbaijani forces in clearing their villages. The Azeris, too, consolidated themselves in areas where they formed a majority.

These population exchanges were already complete by late 1991, when the uncertainty surrounding the future of the Soviet troops in the enclave encouraged the warlords of both sides to try to take as much territory as they could. In the years since the Karabakh agitation began, the fighters had become utterly ruthless. From 1990, they moved from intimidation – stoning cars or stealing livestock – to offensives aimed at liquidating entire villages. Hostages, overwhelmingly women and children, were taken as a matter of course, to be bartered for fuel or cash or prisoners held by the enemy. In the strange morality created by the war, where ideas like revenge or honour were used to justify all sorts of crimes, ordinary families would take hostages of their own to keep as an insurance policy for a son who had gone missing in action.

But while the fighters demonstrated little regard for humanitarian law, a command structure had begun to develop. The ragtag bands of both sides began to fall under designated commanders. The Armenian combatants, who started as vigilante defence units against Azerbaijani pogroms, united under the banner of the Armenian Popular Liberation Army of Artsakh. They were reinforced by volunteers from Armenia. The Azerbaijani militias were organised by the Popular Front.

By late 1991 the Popular Front was urging President Mutalibov to give greater support to the war, but Mutalibov was afraid of creating a national army in case it was taken over by the Popular Front and became a threat to his own position. It was only under continued Popular Front pressure that Mutalibov issued a decree in September 1991 creating a ministry of defence. In October, parliament passed a resolution nationalising all Soviet military hardware on its territory and recalling the estimated 140,000 Azerbaijani conscripts from the Red Army. There was a shortage of experienced Azerbaijani officers; conscripts to the Red Army tended to serve in construction battalions rather than combat units. Continuing political upheaval also delayed the organisation of the force. Within its first six months, the fledgling defence ministry had no fewer than four ministers.

At the same time as the Azerbaijanis and Armenians were manoeuvring to improve their military position, their political approaches were undergoing a transformation as well. The most important consequence of the Soviet collapse was the split between the leadership in Yerevan and the enclave. Armenia's pro-democracy movement had previously merged completely with the Karabakh issue. President Levon Ter-Petrosian, who had led Armenia to independence, had been a member of the Karabakh Committee. After independence, the quasi-governmental Artsakh committee was put in charge of maintaining contact and funnelling relief to the territory.

The rift between Armenians followed the Nagorno-Karabakh assembly's declaration of independence in September 1991, which was confirmed by a referendum later that year. It was in many ways a sleight of hand, intended to conceal the support Armenia offered to the enclave at the same time as it shielded Yerevan from international criticism of Karabakh's leadership. While there was no move to recognise Karabakh's independence, Armenia continued to insist that the territory had the right to autonomy, and Ter-Petrosian went on presenting its case to the international community. Yerevan was used as a conduit for humanitarian aid and food as well as arms; all mail to Stepanakert was routed through Yerevan. However, Armenia gave up all territorial claims on Nagorno-Karabakh, and declared that it had lost all influence over decisions taken by the enclave. This claim appeared more credible after the election of a radical Dashnaktsutiun government in Karabakh.

In December 1991, the newly elected Karabakh assembly voted to

participate as a fully fledged member of the Commonwealth of Independent States. The request was ignored. The next day, deputies followed their declaration of independence by laying claim to the district
of Shaumian, which had been excluded from the final boundaries of
the enclave in 1923. There was an immediate flare-up of fighting in
the area to the north of the enclave. Irredentist tendencies surfaced
again at New Year, when the parliamentary chairman of the Karabakh
assembly ruled out any notion of a peaceful solution that did not
accept the independence of the enclave and Shaumian as a *fait accompli*.

The increasing belligerence of the Karabakh leadership did not go
unchallenged in Azerbaijan. From late December, the Armenians came
under a steady hail of Grad rockets, fired from the heights of Shusha
where Stepanakert was clearly visible. Although President Mutalibov
restated his readiness for talks, he insisted that the only avenue for
negotiation was the issue of greater cultural autonomy within
Azerbaijan. He emphasised that Azerbaijan had become a democracy
where questions of discrimination could be easily addressed by guarantees of human rights for all.

On the propaganda front, both sides traded accusations of external
meddling in the war, with Soviet regiments treated as prime suspects.
The Azerbaijanis complained regularly that Armenians were receiving
financial support from the diaspora. Although this seems a reasonable
assumption, Dashnak organisers in America claim that diaspora financial
support has been minimal. However, a special Karabakh fund does
exist, and there are anecdotes of community fundraisers in Los Angeles raising hundreds of thousands of dollars in telethons and other
events.

As for military assistance, Azerbaijan has alleged that ethnic Armenian guerrillas, trained in Lebanon's Beka'a valley during the heyday
of the terrorist Armenian Secret Liberation Army in the 1980s, have
been used in Karabakh. Armenia has always denied the use of foreign
fighters, but in June 1993 it was forced to admit the death of a Cali-
fornian-born guerrilla in Karabakh. Monte Melkorian, aged 35 and a
university graduate in archaeology, had commanded a force of 3,000
men, and had received his military training with Kurdish separatists in
Iran as well in Lebanon. In August 1993, Gerard Libaridian, a senior
adviser to Ter-Petrosian, admitted that Armenia had sent anti-aircraft
missiles to Karabakh. He denied that Armenia had supplied the separatists with any other weapons such as tanks. The Armenians in turn
strongly suspect Turkey of providing arms to Azerbaijan. The Azerbaijanis
have admitted to receiving advice from retired Turkish army officers,
but deny receiving arms.

While it is difficult to prove allegations of interference by foreign countries, there is no doubt that Red Army troops had outlived their usefulness as neutral peacekeepers in Nagorno-Karabakh. There were persistent Azerbaijani allegations of Soviet army participation in the assault on Khojali, and timing would suggest that there is some truth in their accounts. Khojali fell amid the confusion and panic that accompanied the withdrawal of the last Soviet forces from Nagorno-Karabakh, the troops of the 366th motorised infantry regiment. In February, the commander of the CIS forces, Marshal Yevgeny Shaposhnikov, had decided that Russia would not tolerate its troops becoming ensnared in a bitter war in a foreign country. He came to the conclusion days after the officers' mess in Stepanakert had been hit by Azeri Grad missiles, killing two men. Shaposhnikov's announcement only mentioned concern for his men's physical safety, but it was widely believed that he was afraid of the effects on army morale and discipline of having a unit identify so clearly with one side in an ethnic conflict.

Some of the men of the 366th had been in Stepanakert since 1988, and the Armenians clearly regarded them as their protectors, weeping in anguish as they waved them off. Their faith was rewarded: at least sixty men from the 366th defected, including all three battalion commanders. Two of them were Russian. According to the Karabakh defence ministry, the army left behind about eighty tanks and other military vehicles. All night long, two tanks rumbled up and down the main road of Stepanakert as the militias tested their new possessions.

The partisan behaviour of Soviet troops was not restricted to Armenia. There have been eyewitness accounts of defections to Azerbaijan from the main Soviet base at Gyandzha. There are also mercenaries fighting on both sides. In May 1993, Azerbaijan sentenced five Russian soldiers to death after convicting them of fighting with Armenian forces. But whatever outside help the Azerbaijanis received was ineffective. From Khojali onwards, the Armenians enjoyed a series of decisive victories. The most spectacular was the capture of Shusha in May 1992.

Shusha had been badly shelled that winter in a war of missiles with Stepanakert, and civilians had slept in makeshift unheated shelters for weeks at a time. With only the most tenuous road links to Azerbaijan, food was scarce and produce in shops limited to a few shrivelled vegetables. The Armenians had sabotaged the water supply lines, forcing residents to rush out with buckets when water tankers passed. Despite such hardships, the residents of Shusha were as determined as their foes to stay put and there were still several thousand civilians there at the time of its fall.

In June, Armenian forces secured their conquest by capturing a

strip of land from Lachin, south of Stepanakert, to the Armenian town
of Goris. Thousands of people were forced out of their homes in the
town and in the hill villages beyond. The creation of the so-called
Lachin corridor through Azerbaijani territory gave the Armenian
Karabakhis two advantages. It reduced the pressure of supplying the
besieged enclave solely by air, and it turned the psychological connection to Armenia into a physical reality. By October the Armenians had
widened the corridor from six to eighteen miles. After the capture of
Shusha and the creation of the Lachin corridor, the military situation
in Karabakh remained relatively stable until the following spring. Heavy
but inconclusive fighting continued in northern Mardakert and
Shaumian districts, and there was sporadic shelling of the town of
Agdam inside Azerbaijan proper. But these could not disguise the
essential fact that Armenian forces controlled the situation in the enclave.
Militarily, they had won. In April 1993, the Armenians consolidated
their position, capturing the Kelbadzhar region. But like an earlier
victory – at Khojali, where dozens of Azeris were massacred – the
Armenian military success had ruinous consequences. In New York,
the UN Security Council denounced the offensive, its first rebuke of
Armenia, and in Washington State Department officials began voicing
their unease about Armenian expansion in the region.

In Baku, the humiliation of the defeats, coupled with a worsening
economic situation, made the position of the Popular Front government of Abulfaz Elchibey increasingly untenable. There were several
panicky reshuffles at the defence ministry, but Azerbaijan was unable
to recapture the advantage it had held at the end of 1991. In June 1993,
the humiliations of Nagorno-Karabakh collided with the frailties of
Azerbaijan's democratic institutions and Elchibey was overthrown. With
Azerbaijanis thus diverted, the Armenians launched a new, and even
more lethal, offensive.

The search for solutions

The international community stepped in to seek a solution in Karabakh
only after attempts at mediation by CIS members and individual bro-
kers had failed. Turkey offered to act as a broker, but was never formally asked by either side. Iran made two attempts to act as sole
mediator, only to watch a signed deal collapse in spectacular fashion.
The efforts by the CSCE have been the most ambitious, aimed at
extracting a total solution rather than a mere ceasefire. But they have
been frustrated either by the stubborn belief of the combatants that
even the smallest compromise represents capitulation, or by their own
unwieldy bureaucracy. United Nations participation has been limited.

The first peace package for Karabakh was drafted by Presidents Nursultan Nazarbayev of Kazakhstan and Boris Yeltsin of Russia in September 1991, following negotiations with their Armenian and Azerbaijani counterparts. The Nazarbayev–Yeltsin plan called for a ceasefire, an end to the blockades, the re-opening of communications links and an exchange of prisoners. It was torpedoed by Nagorno-Karabakh's declaration of independence later that month. Azerbaijan refused to acknowledge the right of representatives from Nagorno-Karabakh to participate in negotiations, while Armenia insisted that it could no longer speak for Karabakh and was not responsible for the actions of militias in the enclave.

In November 1991, Turkey volunteered its services as a neutral third party, but it lost all credibility in Armenian eyes in March 1992 when its then president, Turgut Ozal, made some ill-advised remarks about teaching Armenia 'a lesson'. The Armenians were also disturbed by Turkish willingness to explain Azerbaijan's position on the war to its allies in the US and Western Europe. During a meeting with President George Bush in Washington in February, the then prime minister, Suleyman Demirel, had appealed to the US to drop its unreserved support for Armenia in the dispute.

Such gaffes left the way clear for Iran. The foreign minister, Ali Akbar Velayati, embarked on a round of shuttle diplomacy in February 1992. He had hoped to visit Karabakh, but was prevented by a surge in fighting that defied an agreed ceasefire. He returned to the region later that spring when Tehran proudly announced that it had secured an agreement from both the Armenian and Azerbaijani presidents to meet for peace talks. On 8 May 1992, Armenia's Ter-Petrosian, representing the Karabakh Armenians, and the acting Azerbaijani president, Yakub Mamedov, duly gathered in Tehran. They signed a treaty agreeing to impose a ceasefire within the week, to lift the economic blockade of Armenia, to admit international observers to the area, to ease the exchange of prisoners, and to come to a joint decision on the problem of refugees. The accord turned out to be a complete disaster for Iran, and a source of embarrassment for Ter-Petrosian. A day after it was signed, the Armenian forces launched their offensive against Shusha and – in an even more galling move – the enclave of Nakhichevan, which borders directly on Iran.

After the failure of the Tehran talks, there were only rare attempts at peacemaking. Russia and Kazakhstan tried in vain to revive their original plan in September 1992, and France dipped into the conflict to arrange a short-term ceasefire to allow aid to be sent in to civilians. But although Armenia and Azerbaijan professed themselves interested in outside mediation of the conflict, Armenian Karabakhis were in no mood for compromise, rebuffing all peace initiatives. In any case, aside from the CSCE there were no takers.

The CSCE had officially become involved in Karabakh in March 1991 when an eleven-member peace committee was formed under Italian stewardship. While both Armenia and Azerbaijan are members, Karabakhis of both communities have been able to attend the talks only on an unofficial level as guests of Italy. At the time, the CSCE initiative on Karabakh was the most ambitious peacekeeping project to be undertaken by the organisation. If its May 1993 plan was to be implemented, it would require 600 military observers – the first deployment of troops for the CSCE. But the chances of the CSCE negotiating an agreement had been slim from the start, and were shrinking rapidly.

Despite the agreement on armed observers, it was far from certain that any country would be willing to commit any troops to Karabakh. The débâcle over Bosnia is evidence of such reluctance – and Nagorno-Karabakh is even further away and more obscure. The CSCE organisation itself has been hampered by the requirement that decisions be taken unanimously, and the talks have been close to collapse on several occasions. Azerbaijan's refusal to countenance participation in any forum which implied recognition of Karabakh's secession was one obstacle. Another was the willingness of both sides to agree to truces while making little effort to enforce the ceasefire on their troops. The movement in the spring of 1993 came about only after Russia, Turkey and the US intervened informally to secure Armenian, Azerbaijani and Karabakhi participation in the CSCE plan.

The Armenians' success during the preceding calendar year had caused great anxiety in Iran and Turkey. The Armenian forays into Azerbaijani territory, especially around Nakhichevan in May and June 1992 and Kelbadzhar in April 1993, brought the war uncomfortably close to international frontiers with Iran. Turkey, which had determinedly continued to profess its neutrality, faced a population clamouring for direct intervention. It was no longer only a matter of Russian concern that the conflict could overspill its borders, but a question Turkey and Iran could no longer ignore.

The proposal agreed on in June 1993 set a deadline of six months for the implementation of a permanent ceasefire. It also required Armenian forces to evacuate Kelbadzhar, a sticking point for the Karabakhi militants. After that was accomplished, the plan called for a full conference of all eleven members at Minsk to seek a political solution to the conflict. First on the agenda would be the disarmament of local militias and the return of refugees. Azerbaijan's beleaguered government accepted the plan with alacrity. Armenia was also willing, but getting the Karabakhi Armenians' assent was more diffi-cult.

Hardline Armenians believed that Kelbadzhar was vital for protect-ing the Lachin land route to the enclave, which had come under Azerbaijani fire. The Lachin corridor itself is of course entirely Azerbaijani territory. But the Armenians shrugged off critics in the West who pointed out that the seizure of lands outside the Soviet boundaries of Nagorno-Karabakh – in Lachin, Kelbadzhar and the northern Shaumian districts – represented expansion rather than de-fence of an embattled community. Armenian hardliners argued that these were niceties which foundered before the all-consuming ques-tion of survival.

It was a familiar argument, reflecting as it did the ever-present memory of Ottoman-era persecution. Securing the agreement of the Karabakh parliament required a personal visit to the enclave by Ter-Petrosian – his first – and the removal of the enclave's leader, Georgy Petrosian, who had balked at signing. On 14 June, Petrosian's deputy, the apparently more conciliatory Karen Baburyan, finally signed the accord amid protests from his fellow Dashnaks. The event evidently came as a relief to Ter-Petrosian, who said that Baburyan's elevation was in keeping with the newly arrived 'time for peace'. However, it was not to be. In the wake of the signing, Armenian forces launched a new offensive, building on the territory captured south-west of the enclave.

The new offensive through Azerbaijani territory to the south was aimed at clearing a swathe of territory up to the Iranian frontier, and cutting Azeri supply routes to the enclave. In August 1993, the Arme-nians advanced to within just three miles of the Iranian border, earn-ing a sharp rebuke from Tehran and the UN Security Council. Tens of thousands of Azeris from the towns of Jebrail and Fizuli fled in terror into Iran, in motley convoys of buses, horse-drawn carts and tractors. The offensive seemed aimed at seizing as much territory as possible to put Armenia in a favourable position at the talks – when they eventually took place.

The reluctance of the Karabakhi Armenians to participate in the peace process has been at the hub of the doomed efforts to end the war. The Azerbaijani government, too, has not advanced much from its earliest offers of cultural autonomy and the same civil rights guar-anteed to all Azeri citizens – despite the fact that it has lost all its territory in the enclave and has absolutely no credibility with Arme-nians. The primitive political culture of all sides has, from the begin-ning of the Karabakh dispute, reduced the possibility of a settlement. This has become apparent in the conviction that historical evidence

– even if inaccurate – outweighs concepts of international law, and in the inability to comprehend that there are intermediate stages between total subservience and total independence. Such failings are especially tragic because of the claim of the original protagonists – the Karabakhi Armenians – that their actions represent a democratic striving for self-determination. While the Soviet authorities failed to take decisive action, Karabakhis of both communities indulged in a spiral of atrocities that increased mutual hatred to the point where rational debate was impossible. In the meantime, the fortunes of Armenia's and especially Azerbaijan's post-Soviet leadership have been so closely bound up with the war that it has been difficult for them to take too conciliatory a position.

Quite apart from Karabakh, the international community has demonstrated its inability to solve the new, internal conflicts that have emerged with the end of the Cold War. There has been a near total lack of vision of the kinds of accommodations that could be made between Azerbaijanis and Armenians over Karabakh. The UN lacks funds, and the European Community and Nato do not have the appropriate mandates. The CSCE, which has had little experience of peacemaking, has been inexcusably slow in Karabakh. Until the spring of 1993, no negotiated ceasefire had ever been observed for more than fifteen days. The CSCE process has proved so cumbersome that it has required direct intervention from the US, Turkey and Russia. There has also been criticism of the choice of an Italian chairman for the process, when countries with significantly more influence in the region have expressed an interest. Similarly, the exclusion of such an important neighbour as Iran could render any decisions irrelevant.

All of these failings have contributed to the impasse over Nagorno-Karabakh. Although there is some hope so long as the CSCE process is not abandoned completely – and after the Armenian seizure of a swathe of Azeri territory near the Iranian border a ceasefire did hold for some time – there is a much greater chance of the war spreading.

The military situation in Karabakh at the close of 1993 bore little resemblance to what I had found on my first visit. The misery of the helicopter field at Kholotak was reduced to a memory; Armenians now travelled in comfort to the enclave by scheduled buses. Life was returning to Stepanakert and Armenian villages; refugees were finding their way back to their homes or to new accommodation in the former Azeri captial of Shusha. But the areas once populated by Azeris told an entirely different story. Agdam, Jebrail and Fizuli, places that had once housed tens of thousands of people, had been transformed into ghost towns. Their inhabitants had fled in terror across the Iranian border and then to safety in Azerbaijan. The towns themselves were comprehensively looted and burnt by Armenian forces after their capture.

The danger for Karabakh is that this deliberate destruction – and that of towns outside the actual borders of the enclave – is a sign of the future. With easy availability of sophisticated weaponry, the conflict has grown ever more deadly. At the same time the possibility of a negotiated peace recedes further into the distance. There is little trust in Baku, Yerevan or Stepanakert in international negotiations. Azerbaijan has responded to its defeats in Karabakh with a growing sense of betrayal by a world community unable or unwilling to bring the Armenians to book. The Armenian side appears to lack any strategy but to hope for a series of victories so punishing that they can win independence by bringing a once powerful opponent to its knees. Both sides are trapped within the logic of war.

Notes

1. Alijarly, Sulejman (1992), 'The republic of Azerbaydzhan: Notes on the State Borders in the Past and the Present', unpublished paper. London.

2. Bourhoutian, George A. (1983), 'Ethnic Composition and Socio-Economic Conditions of Eastern Armenia in the First Half of the Nineteenth Century', in *Trans-Caucasia: Nationalism and Social Change*, University of Michigan, Ann Arbor, p. 78.

3. Walker, Christopher (1991), *Armenia and Karabagh: The Struggle For Unity*, Minority Rights Publications, London, p. 118.

9

The North Caucasus: Small Nations Stirring

There is no mistaking Grozny for a Russian town, although that is where one would find it on the map: in one of the cluster of republics along the federation's southern border. Liberty Square, where all the official buildings are, is full of scenes from another continent. Everywhere one sees men in various menacing guises, loitering with a disregard for time that seems closer in spirit to Peshawar, say, than to Moscow. The village elders with heavy sheepskin cloaks and cutlasses, the suspected mafiosi with the gold teeth, fedora and black coat of movie gangsters, the bored soldiers – these are the people with power in Grozny. The city, capital of the republic of Chechnya, is sufficiently small for them all to know one another.

Many of the men appear to be permanent fixtures in the various entourages that traipse through the square. They preen themselves in front of some of the finest cars in Russia – Mercedes, Saabs and other imports – or wander over to the other bodyguards and hangers-on gossiping in the sunlight. Casting an occasional glance up at the government headquarters, they clasp each other's shoulders in a quick hug in the Islamic style of greeting, mutter 'salaam', and move on. On Thursday mornings the square is reserved for the dancers, who, according to local Sufi or mystical traditions, move at speed in dizzying circles and patterns meant to induce a religious ecstasy.

Few women dare to part that daily crowd of men to enter the buildings on the square. One who does is Aisa, and she reports directly to Grozny's most important citizen, General Dzhokar Dudayev, in what was once the Communist Party building. Aisa, despite her imperfect English, is General Dudayev's favourite interpreter, and has a job in the information ministry of Chechnya. Because of this, she is often the first person journalists and other foreigners meet in Grozny and it is through her eyes that they begin to know Chechnya. But Aisa, despite her position, is self-effacing.

She insists that she does not understand the intricacies of government. Her careful courtesies to Dudayev's bodyguards, she says, are just a woman's way. Aisa professes little taste for politics. 'I'm just like other women. I work because I like to buy pretty things.' She moves through the corridors of power in a vapour of Poison perfume from a bottle removed periodically from her handbag. Like other Chechens, Aisa is vague about the rivalries in the republic, the first to declare independence from the Russian Federation in the autumn of 1991. 'The opposition' is a shadowy thing. Aisa is afraid to name openly the forces who are opposing Dudayev. Even to be seen talking to a critic of the general by his bodyguards would be dangerous. It is safer to remain apart.

Aisa's life outside the office is subject to similar constraints. Her hair is fully covered with a scarf. She is more careful than many women in Grozny, whose concession to Muslim conventions of modesty can be as nominal as an Alice band. Although within Russia divorce is commonplace, since her husband left her Aisa has referred to herself as a widow. Divorce is shameful for Chechen women, doubly so for someone like Aisa whose family had been well-placed in the communist bureaucracy. She and her daughter live with her parents.

Home is a vaguely Middle Eastern complex with a degree of space unheard of in Moscow. Four branches of the family live behind the flat stone wall and metal gate. In addition to the central courtyard, each family has its own kitchen and living quarters and its own television set. On most evenings, all four are going separately even though there are only two channels to choose from.

This is where Aisa spends most of her time outside work. Few women walk out alone in Grozny, and certainly not at night when there are nearly always sounds of gunfire. There are one or two restaurants, but a visit would be unthinkable unless Aisa and her friends were to sit in the special women's cell at the back, to wolf down a joyless meal away from the eyes of men.

Aisa's cloistered life is not uncommon in Grozny. To her employer, General Dudayev, it is exemplary in its devotion to local customs and religion. For Chechens, as for most of the peoples of the north Caucasus, Islam is inseparable from ethnic identity. It is inconceivable to be Christian and Chechen. Aisa's separate way of life is thus a triumph: evidence of the survival of the Chechen identity in defiance of Russian rule. The annexation of the Caucasus range in 1864 was accomplished only after decades of war against different mountain tribes. For Russians, the struggle assumed epic proportions. The heroic resistance of the mountain peoples that captured the imagination of Russian writers like Tolstoy and Lermontov was instrumental in according to the region the image of romance and danger that persists today. Throughout the Caucasian wars, the region was bound closer still to Russia by the settling of Cossacks along the Kuban and Terek rivers. Their descendants and more recent Russian settlers now outnumber locals in some of the administrative territories established during the Soviet period.

But even after 1864, during a campaign of assimilation that was handed down from the Tsarist viceroys to Communist Party apparatchiks, there were regular risings against foreign and non-Islamic rule. Islam and the jealous guarding of a distinct language and culture bred in the high passes of the mountain range were the inspiration for the long years of struggle by the Chechens and other nationalities. This attachment to ethnic identity and to religion remains strong in the post-Soviet era.

Seven decades of communist rule entrenched the Tsarist legacy of persecution. Under Stalin, administrative structures were imposed which divided the mountain peoples and prevented them acting together in their own interest. It magnified differences of dialect to build up the idea of separate nations, and then confirmed the split by concocting separate literary languages. With the Chechens, the policy served as a wedge between them and the Ingush. In the most horrific crime of Stalin's era, entire nations nearly perished during the wholesale deportation of the Chechens, Ingush, Karachai and Balkars. These two fundamental injustices – the divide-and-rule policy and the deportations – have been a powerful force in the reassertion of ethnic identity that has occurred since the late 1980s. But while bitter memories have helped to strengthen ethnic consciousness, they are also the source of the disputes that plague the region.

Who's who

Of the six Caucasian republics within Russia at the time of the dissolution of the Soviet empire, Daghestan in the east was the largest, both in population and in sheer size, and its demographic composition the most diverse. Its borders stretch along the coast of the Caspian Sea to form a frontier with Azerbaijan in the south, with Chechnya in the west and Georgia in the south-west. The 1.8 million inhabitants at the time of the 1989 Soviet census included thirty-three recognised nationalities. Even within these groups there are a multitude of dialects, variations in language and custom that are a product of the remoteness of mountain villages. The largest nation, the Avars, is divided into fourteen tribal groups, comprising 27 per cent of the population. Russians make up 9 per cent.

Until recently, Daghestan remained a relatively loyal corner of Russia and relations among ethnic groups were peaceful. Makhachkala, the capital, and Derbent, once a centre for Islamic study, benefited directly from scholarly interest in Daghestan's extraordinary demographics with its own branch of the Academy of Sciences. But from the 1990s, the individual nationalities in Daghestan have formed separate organisations to campaign for a greater share of the republic's wealth, or even secession. Although there is no strong movement for Daghestan's independence, these demands have awakened fears about stability.

Loyalty to Russia is stronger still in North Ossetia in the central Caucasus. The Ossetian capital, the old fortress town of Vladikavkaz, or Lord of the Caucasus, controls the high pass through the mountains to Georgia, a route whose strategic importance was recognised centuries ago. The main road linking Georgia to Russia still runs through the Daryal pass in Ossetian territory.

The Ossetians remain a people apart in the region. Their origins are obscure, although they are thought to descend from the Alan tribes which were engulfed by the Huns and driven westwards with them in the 4th century. They are still viewed as newcomers to the region. However, their contemporary isolation owes as much to their Orthodox Christianity (although some Ossetians are Muslim) among their Muslim neighbours and their linguistic singularity – their language is distantly related to Farsi – as to their affinity for communist rule. The Ossetians tied their fortunes to Russia early in the colonial period, seeing it as an ally against their Caucasian neighbours. But despite their loyalties, they also suffered the indignities of colonial rule. In the Soviet period, their lands were divided between Russia and Georgia.

Ossetians made up 53 per cent of the republic's population of 633,000 in 1989, but that balance has since been dramatically altered. North Ossetia has absorbed the refugees from the war between Georgia and their compatriots in South Ossetia, but lost the Ingush who had made up 5 per cent of the population following a separate territorial dispute.

Russians hold the balance of power in three republics. All three are in the north-west, where the resistance to the Russian invaders was less effective than in the eastern theatre of the Caucasian wars. After their defeat by the Russians, hundreds of thousands of Adygs and Cherkess fled their homes for Turkey. In the Kabardino-Balkar republic to the west of North Ossetia, Russians make up 32 per cent of the population. The republic of 750,000 is an anomaly. It was designated a homeland for two unrelated nationalities: the Kabardians, who are an indigenous mountain people and make up 48 per cent of the population, and the Turkic-speaking Balkars who make up 9 per cent. The Kabardian and Balkar cultures are far apart, and their languages mutually unintelligible. In recent times, these differences have caused tensions. The situation is similar in the Karachai-Cherkess republic further west where the Karachai, who are closely related to the Balkars, and the Cherkess, an indigenous Caucasian group, co-exist uneasily with a large population of Russians and Cossacks. In the Adygeya republic, centred around the oil town of Maykop, the indigenous population is vastly outnumbered by Russians and other Slavs. Adygs, whose language is related to the Cherkess' and Kabardians', make up only 22 per cent of the population, a fact which has bred resentment and clashes with Russian groups.

And finally, the Chechens, the traditional leaders of the north Caucasian peoples. Until 1991, the Chechens were grouped together with their ethnic cousins, the Ingush, in the second largest republic both in terms of population and of territory, to the west of Daghestan. The Chechen-Ingush republic, with its important oil refineries, had 1.3 million inhabitants in 1989, 55 per cent of them Chechen, 12 per cent Ingush and 22 per cent Russian. Since the Chechens broke away to declare independence, the Ingush have been reconstituted in their own autonomous republic centred around the town of Nazran.

From the time of the conquest, the Chechens have led the struggle against Russian rule. Other nations of the Caucasus proved relatively easy to subdue: the Kabardian nobility through marital alliance with Ivan the Terrible in 1561 and the Ossetians through treaties during the late 18th century. But then, as now, the Chechens proved a formidable enemy. There were rebellions in Chechnya and Daghestan whenever the mountaineers saw an opportunity: during the Russian–Turkish war of 1877, the failed revolution of 1905 and the civil war that followed the Bolshevik revolution. The Russian treatment of the Chechens has reflected that struggle: in the purges of the 1930s, and the deportations during the Second World War. After the collapse of Soviet power, the Chechen leader, General Dzhokar Dudayev, became the most prominent advocate of independence from Russia in the region, and a force behind efforts to build Caucasian unity.

Politics of empire

The over-arching issue for the Caucasian peoples is that of unity. Although the 4.7 million north Caucasians differ in language and ethnicity, they have practices in common. They remain predominantly rural societies, and share codes of honour, folklore, and, apart from the largely Orthodox Ossetians, the Sunni Muslim religion. Any hope of real independence from Russia depends on instilling a wider national consciousness in ethnic groups whose identities and loyalties have traditionally been formed locally, at the level of clan or village. It is exceedingly doubtful whether a patchwork of tiny independent states could ever remain viable. Unity in turn is the main issue for Russia, which views the prospect of losing control of its strategic southern flank with trepidation. An independent Caucasian republic, no longer subordinate to Russia but a member of the Commonwealth of Independent States in its own right, would go against the Soviet nationalities policy that has prevailed since Stalin's time.

Though remote and underdeveloped, the northern Caucasus is strategic. It is a crucial buffer as well as a filter between Russia and Turkey and Iran, a fact as salient at the start of the 21st century as it was for Ivan the Terrible in the 16th. The region has served as protector both for Russia and for the Muslim world beyond. Even as recently as the Second World War, unrest in the north Caucasus forced Moscow to abandon designs on Iran. Ethnic links make it impossible for Georgia, with its Abkhazian and Ossetian minorities, to contemplate a peaceful future without the co-operation of their brethren in the north Caucasus. Contacts between north and south Ossetians and between Abkhazians and the Adygs, Kabardians and Cherkess have increased since the fall of the Soviet Union. Communities of mountain peoples in Turkey and other outposts of the old Ottoman empire provide further links to the Muslim world, preventing the region from remaining staunchly Russian.

With Georgia, Azerbaijan and Armenia declaring independence in the 1990s, the Caucasus range became an international border again. There are dozens of incidents that illustrate how the region compromised Russian security. The civil war that followed the 1917 Bolshevik revolution washed over and beyond Russia's border region, and Daghestani volunteers fought in Azerbaijan on behalf of the anti-Bolshevik Musavists. Even more disturbingly, they had foreign advisers and assistance, mainly British. What would the loss of the north Caucasus mean to Russia? A strong, oil-rich, Muslim block on its southern flank which has already demonstrated an unfriendly turn of mind. It would further diminish Moscow's control over the Black Sea, its gateway to the Mediterranean. Moreover, the mountain range towers over the most fertile agricultural lands of Russia, the black soils of the Stavropol and Krasnodar districts.

But an independent northern Caucasus poses an internal threat as well, and a dangerous example to the two dozen other autonomous republics, regions and areas in parts of Siberia and the Far East that are technically within Russia's borders. Although all but Tatarstan and Chechnya signed the federative treaty with Russia on 31 March 1992, the republics were greatly influenced by General Dudayev's success in declaring independence with impunity. It was seen as a sign of Moscow's weakness, further undermining a federation which was losing its grip on far-flung but resource-rich or strategic territories.

The Caucasian peoples have never been ruled by a single unified government, aside from a brief interlude during the civil war. Nationalist and Islamic leaders proclaimed the United Mountain Republic, which was soon beset by both the White and Red armies. In 1921, not long after its fall, the Mountain Autonomous Republic was created, incorporating the Chechens, Ingush, Ossetians, Karachai, Cherkess, Kabardians and Balkars. Daghestan was a separate entity. There was little pretence that the republic was a genuine reflection of the aspirations of the Caucasian nationalities. At its founding congress, the executive committee had thirteen members: nine Russian, two Ossetian, one Ingush, and one of uncertain origin.[1]

But even this display of autonomy, artificial as it was, did not last. In September 1921, the Kabardians were given an autonomous province; in January 1922, the Karachai were allotted an autonomous province together with the Cherkess while the Balkars were merged with the Kabardians. One year later, the Chechens were given an autonomous province of their own, and in July 1924, the Mountain Republic was disbanded completely when the Ossetians and Ingush were separated. The administrative reshufflings continued throughout the 1920s and 1930s. The tendency for a heavy hand against the Chechens swiftly became apparent: for Checheno-Ingushetia, there were Russian first secretaries, while the leaders of Daghestan were Caucasian. The administrative divisions were followed by a linguistic policy that, while introducing written languages and formal education to a population where illiteracy was widespread, discouraged the use of Arabic and Turkish which had allowed the nationalities (or at least the clergy and other educated groups) to communicate freely. Turkish, viewed with suspicion in Russia as the language of an unreliable neighbour, was outlawed in 1928, and Arabic in 1944.

The administrative division of the Caucasian peoples defied ordinary logic. It was a divide-and-rule policy that put disparate peoples together and divided closely related tribes. Sometimes geography was used as a pretext. The Karachai and Balkars, two peoples closer in language and tradition than even the Chechens and Ingush, were separated at the stroke of a pen. The reason: a high range that ran through their adjoining territories. Similarly, the Ossetian territories were parcelled out between Georgia and Russia with geography as the stated reason. The only possible conclusion is that the administration of the northern Caucasus was meant to keep the region weak and unstable – a classic colonial attitude.

When, in the late 1980s, the non-Russian nationalities began to assert themselves by forming popular fronts and demanding independence from the Soviet Union, the smaller Caucasian peoples responded by forming an unofficial group of their own. The Confederation of Mountain Peoples was founded during a conference at Sukhumi in 1989, largely at the instigation of the Abkhazians who were seeking support in their conflict with Georgia. Aside from the Abkhazians, the confederation had fifteen member nations. The larger nationalities like the Chechens and Avars were represented along with smaller groups which had not been allotted specific territories under Soviet rule, and the Ossetians, the least independence-minded group. Initially, none of the fifteen national groups from the north Caucasus were as ambitious as the Abkhazians in their demands for autonomy. The confederation's aims were modest, focusing on local culture and Islamic custom. The conference also passed a resolution declaring its intention to play a supporting role to the Communist Party. But gradually, with the demise of the Soviet Union, and largely at the instigation of Chechnya's General Dudayev, the independence-minded leader who was assuming a larger leadership role in the region, the confederation has become an instrument of Caucasian national will. It has become a skeleton for a supranational government. In January 1993, representatives of political parties, national and social groups decided to turn it into a permanent body to promote peace in the region. The move was seen as a deliberate revival of the council of elders that had existed before the conquest, and which used to mediate in disputes.

However, the current confederation carries within it the seeds of its own destruction, although like the original pre-Tsarist councils it was created to promote peace. In exploiting the grievances of the Soviet era, it risks inflaming the old grudges that the smaller peoples have against each other – all the products of foreign rule. The confederation has tried to settle the territorial disputes that threaten to set its sixteen members against one another – but with mixed results. All of these disputes, and there are about a dozen, date from the Stalinist era, when people were settled on lands left behind by deported nations. In a region where arable land is scarce, these losses still rankle.

The confederation did succeed in 1990 in reaching a compromise between Chechens resident in Daghestan and the tiny Lak nation of 92,000. The Laks had been forcibly moved, with the loss of 2,500 lives, to border lands left by the Chechens when they were deported in 1944. After three years of mediation, the Subarz or New Moon Lak Popular Front agreed to abandon Novolakskoye district to be resettled on lands in the south of Daghestan. It was the first land dispute in the region to be settled amicably, and the first time that a nationalist organisation has facilitated compromise rather than conflict. But the confederation failed entirely during two years of mediation to avert bloodshed in a similar dispute between the Ingush and the Ossetians. That conflict exploded into full-scale war in the autumn of 1992, and ended with thousands of Ingush losing their homes and being driven out of North Ossetia.

It is in its interventions outside the north Caucasus that the confederation has become a real challenge to its neighbours. In August 1992, under Chechen guidance, volunteer fighters were sent to Abkhazia to help repel a Georgian invasion. The arrival of the Chechen, Adyg and Kabardian fighters coincided with a turn-around in Abkhazian fortunes. Not only did the volunteer forces stave off a near-certain rout, they were instrumental in the capture of the republican capital, Sukhumi. The deployment of fighters in Abkhazia cemented the unity of what had until then been a purely political alliance. It showed that members could act in concert on behalf of a threatened partner. And the ability of fighters from different nations to act together provided a useful example for the eventual formation of a united mountain people's army.

The interference of north Caucasian fighters in the Abkhazian war underlines again the crucial role the smaller nations play in the stability of the entire region. Along the Caspian Sea coast, there are the makings of a territorial dispute similar to the Georgian–Abkhazian conflict. This time, it involves Azerbaijan and the Lezgin nationality. The Lezgin of Daghestan, who number 240,000, founded the Sadval (Unity) organisation in 1990 to press for border changes that would allow them to unite with Lezgins in Azerbaijan. They claim that Lezgins across the border, who official estimates say number 175,000, are under threat of assimilation, as a Sunni minority within largely Shia Azerbaijan. The peoples were divided when the Soviet borders were fixed in 1922, and the first demands for unification were made in Daghestan in the 1960s. There was a parallel movement founded in Azerbaijan in 1992 which organised rallies on both sides of the border and reportedly announced the refusal of Lezgins to serve with Azeri forces in the war in Nagorno-Karabakh. Given the conflict with its Armenian minority, the Lezgin issue has been treated with extreme care by Russian and Azerbaijani officials. In August 1992, the Russian foreign ministry acknowledged the concern among the local population along the border, and pledged that there would only be a minimum of frontier controls to prevent smuggling.[2] However, it remains uncertain how far such reassurances will go towards meeting Lezgin demands for autonomy.

Chechnya

In Moscow's newspapers and on television, the leader of independent Chechnya, General Dzhokar Dudayev, is portrayed as a dangerous lunatic. Amid all the Russian prejudices against Caucasians, there is a particular contempt for Chechens. They are depicted by the media as a nation of thugs and criminals, relying on strong-arm techniques to safeguard their claim on the takings of Moscow's drug dealers, prostitutes, arms merchants and smugglers. Although there is almost certainly a Chechen presence in Moscow's underworld, this fact is blown out of all proportion by a mentality still coloured by the hard-won Russian conquest of the mountain people in the last century. The exaggeration also serves to justify Moscow's current efforts to keep the smaller nationalities under its control. As a Chechen foreign ministry official complained:

> Some journalists who come to the Chechen republic only see the limousines, they can't see the poor people, or the people fighting for their freedom. The main purpose of this idea of the Chechen mafia is to hide the struggle of a people for independence.

At first glance, General Dudayev does indeed appear strange. His grip on affairs is so complete that it is impossible even to get a hotel room in Grozny without his personal intervention. Visitors seeking an audience stand waiting for six hours at a stretch in a corridor of heavily armed bodyguards, pacing and smoking. When they do reach the inner sanctum, Dudayev is invariably behind his desk, a strategy to hide the fact that he is very short. Wary but smiling in civilian clothing, he greets visitors from beneath the new green velvet Chechen national flag. The emblem of freedom shows a seated wolf on a mountain top in the light of a full moon. The green represents Islam, and the wolf the uncompromising independence of the mountain people. As Dudayev himself proudly acknowledges: 'We Chechens are proud and brave and cannot tolerate when someone keeps us as a slave. Of course, we are hot-tempered, but not when someone treats us kindly.'

The wolf symbol seems appropriate for a man who has acted alone, and dangerously, since the start of the 1990s. Dudayev was born in February 1944 during the worst period of Chechen history: the mass deportation to Central Asia. He spent the first thirteen years of his life in exile in Kazakhstan. But he overcame the stigma attached to his origins, and went on to establish a successful military career by any standards. After enrolling in flying school and graduating from the Gagarin air force academy, Dudayev served as a fighter pilot in Siberia and Ukraine. He ended his career as commander of the air base at Tartu, Estonia. Dudayev is married to a Russian, and it was not until

1989, when he allowed an Estonian flag to be raised at the base, that he betrayed any sympathy for national aspirations.

He became a Chechen national leader almost by accident. In November 1990, Dudayev attended the founding meeting of the All-National Congress of the Chechen People as a guest, but he so impressed delegates with his speech that he was elected their chief. The congress soon became the most influential political grouping in the republic, eclipsing the new and poorly organised Islamic, cultural and national parties. Party structures are alien to the Chechens and, as a consequence of Soviet rule, viewed with suspicion. The Chechen congress had an executive core of sixty members with enough clan leaders represented to ensure a broad support base. The Ingush were not represented, an omission that would have repercussions later.

Almost immediately, the congress began to call for the disbanding of the Supreme Soviet, which had been elected in 1990 – before emerging democratic groups had had time to win popular support – and was controlled by the communists. The Supreme Soviet dismissed the congress demands for sovereignty and responded to its campaign with a crackdown. The authorities banned congress newspapers and leaflets, and subjected its leaders to harassment.

The balance of power shifted after the bungled coup against Mikhail Gorbachev on 19 August 1991. The authorities in Checheno-Ingushetia were timid, and failed to assemble a coherent response to the dramatic events. The chairman of Grozny's Supreme Soviet, Doku Zavgayev, was in Moscow, and his deputy went into hiding, leaving no-one to convene parliament. Local television and radio were taken off the air. Only when it became clear that the coup had failed did Zavgayev return to Grozny to call an assembly of the Supreme Soviet. It dutifully condemned the putsch.

In the meantime, however, his absence had allowed General Dudayev to claim the spotlight. As news of the coup spread, he called for civil disobedience and an indefinite general strike. On the first day, taking Boris Yeltsin's anti-coup declaration in Moscow as an invitation, he made a speech denouncing the committee for the state of emergency as 'a coup d'etat by a group of government criminals'.[3] After Zavgayev's return, Dudayev led a rally at Liberty Square, condemning the entire leadership for its cowardice. The Chechen congress passed a resolution calling for the resignation of Zavgayev and the disbanding of the Supreme Soviet. Emboldened by the euphoria that followed the defeat of the coup, the congress called for the transfer of power to its executive committee pending fresh elections, and for a commission to investigate the police, KGB, and procurator's office for their behaviour during the uncertain days of August.

The general strike launched by Dudayev originally as a protest against the putschists eventually toppled Zavgayev, and brought an end to Russian rule. It lasted ten weeks, and became increasingly violent. Busloads of villagers descended on the capital, transforming peaceful rallies into uproarious affairs. Armed supporters of Dudayev seized government buildings, the telephone exchange, and the television centre. They stormed the Supreme Soviet while it was in session and disbanded it, and then blockaded the airport to prevent the communist leadership from fleeing to Moscow. On 15 September, the demonstrators won their first victory. Zavgayev was sacked to make way for a provisional council that was supposed to organise new elections. But Dudayev was still not satisfied. He declared his own executive council to be in charge until elections could be held – at a date one month earlier than the authorities had envisaged. It was a tactic designed to prevent Moscow from interfering in the vote.

In other parts of the country, the August putsch had spurred those republics which had not yet declared independence from the Soviet Union to do so. But Yeltsin and the ethnic Chechen parliamentary Speaker, Ruslan Khasbulatov, had made it plain that numerically small peoples did not share the same rights as, for example, the Georgian or Baltic nations. Midway through the weeks of demonstrations, Moscow's attitude towards Dudayev changed. The gratitude for the support shown to Yeltsin during the coup turned to hostility. Immediately after the failed coup, Chechen protesters had been singled out for standing up for democracy, and Zavgayev had been listed by name among those leaders who had betrayed the cause of perestroika. Yeltsin had even threatened to sack him and his followers. But as it became clear that Dudayev's aims were greater than the replacement of a stagnant political leadership, Chechen aspirations were seen as suspect.

Dudayev became a target of Russian conservatives like the former Russian Vice-President Alexander Rutskoi. On his advice, the Russian parliament passed a resolution on 8 October 1991, condemning illegal armed formations in Chechnya and urging that the elections be held on the basis of existing legislation – that is, at the later date preferred by the discredited republic authorities. Rutskoi's attacks on the Chechens became more forthright; he urged Yeltsin to take 'specific measures to detain these criminals' and seize their weapons. To the Chechens, disarmament was a clear threat, a reminder of the measures that had preceded the repression and deportations of the 1930s and 1940s.

Dudayev reacted by announcing a general mobilisation of all males aged 16–55, later claiming that 62,000 men had come forward. Volunteer battalions from other areas of the north Caucasus also arrived in

Grozny, as Dudayev had aroused strong feelings of loyalty. Matters came to a head on 19 October, when Yeltsin sent a message to the executive committee condemning their actions as anti-constitutional. He ordered them to submit to the authority of the old guard's provisional council within three days. It was, said Russian deputy Hussain Akhmadov, 'the last belch of the Russian empire'.[4] On 23 October, as a warning to other autonomous republics, the Russian procuracy in Moscow issued a statement banning organisations and media whose campaigns would 'violate the integrity' of the Russian federation.

Dudayev went ahead with his plans. Presidential and parliamentary elections were held on 27 October. Since no women had stood for election, the new parliament was exclusively male. It was split between Dudayev's Vainakh (Our People) party, Greens and Islamists, but the general himself won an outright victory taking more than 85 per cent of the vote in a four-man race. Dudayev set the tone for his new regime by using a Koran for the swearing-in, and granting himself emergency powers for one month. Less than a week later, on 2 November, Chechnya announced its independence, a declaration which split the republic and orphaned the Chechens' partner nation, the Ingush. The Ingush opted to remain with Russia.

The events that followed were to prove deeply humiliating to Yeltsin. He refused to recognise Chechen independence, a snub Dudayev returned by refusing to recognise Russia. Immediately after the declaration, Yeltsin announced a state of emergency, dispatched troops to Chechnya and ordered the general's arrest. Unfazed, Dudayev prepared for violence and conspired to have 640 hardened prisoners escape from Grozny's jail overnight. The prisoners immediately announced that they would help defend the republic's independence, a declaration that underlined the Chechens' determination not to give in. But then on 10 November, two days after he declared a state of emergency, Yeltsin was forced to pull back from the brink. The Russian parliament failed to sanction his state of emergency, and he had to concede to a troop withdrawal. The soldiers were bused out of Chechnya after only minor exchanges of fire. The botched invasion was reportedly instigated at the suggestion of Ruslan Khasbulatov. Soon afterwards relations between Khasbulatov and Yeltsin deteriorated sharply, and the Speaker became a focus of conservative opposition to the Russian president.

But the war of nerves between Yeltsin and Dudayev continued. The soldiers were withdrawn only to North Ossetia, still within easy striking distance of Chechnya's wayward general. Russia imposed an economic blockade against Chechnya which, though relatively porous, still inconvenienced the administration. Although the crisis had passed, the prisoners stayed on the streets of Grozny. Among them were several murderers, and according to their leader – a 'security specialist' and karate enthusiast – about half had been jailed on illegal weapons charges. This, in the Chechen view, was merely a Soviet crime, because weapons-bearing was part of the mountaineer's culture. Fully armed and threatening, the prisoners were to remain in Chechnya's National Guard, despite token efforts by Dudayev to negotiate a return to jail. They became the nucleus of his ever-expanding bodyguard.

Chechnya's victory in its first showdown with Yeltsin was an inspiration to independence-minded people in the north Caucasus. And Dudayev's provocative actions since his declaration of Chechen independence made it clear that his ultimate aim was the dismantling of a colonial empire. Chechnya's survival of its confrontation with Yeltsin was but the first step towards Dudayev's main ambition: independence for the autonomous regions, followed by confederation and then a federation of mountain peoples.

Dudayev's real threat to Yeltsin was embodied in this dream, rather than in his talent for confrontation. Dudayev had said consistently that he was not content with his own 'scientific revolution' or with leading just a single nation to independence: 'If even one of our Caucasian republics belongs to Russia we will have no peace.' He has infected the Mountain People's Confederation with this spirit, turning it, in effect, into a popular front through which all the independent leanings of the non-Russian nationalities in the region could be expressed. Dudayev's danger lay in his readiness to intercede outside Chechnya's borders: sending troops to Abkhazia, and threatening clashes with the Russian troops drafted in to the Ingush–Ossetian conflict.

Chechnya's independence has not been recognised by any foreign state or former Soviet republic, for fear of offending Russia, and Dudayev himself has been turned down for visas to Western European countries. However, Chechnya has negotiated economic agreements with Kazakhstan and Ukraine to circumvent the patchy Russian economic blockade imposed in November 1991. The general imported truckloads of sugar from Turkey shortly after independence. He has also claimed that his small, unrecognised republic has had offers of support from the conservative Gulf states of Kuwait and Saudi Arabia, further undermining the balance of power on Russia's southern flank.

Despite the reluctance of countries to recognise Chechnya, Dudayev established a foreign ministry and despatched several envoys on lengthy trips abroad aimed at securing support for independence. Finland, the Baltic states, Turkey, Jordan and Syria in particular have been said by Chechnya to be close to extending recognition. But there was also the doomed visit to London in 1993 of two brothers who were to have organised the printing of currency, passports and stamps – vital symbols of nationhood. The emissaries were brutally murdered, dismembered and stuffed in a cupboard, an act that Dudayev and other Chechen officials publicly blamed on Russian intelligence agents. The Russians blamed the murders of Ruslan and Nasabek Utsyev on a shakedown in the Caucasian mafias, pointing to the arrest of an Armenian businessman resident in London. The tabloids had a field day with this explanation, exulting in pictures of luxury flats and the usual tales of mistresses and gambling debts.

Within Chechnya, Dudayev has adopted an ecumenical approach to government. He included both former communists and nationalists within his cabinet, arguing that 'there is only one principle in making a cabinet: education, experience and knowledge'. He recruited a minister of foreign affairs from Jordan where there is a large Chechen community in exile (the men are traditionally recruited to the palace bodyguard). He went to Moscow to hire the rector of the university, enticed a champion wrestler to take charge of his personal security, and a dancer to oversee cultural affairs. Dudayev appointed a Crimean Tatar as minister of energy and claimed to have Russian and German as well as Turkish advisers.

His balancing act extended into his earliest policy decisions. Although the general changed the day of rest from Sunday to Friday to indicate his support for a return to Muslim traditions, he showed no sympathy for demands for the establishment of Sharia religious courts. Despite his habit of confrontation with Moscow, he tried to forestall the exodus of Russian workers under way since 1989. On several occasions, the general assured the 300,000 Slavs who made up a quarter of Chechnya's population that all nationalities were equal in the republic. Both Russian and Chechen would be languages of state.

But the acclaim that greeted the hero of independence wore thin within months. There was criticism of Dudayev for abandoning the poor people who had formed the bedrock of his popular support in favour of developing ties to the criminal mafias. The communist nomenklatura remained loyal to Zavgayev. The intellectuals were extremely sceptical about the prospects of independence, and the Russian blockade and Dudayev's inexperience of government were beginning to take their toll. Despite his team of worldly advisers and a professed interest in foreign investment, Dudayev failed to undertake privatisation. He imposed a 40 per cent tax on profits, and channelled the revenues not into development but into the general budget, increasing the potential for corruption. He re-imposed the cumbersome system of a daily activities report from the oil refineries, a practice which had been abandoned in the late 1980s. The guiding light of his government, according to one opponent, was 'the command administrative system, but without the communist ideology'. Although there is no denying that the mafias have prospered under Dudayev's rule, it remains unclear whether he is a mafia don himself – as argued in Russia – or a prisoner of far more powerful, shadowy forces. The economic difficulties which resulted from the collapse of Soviet power and the blockade created opportunities for mafias.

As the months passed, the village and clan elders who had supported Dudayev against the communist authorities grew displeased. The executive committee which oversaw the takeover was unhappy at being edged out of power by the elected parliament. Among the members of the intelligentsia who had supported Dudayev's struggle to get rid of the previous authorities, there were concerns that he was setting Chechnya on a collision course with Russia. Dudayev seemed to enjoy thumbing his nose at Yeltsin in the months that followed the army's forced retreat: offering asylum to the East German leader Erich Honecker when his presence in Moscow became embarrassing and granting a permanent refuge to the deposed Georgian leader, Zviad Gamsakhurdia. There was also disquiet about the *de facto* split with Ingushetia, which had come about by default after Dudayev's independence declaration, and was sealed after the Ingush voted on 30 November 1991 to stay in Russia. Although Dudayev recognised the new republic at once and was among the first to congratulate the Ingush, among ordinary Chechens there was a feeling of betrayal.

Most of the misgivings about the course Dudayev had taken were voiced privately. In April 1993, they surfaced in an impeachment motion and a series of protests so unsettling for Dudayev that he imposed a curfew, dissolved parliament and imposed personal rule in order to survive. But the protests continued, with Dudayev's opponents gathering arms and occupying a main square in the capital. As the protests gathered pace, they became increasingly violent, leading to full-scale clashes and several deaths.

Before the failed rising, the combination of curfew, roaming criminals, upstart bodyguards and external threat made it nearly impossible to criticise Dudayev without being branded a Russian stooge. He was wont to lump all critics together with the open hostility towards his regime from President Yeltsin, arguing that: 'the opposition is terroristic and based in Moscow.'

There was certainly some truth in the general's assertions that Moscow was seeking to discredit his regime with a dirty-tricks campaign. In March 1992, several heavy trucks with weapons were seized at the border, adding to suspicions of a conspiracy hatched in Moscow with the participation of Zavgayev and Khasbulatov. All thirty political parties in the republic disclaimed involvement in the coup plot, which was launched from Zavgayev's home district where he presumably still enjoyed some support. According to Chechen government sources, the insurrection was aimed at getting Grozny to sign the federative treaty that was agreed later that month.

The administration created its own enemies, especially with the high-handedness of its bodyguards. They became a visible symbol of the abuse of power that was allowed to flourish under Dudayev's rule. 'The administration's bodyguards, the pilots say, have acquired a habit of rushing, armed, into the airport and onto planes, insulting the crew and ejecting the passengers.'[5] The airport manager at Grozny once told me that he had lost count of the number of times that brigands had driven on to the tarmac in their imported cars, firing into the air, and taking delivery of parcels from the flights.

Fears for law and order in Chechnya, which are given generous space in Russian newspapers, grew more pronounced after a number of raids on Russian arms depots, in what has become a traditional Caucasian method of armament. Nearly twenty people were killed in one storming of a Russian army garrison, and the government professed ignorance over whether the weapons had been taken by the National Guard or by uncontrolled elements. Such tensions have quickened the pace of the Russian exodus from Chechnya, along with the slow withdrawal of the former Red Army garrisons. Tens of thousands of Russian civilians were believed to have fled immediately after the Dudayev takeover, abandoning lucrative and strategic jobs in Grozny's oil industry. There is friction between Chechens and Russians in two border districts, which were handed to descendants of Cossacks after the Chechens were deported in 1944.

Islamic revival

Tolstoy-yurt, by its very name, is symbolic of Tsarist and then Soviet attempts to obliterate Islam as a unifying force for the north Caucasian nations. The village, in the hills about an hour's drive west from Grozny, was originally named Doka-yurt, *yurt* meaning village, after a local Sufi saint. It is one of dozens of shrines in Daghestan and Chechnya, modest places of pilgrimage that have replaced the mosque as a centre of religious life. The fact that the shrine exists still is a testimony to the endurance of faith in the north Caucasus. All the nations of the north Caucasus remain Muslim to a degree: the Abkhazians are a mixture of pagans, Christians and formally lapsed Muslims, and Islam is confined to the remnants of the old aristocracy in North Ossetia. The Daghestanis,

Chechens, Ingush and Karachai tend to be more religious. Islam came to lowland areas of Daghestan as early as the beginning of the 8th century, but peoples living in the more remote mountainous areas were relatively late converts, embracing the religion in the 17th, 18th and 19th centuries. The last Ingush village was converted in 1864.

Under Soviet rule, Muslims in the Caucasus were subjected to an anti-Islamic campaign which began in 1928. Mosques were closed, shrines destroyed, Sharia courts disbanded and religious leaders executed. After all potential for dissent was eliminated, the Soviet authorities created a new religious board for the north Caucasus in Daghestan in 1945. The body monitored the pliable and often badly educated Muslim clergy who had managed to survive, and who were distrusted by the majority of the population because of their links to the KGB.

The purges and the puppet religious leadership diminished spiritual life for generations. While institutional religious life continued in Daghestan, it became alienated from the majority of the population because of the mistrust of the clergy. Thus scholarly knowledge of the religion in Daghestan remained, but popular practice fell away. In Chechnya, on the other hand, the authorities clamped down hard on public expressions of religion. While official religion suffered, a parallel Islam endured quietly through village shrines and small prayer assemblies. No mosques were built in Chechnya until 1978; at the time of independence there were just two in Grozny. After perestroika enabled young people to examine their own culture, many were disturbed by how far the conventional face of religion had been degraded. As Abdullah Khadjiev, the young editor of Daghestan's first Muslim newspaper, *Islamic Novosti*, explained: 'The spiritual leaders of Islam are illiterate now and limited in knowledge, and that contributes to the bad image of Islam.'

But Islam survived the Tsarist and Soviet onslaughts – largely because of the influence of the Sufi orders. The two main orders in Chechnya and Daghestan, the Naqshbandiya and Qadiriya, are egalitarian and have a tradition of secrecy and decentralised structure which accommodates conspiratorial work. The Sufi orders despised the Tsarist and communist authorities as equally alien non-Muslim regimes. The brotherhoods were more influential among tribal societies like the Chechens and some Daghestani peoples. These were also the peoples who showed the strongest resistance to alien rule. The Kabardians, who had a huge aristocracy and were seen as the most chivalrous and gallant nation of the north Caucasus, were vulnerable to Russian overtures. They were the first nation to align with Russia after Ivan the Terrible took a Kabardian princess as his bride. For the Kabardians,

Islam was like a thin veneer. Their disdain for the Sufi brotherhoods was shared by the Cherkess and the Ossetian Muslim nobility. But the Chechens and the more mountainous Daghestani peoples had no aristocracy and a much more egalitarian system of village councils. They flocked to the brotherhoods and to the clergy. Before the revolution, clerics made up 5 per cent of the population of Daghestan. There were more than 2,000 mosques and 800 *madrassahs*, or seminaries. In Chechnya, 60,000 men declared themselves to be members of a Sufi order.[6] During the Caucasian wars, Chechens and Daghestanis took a leading role followed by the Ingush, Adygs, Balkars and Karachai – albeit in lesser numbers and with less enthusiasm. The Kabardians, Cherkess and Ossetians did not fight against Russian rule.

Nowhere was the melding of faith and political organisation more evident than in the heroic struggles of the Caucasians against the Russian invaders. Imam Mansour, a Naqshbandi, was one of the earliest rebel leaders, taking his men to a series of victories over the Russians from 1785 to 1791. He left no successor, and the rebellion was dormant for some forty years. Then his mission was taken up by the 'lion of Daghestan', Imam Shamil. Shamil was an Avar, but his rebellion relied more on support from Chechens than from his own countrymen. It was Shamil's organisation, a network of thirty-one naibs, administrators and military commanders, and a separate Islamic justice system, that gave a structure to decades of sporadic guerrilla struggle against Russian forces. Although his Russian opponents called Shamil's movement Muridism, after the word for disciple, it did not represent a separate Caucasian tendency or a sect of Islam. His combination of spiritual and temporal power and evocation of a holy war was in the tradition of the Naqshbandi brotherhood.

Over the years, word of Shamil's resistance spread to Western Europe, where he won respect for his brilliance as a guerrilla commander and for his bravery. Because of the regard in which he was held, the Tsar hesitated to have him executed after his capture, and the defeat of his rebellion in August 1859. He feared creating a martyr of Shamil, which could provoke a further Caucasian conflagration. Instead, Shamil was banished from the Caucasus to a relatively comfortable captivity in Kaluga and Kiev. After many requests, he was allowed to make a pilgrimage, or *haj*, to Mecca in 1871. He died in Arabia and was buried in Medina. As a measure of the Tsar's success in subduing his biggest foe, Shamil's son studied in St Petersburg and rose to the rank of general in the Russian army.

The lesson of Shamil was that Islam and national sentiment could overcome ethnic divisions and unite all the Caucasian peoples. The process was repeated in the fighting against the Bolshevik army in the high Caucasus during the civil war. The campaign ended in the fight to the death of 10,000 mountaineers who had openly committed themselves to *Ghazawat*, or holy war. As Alexandre Benningsen and S. Enders Wimbush noted in their study of Islam in the Soviet Union, the passions aroused by the declaration of a holy war were all-consuming:

> It was most likely that the brotherhoods were fighting without any precise goal in mind, except to expel the Russians — simply because they could not submit to the new Soviet regime with its old Russian character and its new militant atheism.[7]

That continuous tradition was embodied in the character of Doka, who became immortalised at Doka-yurt. Although he exemplified a much more gentle tradition, it was still crucial to preserving ethnic identity. Sheikh Doka, or Abdul Aziz Sheptukayev, was executed as a traitor at the beginning of the century. He was said to have healing powers, able to cure stutterers with a glance and rheumatism with the laying on of hands. His grave, a fenced-off mausoleum in an otherwise simple cemetery, became a pilgrimage site for the faithful. And the pebbles and tokens left there by visitors were evidence that pilgrimage to sites such as this had increased in importance as conventional methods of worship suffered.

Within weeks of Dudayev's rise to power in Chechnya, a new mosque was built near Doka's birthplace, a small whitewashed hut with a corrugated metal roof and no minaret. The jumble of carved walking sticks amid the shoes left at the entrance one Friday spoke of the inroads the state has made against Muslim identity. Islam appears to have skipped a generation and a half at Doka.

Only the very old and the very young attend the mosque. Religious knowledge has been passed on in a random way by fathers or grandfathers who still remember how to pray. Among the old men is Salman Doka, a descendant of the saint. The children at the mosque began receiving formal instruction in religion and Arabic in the autumn of 1991. Since then, there have been proposals for an Islamic summer camp for children. But as the acting priest of Doka has admitted, it has not been the adherence to the letter of Islam that mattered so much as its importance as a symbol of Chechen identity: 'Religion in every time is very important, but as for us we are so far from Islamic ways. We have particular ways, our own ways. It doesn't look like any other religion.'

The renewal of interest in Islam in neighbouring Daghestan is also concerned more with reclaiming culture than with embracing the Tehran-style fundamentalism which so concerns Moscow and the West.

In Daghestan, perestroika has led to a multiplying of mosques in mountain villages, as well as the founding of a *madrassah*, or seminary, and of libraries and hostels. Among the emerging Islamic institutions is the irregular tabloid newspaper, *Islamic Novosti*. Its part-time editor, orthopaedic surgeon Abdullah Khadjiev, intends the paper to fill a huge gap in knowledge about Islam and traditional Daghestani culture: 'During the whole period of Soviet power, Islamic thoughts and ideas were banned. The ban aroused a hunger in the people and they need an educational Islamic paper. We have separated from our history.' As if to reflect its informational bent, the back page of the first issue was dominated by a picture of the American pop singer, Paula Abdul – a symbol of Muslim achievement, according to Khadjiev.

The deportations

Islam has been one constant in the preservation of ethnic identity in the north Caucasus. The other powerful symbol which the new nationalist leaders have used comes from the Stalinist era, a wholesale persecution still in living memory: the deportations. The displacement of the entire populations of Chechens, Ingush, Balkars and Karachai, even those living outside their native territories, marked the second exodus of the north Caucasians. The deportations to Kazakhstan and Kyrgystan were a potent reminder of the flight of half a million Circassians to Turkey at the time of the Russian conquest, and the subsequent annihilation of the once numerous Ubykh peoples of the Black Sea coast.

The Karachai, numbering 70,000, were the first nation to be deported in November 1943, followed by 200,000 Chechens and 90,000 Ingush on 23 February 1944, Red Army day. The 35,000 Balkars are believed to have been deported that March. The deportations had been planned for several months in advance. Although ordered by Stalin, all were executed according to the instructions of a three-man committee led by a KGB general, Ivan Serov. The Caucasians were taken completely by surprise. Still, some people managed to escape into the hills, and there were outlaw gangs of Chechens and Balkars in the mountains until 1951.

Officially, the deportations were necessary for wartime security. The Soviet authorities held that the Caucasians were unreliable and a potential fifth column. This was absolutely untrue. There has never been evidence of widespread collusion between Caucasian peoples and Nazi Germany. Historians disagree about the real reason for Stalin's persecution of some of the north Caucasian peoples, but the choice of the Chechens and Ingush strongly suggests that it was aimed at destroying a natural leadership in the region, as the Chechens were at once the most numerous and most rebellious nation. A Chechen uprising against Russian rule in 1939 was even furnished as evidence of their collaboration. The other peoples deported in the region as a whole – the Karachai, Balkars, and Meskhetians of Georgia – were all Turkic. Their selection reflects the traditional Russian unease about its southern neighbour, as well as a fear of Turkish alliances with Nazi Germany. The timing of the deportation in itself is proof that Stalin's pretext was a fiction: by 1944 the Nazis were already withdrawing from the region, making a nonsense of the idea that the Caucasian peoples could constitute a wartime threat.

Although the Caucasian campaign of the Second World War was important, it was reduced to a sideshow by the battle of Stalingrad. During the summer of 1942, when the campaign began, all Soviet oil came from the Caucasus and there was panic about the prospect of Baku's oil fields falling under Nazi control. Poti and Batumi were the only ports still in Soviet hands; and with Ukraine occupied, the region was crucial to food supplies. With these strategic interests in mind, the German army poured thirty-five to forty divisions into the Caucasus. But after a series of victories – the capture of Stavropol and the Maykop oil fields – the German advance was halted in December 1942. The Nazis were fifty miles from Grozny and Chechen lands. Even those lands which fell were only briefly occupied by the invaders: the occupation of Karachai territory lasted just four months, from August 1942 until January 1943.

Aside from strategic interests, the other pretext offered for the deportations was the Nazi scheme to form a Bergmann, or mountaineers' battalion, as well as to recruit subversives from among the prisoners of war. In addition, there were reports that Said Bey, Shamil's grandson, had visited Berlin in 1942 to discuss plans for a Nazi-sponsored homeland. Although the Nazis did intend to create a Caucasian battalion, this was in line with a policy that sought to exploit the discontents of all subjected nationalities, such as the Ukrainians or Baltic peoples. As for mass collaboration, the overwhelming majority of Caucasian men served in the Red Army. At the time of the deportation, fourteen Karachai were to be rewarded as heroes of the Soviet Union. They were sent to Kazakhstan anyway; only one of the fourteen ever received his honour, and that posthumously. He received the title in 1967 after lobbying from Belorussia, where he had been in a partisans' unit during the war, according to information from new archives made available to the Karachai historian, Maria Osmanova Baichorova. That tally of honours for a nation of traitors compares well with Daghestan, whose loyalty was never questioned. Daghestan produced forty-nine war-time heroes out of a population ten times larger than the Karachai. The main difference between the behaviour of the north Caucasians during the war and that of other nations was that it was practical to deport the Caucasian nations.

Baichorova is a historian at the Cherkessk museum, the largest town in the Karachai-Cherkess republic. She is a member of the special committee that has been investigating the deportations of the Karachai since 1991 with a view to assessing the need for compensation. She was 6 years old when the deportations took place.

> I can remember everything. A big Studebaker lorry came into the yard in the evening. The soldiers searched the entire houses and gave us an hour to collect our belongings. We lived then in a Russian Cossack village and our neighbours helped us to pack. We could take food and some furnishings but not our animals. I remember my older brother, Magomet, used to play the balalaika. And when the soldiers found it, they ordered him to play. He was crying but he played the balalaika. What a mad moment it was, what a mad moment.

After the people were assembled and driven to a rail head, they were loaded, four or five families in each carriage, on to goods trains bound for Kazakhstan or Kirgizia. Then the carriage doors were sealed on the thirty or forty people who had been herded inside. Conditions on the train were horrific. The cars were unlocked only once a day when people were fed, and in such crowded and filthy conditions disease was rampant. The trains took weeks to reach their destinations, and trails of corpses were abandoned by the railway line. According to Baichorova, the deportees were never told where they were going and no arrangements were made for housing them once they arrived in Kyrgystan.

They were supposed to have been billeted randomly, but found that they were shunned by Kyrgyz. This was as much for the political stigma as for the tales that had preceded the Karachais' arrival, portraying them as a nation of barbarians from the high Caucasus. Many Karachai families were reduced to begging; Baichorova remembers that a special trick among children was to say their names were Lenin or Stalin so that they could earn extra money. But despite the abject conditions of exile, there were acts of resistance: an Ingush rising in 1945, work strikes by Chechens, and a mass breakout of 4,000 prisoners at a camp in Krasnoyarsk, Siberia in 1954.

It is impossible to overstate the effects of at least fourteen years of banishment. These were small and close-knit societies, whose people had a passionate attachment to culture and place. There are no definite figures on how many people perished during the deportations and the harsh exile in Central Asia, but Conquest compares rates of population growth from 1944 to 1957 to the period of 1926–39. Even accounting for the deaths due to the Stalinist terror, the rates of growth fell drastically during the years in exile, indicating the scale of the tragedy. The Chechen population grew by just 2.5 per cent during the punishment years, compared to 28 per cent during a decade of purges. The Balkar population was static compared to an earlier growth rate of 28 per cent.[8] The Karachai population increased by 8 per cent compared to 37 per cent, and the Ingush by 15 per cent compared to 24 per cent.

Aside from banishment, the entire history of the north Caucasus was systematically altered. Territories were wiped off contemporary maps, and the names of towns and villages were Russified or otherwise changed. The deportations were not even announced until 26 June 1946, well after they were completed, and there was no information on the fate or destination of the deported people until 1955. And even in these brief notices, there was no mention of the Karachai or Balkar peoples; officially they had ceased to exist. In their absence, the lands of the deported people were divided up among arriving settlers. Karachai land was given to Georgians; Chechen land to the Laks, a small Daghestani ethnic group; and Ingush land to Ossetians. Their heroes were also reviled. Shamil, though he had been admired by Marx as a freedom fighter, was transformed in Soviet ideology into a reactionary and an agent of imperialism 'in the service of British capitalism and the Turkish sultan'. The story of the annexation of the Caucasus was given a completely different twist. Conquest quotes the theoretical organ *Bolshevik* from July 1950:

> In the eighteenth and beginning of the nineteenth century the problem of their future fate faced the people of the Caucasus with particular acuteness. They could be swallowed and enslaved by backward feudal Turkey and Persia or be annexed to Russia ... Inclusion in Russia was for the people of the Caucasus the only possible path for the development of their economy and culture ... Despite the arbitrary acts and cruelty of the Tsarist colonisers the annexation of the Caucasus to Russia played a positive and progressive role for the people of the Caucasus.[9]

It was more than three years after Stalin's death that the beginnings of reparation were made to the deported peoples. On 4 July 1956, a Karachai delegation went to Moscow to appeal to Khrushchev to put the deportation issue on the agenda of the 20th party congress. He did, and in the so-called secret speech that attacked Stalin's excesses, Khrushchev offered what was then the fullest official explanation of the deportations. However, it was not until February 1957 that a law was passed restoring the territories of Checheno-Ingushetia, Karachai-Cherkess and Kabardino-Balkar.

There was little effort to ease the way for a homecoming. Returning Chechens were met by signs reading 'Keep Chechens and Ingush
out of the Caucasus' and a three-day rampage by Russians who had
been settled on their lands, and were now unwilling to leave. The
Chechens were forced into second-class accommodation that would
not displace the newcomers. Other returnees remained permanently
dispossessed by boundary changes. And they all carried the stigmata
of the 'traitor'. Despite the official pardon of the Caucasian deportees,
Soviet historians continued to dwell on their 'unreliability'.

The slurs against the Karachai were repeated in academic and official journals as recently as the late 1980s. Central to the defamation
campaign was the false accusation that the Karachai had participated
in a wartime massacre of children, even though subsequent excava-
tions had shown this to be untrue. The evidence of the slaughter of
innocent children, which had so incensed Russians, turned out to be
a mass grave of two dozen people, mostly adults, who had been shot
by the Germans. However, as recently as 1989 a regional party committee recommended that a book, *In the Name of the Cheka*, in which
the Karachai are shown as cannibals, bandits and traitors, be studied
in all kindergartens.[10]

For nations such as the Karachai and the Balkars, the deportations
have become an issue central to their political life. This is in part due
to the relatively late rehabilitation of the Karachai, who were the last
nation to set up a committee to discuss compensation for the
deportations. But their political movements have yet to progress towards a consideration of their status within Russia. For Chechens, the
struggle with Russia is firmly in the present. The deportations are
marked in Grozny as an official holiday. Schools and offices are closed,
and television broadcasts are given over to live coverage of a memorial
service. But although the deportations have ceased to occupy such a
central place on the Chechen political agenda, they have of course
inflicted the same hindrances. The lack of educational and other opportunities for the generation of governing age is felt deeply.

Among those Chechens deported was Solombek Khadjiev, aged 2,
and now leader of the opposition to Dudayev. Khadjiev was Soviet
petroleum minister for the last eight months of the union's existence
before heading Grozny's petroleum research institute. He is one of the
few Chechens of his generation to have overcome the tremendous
disadvantage of belonging to a 'punished' nation. Another more prominent survivor is the former Russian Speaker, Ruslan Khasbulatov,
who is the same age. Khadjiev was among the first batch of Chechens
to be allowed to enter university. Others, less fortunate, were denied
further education. He remembers: 'We had only seven or ten years of

school, depending on the village and availability. We were not allowed to go to a different village. There were no buses to the school and we walked eight kilometres in each direction.' The denial of educational opportunity, he says, goes some way towards explaining the stereotype that Chechens are easily led into crime, as well as the reason why an area as rich as Chechnya should have one of the highest unemployment and poverty rates in all of Russia.

The oil industry – Chechnya's future?

The centre of Chechnya's oil industry lies along the road between Grozny and the Ingush city of Nazran, and the pipes and stacks of the refining plant dominate the skyline. Like other Soviet institutions, Grozny's oil industry has its own museum, explaining the history of oil in the Soviet Union, and the growth of the refining industry at Grozny. On the wood-panelled walls of the museum of the petroleum research institute are thirty-two photographs of former directors. Only two are Chechen, and one Ingush. Even after Chechen independence, the workforce remained 70 per cent Russian. The legacy of a 'punished nation' could not be more clear. But the oil industry is the main hope for Chechnya becoming economically viable. In his speeches at the time of Chechnya's independence, Dudayev often mentioned the 'golden tap'; the reference to Chechnya's oil always raised a cheer from the crowds.

Oil was discovered in Chechnya in 1823. The British built the first refinery at Grozny, and a number of lavish mansions in an otherwise featureless city are a reminder of the days of the foreign oil barons at the turn of the century. In 1928, the Soviet Union's first petrochemical research institute, in effect the nucleus of the country's oil industry, was founded at Grozny. The engineers it trained went on to build about half of the refining plants in other parts of the country. Although Grozny still produces 3.5 million tonnes of petroleum a year, it is more important now as a refining centre, processing 6.5–7 million tonnes of crude a year, which arrives via pipelines from Kazakhstan as well as from Tyumen in the Urals.

For its own needs, Chechnya needs only one million tonnes of oil a year, so the 2.5 million tonne surplus could provide the basis of its economic development. It is also seeking out markets for its petrochemical products in Germany and Turkey. However, there is an expiry date on Chechnya's wealth. Its estimated reserves are only 50 or 60 million tonnes, which would be exhausted in about fifteen years. There have been discussions with American and Japanese firms about exploration, but the political instability in Chechnya has so far deterred investors. So too have reports of Chechnya's petrol pirates, who drill holes in pipelines to siphon off supplies to sell at immense profit in Russia. As for legitimate oil sales, the only route out of Chechnya is through Russia, leaving the republic vulnerable to the whims of its large neighbour.

Territorial dispute: the Ingush and the Ossetians

In November 1992, a year after Chechnya's independence, Russia mobilised 3,000 troops and declared a state of emergency in North Ossetia and Ingushetia, where there had been worsening violence in a land dispute. The clashes were the first outbreak in Russia proper of the ethnic violence which had plagued the post-Soviet order. The genesis of the dispute, like other territorial conflicts in the region, lies in the Stalin-era deportations, which resulted in large populations of nationalities living outside their titular boundaries.

When the Ingush returned from exile in Kazakhstan and Kirgizia, their territory had shrunk by 113,000 hectares. Some Ingush settled near their old lands in the Prigorodny and Malgobak districts of North Ossetia. When the frustration at the loss of the territory boiled over there were 45,000 Ingush living in the republic. In addition to lands in the two districts, a section of the Ingush returnees in North Ossetia also claimed the right bank of Vladikavkaz as a national right. The demands for restitution, first voiced in 1990, were heading for violence fully a year before Yeltsin declared a state of emergency on 2 November 1992 following the kidnapping of eighty Russian interior ministry troops in the border village of Chermen.

Chermen had been an entirely Ingush village before the Second World War, and those Ingush who lived there after 1957 still insisted on calling it by its old name: Bazorkina. Chermen/Bazorkina's population had been evenly mixed. But by late 1991, Ingush began migrating to their own republic following a campaign of intimidation that included threats and visits to their homes by gangs of Ossetian thugs. For those who tried to stay on, the end was tragic. A year on, there were virtually no Ingush left in North Ossetia. There were reports of columns of Ingush refugees perishing in the snow in the highlands after the Ossetians blocked the roads.

The land dispute had taken on new urgency after Chechnya declared independence. The Ingush leadership had parted company with the Chechens in the summer of 1991, arguing that settlement of their land claims took precedence over independence. In that, the leadership believed it had Yeltsin's support. The Ingush believed that he had promised a sympathetic hearing of their claims against the Ossetians during a visit to the region in September 1991. Swayed by that hope, more than 90 per cent of the Ingush voted to remain inside Russia during a referendum on independence in November 1991. Then, when it became clear that Yeltsin would not act on his promises, if indeed he had made a promise with such sweeping implications for similar disputes, the Ingush leadership became bereft of ideas.

I visited the village of Chermen during the autumn of 1991. By then, older men, as well as young hotheads, were full of fighting talk. Among them was Isa Tarkoyev, aged 55, who had made a daily ritual of visiting his erstwhile properties. I met him outside the low blue stucco cottage that his father had built in the 1930s, and although Isa now had his own, much larger, home, the loss still rankled. For Chechens and Ingush, there is no greater shame than the departure of a younger son from the family home. A son who fails to maintain his father's house is seen as bringing dishonour upon the family name. With this in mind, Tarkoyev was seething at the Ossetian owner's refusal to sell. 'They take my land and then they stretch out their hand in friendship,' he said, shaking his head in disbelief.

What is interesting is the Ossetian leadership's apparently concili-atory stance at that same time. In contrast to the bluster in Bazorkina, the authorities in Vladikavkaz seemed anxious to avoid confrontation, Although there was no question of redrawing land borders, the Ossetians were prepared to offer monetary compensation and to help in reset-tling, according to Taymuraz Kusov, president of the nationalities com-mittee:

> There could be negotiations about people who were personally driven away from these districts. If some of them can't get land back, we are ready to help them return. If it is a question of Ingush houses, we are ready to discuss that question too. In such a case, we may help build a new house and resettle some of them.

The Russian operation in North Ossetia a year later coincided with signals of a new hardline approach to the nationalities question. In the same month, Yeltsin sacked his adviser on ethnic affairs, the liberal Galina Starovoitova, who had championed the Armenian cause during the early days of the Nagorno-Karabakh agitation, as well as serving as his original envoy to the north Caucasus. He deputed a close ally, Sergei Shakhrai, to take charge of the region, and granted him sweep-ing powers.

It was perhaps inevitable that Chechnya's general should see the changes and the arrival of Russian troops in neighbouring territories as a threat. A year earlier, he had predicted such clashes and had accused Moscow of cynically exploiting the land claims issue. North

Ossetia has always occupied an odd place within the Caucasus. The Ossetians are Indo-Aryans, and rather than speaking a Caucasian or Turkic dialect, their language is distantly related to Persian. In Russia, as in Georgia, the Ossetians have shown a loyalty to Moscow that sets them apart from their neighbours. This affinity is visible in the main square of Vladikavkaz, where a statue of Lenin strides into the middle distance, long after such displays fell out of favour in neighbouring republics. 'The Russians have provoked the situation between the Ossetians and Ingush about territorial claims. The Russians have armed the Ossetians', Dudayev told me in late 1991. But the Ingush also had arms funnelled through to them.

North Ossetia was particularly vulnerable to the arms build-up. It was the smallest of the autonomous republics but under tremendous demographic pressure. Aside from its 600,000 inhabitants, North Ossetia was straining to absorb 100,000 refugees from the war between Georgia and South Ossetia. The authorities were also struggling to build housing for some 20,000 soldiers who were to be resettled in Vladikavkaz from Germany. But if Dudayev was fearful of an external hand in the Ossetian–Ingush dispute, he also thought such interference could be Russia's undoing:

> I am confident that if something happens here it will be a great war in all the Caucasus and Trans-Caucasus. A stable situation in the Caucasus depends on a stable situation here. If any Caucasian nation notices any Russian provocation, they will all rise to support us.

Knowing Russia's hostility towards him, the general had particular reason to fear the deployment of Russian troops in that the lack of fixed boundaries between Ingushetia and Chechnya left his republic open to invasion. A fortnight after Yeltsin's declaration of emergency, Dudayev signed a decree declaring a state of emergency in western Chechnya, which abuts on the disputed region, and appointed a new defence council.

Dudayev's analysis of the Ingush–Ossetian dispute was prophetic. Months after the initial clashes, Ingush leaders began to complain that Russia was uninterested in a political solution to the conflict, or in disarming the Ossetian gangs which had taken part in the fighting. Several Ingush officials resigned their posts in protest. But still, there was no initiative from Moscow to reverse the forced population transfer or to begin to address Ingush demands. The troops remained in Ossetia, a constant reminder to Chechnya and the independence-minded republics of Russia's greater power, and of its disinclination to disengage from the region.

Daghestan: a test of unity

It is a slushy and wet Wednesday morning and the lecturer is working hard to coax a few words from the final-year English students at the pedagogical institute. The college has a new policy of encouraging students to express opinions on current events, and today's topic is the 'nationalities question'. As usual, the older students are reticent. At last, after several spurned opening questions, one boy at the back raises his hand. 'This is a very painful problem, we don't like to touch this problem', says Mansour. His classmates join in. 'This period of freedom has awakened problems of ancient times. Democracy has already proved itself to be ineffective in solving our national problems.'

The 'nationalities question' is potentially more explosive in Daghestan than anywhere else in the former Soviet Union. An autonomous republic the size of Scotland, it includes thirty-three Caucasian nationalities, in addition to immigrants from other parts of the country. Some of these nations are so tiny as to exist nowhere else: the Laks, for example, a nation of 120,000 who have traditionally been tinkers, repairing samovars, and the 19,000 Tats, assimilated elsewhere, a Farsi-speaking, primarily Jewish community. Daghestani society is rural and the larger indigenous nationalities all have a land base.

Under communist rule, government posts were judiciously divided according to nationality, ensuring that Avars, Kumyks, Lezgins and Dargins – the largest of the indigenous nationalities – did not get too much power. The system of ethnic quotas permeated all spheres of life. The authorities were as careful to fund theatres for the Dargins, who in 1989 made up 16 per cent of Daghestan's 1.8 million people, as they were for the Avars, who are the largest group.

For many years, the rigid quota system appeared to work, dampening down potential discontents. The rate of intermarriage in Daghestan was 25 per cent until the mid-1980s – by far the highest in the entire Caucasus, and a convenient indicator of relaxed ethnic relations. But as Enver Faridovich, head of the sociology department at the Academy of Sciences, noted, even the most idealistic of policies suffered in the breakdown of the Soviet order:

> We cannot say that there was not any national policy. It was conducted in such a way that you cannot criticise it. It was honest and just. It lacked only one thing. It was organised by the state. During the last years of stagnation there was a strand of corruption everywhere, and even a nationality policy that had been all right was beginning to become breached.

The system has come under attack since the beginning of this decade, when every nationality in Daghestan formed a popular front to press for more power, and in some cases a confederal system of government. At the top of the agenda is land. Daghestan means 'land of mountains'; a geography that encouraged so many different language groups to develop in isolation. But its population is growing and the fertile land near the shores of the swollen, grey Caspian Sea is in short supply. Economic problems are undermining the efforts for ethnic harmony that characterised Daghestan. 'This fraternity that lasted for so many years probably wasn't sincere', says one woman in the class. A Kumyk, she is the first to admit, in front of a disapproving teacher, that she supports a popular front.

The Kumyks, who speak a Turkic language, are the third largest indigenous ethnic group in Daghestan. Their popular front group, Tenglik, meaning 'equality', was the first to emerge at the end of 1989 and remains the most radical. Among Tenglik's demands is the establishment of a sovereign Kumyk republic along the Caspian Sea coast. According to Tenglik, Kumyks have suffered in Daghestan's division of spoils, and have been discriminated against in obtaining higher education. At the root of Kumyk discontent is the migration from the highlands of Avar and Dargin farmers from the 1950s to the 1970s. They were settled in valleys populated by Kumyks, and were granted higher prices for their produce to help them settle in. Kumyk demands have led to small-scale clashes. In October 1992, Tenglik activists blockaded the railroad for two or three days at a time. In response, the Avars have set up a popular front of their own, named after Shamil.

The proliferation of popular fronts represents the biggest threat to Daghestan's territorial integrity, a replica in miniature of the nationalist forces which tore apart the Soviet Union. So far, the Kumyk agitation has proved the most dangerous and the most prone to violence. It is obviously impossible to contemplate the division of such a small territory as Daghestan into separate statelets for its main nationalities: the Avars, Lezgins, Kumyks and Dargins. But the limited lands and poor economic prospects in Daghestan make it difficult to satisfy competing economic demands. Unless the aspirations of the Kumyks and other groups can be accommodated in new power-sharing arrangements, Daghestan's prospects do not look good.

Redefining borders: the Karachai-Cherkess republic

Like Daghestan, the Karachai-Cherkess republic represents another area which, although so far largely peaceful, contains all the elements for an ethnic conflict. In the Karachai-Cherkess republic, the issue is not over competing claims to land, but over the suitability of an administrative region which combines three different nationalities against their will. No nationality forms a majority in the republic. Russians make up 42 per cent of the population, followed by 32 per cent for the Karachai, and less than 10 per cent for the Cherkess. Although established as a joint autonomous region in 1922, the Karachai and Cherkess people were separated from 1926 to 1943 in recognition of the fact that the Turkic Karachai are unrelated to the Cherkess. But after the region was reconstituted in 1957, the two peoples were re-combined. That equation, and the fact that until 1991 Karachai-Cherkess had been subordinate to the Stavropol region rather than constituting an autonomous republic, provided the first stirrings of the nationalist movements.

While the landscaped streets, educational institutes and Academy of Sciences of Makhachkala indicate the economic advancements under Soviet rule, the cities of Karachayesk and Cherkessk speak of neglect and of attempts to stamp out the identity of the Caucasian peoples who live there. Both main communities complain of the lack of instruction in native languages. In the larger city, Cherkessk, the air is full of dust from unpaved roads. There is little industry, and the tourist trade in Karachayesk that had helped sustain the economy has vanished with the end of party-sponsored group holidays. The main road in Cherkessk is bare of trees; every building is topped by neon-lit communist slogans and emblems. Years after the event, the posters for the 28th party congress are still hanging.

The Karachai began the clamour for a division of the autonomous republic the same year as the congress in 1988. The injustice of the deportations provided the impetus for their campaign. In 1991, a conference to consider reparation erupted into a noisy demonstration during which a statue of Lenin was torn down, and Islamic flags raised. In response, Karachai-Cherkess was upgraded from a region, administered by Stavropol, into an autonomous republic, directly subordinate to Moscow with greater autonomy for the local legislature. But the leaders of the Karachai pressure group, Jamagat, were unimpressed. They argued that the nation could never be fully rehabilitated unless it enjoyed the same separate status as it had during the pre-war years. 'There is no rehabilitation without reconstruction', maintained Kazi Tenayevitch Leipanov, the Jamagat leader.

The Karachai claimed that the failure to restore their own republic was in itself an indication that they were still not fully trusted by the Soviet authorities. They maintained that they were destined to be subordinate to Russians in any joint republic, citing as evidence the absence of a single Karachai as secretary of the Karachayevsk party committee, head of police, prosecutor, judge, or KGB employee for thirty years.[11] They feared that they would remain vulnerable to being played off against the far smaller Cherkess population, to both nations' disadvantage. Their discontent set off reactions among all the ethnic groups in the republic.

In November 1990, the Cherkess reacted to the Karachai demands by forming their own popular front, the Adygeya-Khasa, which opposed demands for separation. The Cherkess viewed the divisive approach of the Karachai as one that ultimately suited Moscow's interests. Instead, the Cherkess held that they were entitled to compensation for wrongs that pre-dated the grievances of the Karachai: the decimation of their nation in the Russian conquest. The Adygeya-Khasa leaders demanded a full review of the history of the Russian conquest and an apology to the Cherkess.

The new assertiveness of the Karachai and Cherkess triggered further separatist movements. Two smaller nationalities, the Nogai, who are the descendants of the Mongol Golden Horde, and another Circassian group, the Abasin, also began to demand a new confederal structure for Karachai-Cherkess, with separate statelets for each nation. Together, their populations make up only 9 per cent of the republic. But far more significant was the reaction from the local Cossacks, who form a sizeable part of the Russian population. The Cossacks also began to organise in 1990, alarmed at the prospect of diminishing Russian influence after the republic was granted more autonomy. Some of the Cossack demands were merely provocative, such as the campaign to change the name of Cherkessk to Batalpashinsk to commemorate an 18th-century Russian victory over the local population. But the Cossacks were genuinely afraid of the rise in nationalist sentiment. They feared that their villages in the Zalenchuk district would be separated by a Karachai-Cherkess split and responded by seeking a further carving-up of the republic. They asked that their *stanitsy*, or villages, be ruled directly from Krasnodar, a contiguous territory. Such a move would be a reversion to the administrative structures that existed while the Karachai were in exile. It was, the local *ataman* (Cossack leader) argued, a natural right. He held that the Cossacks were a minority distinct from Russians by virtue of their repression after the Bolshevik revolution, and one under threat by rising national consciousness in the surrounding Muslim population. The sense of unease was added to by the migration of Russians from the former Soviet republics that began in the late 1980s.

For the short term, the crisis in Karachai-Cherkess has been averted. The Karachai movement had aroused such fears that any talk of restitution was shelved. In an April 1992 referendum, 76.8 per cent of the population voted to maintain the republic's present borders, although both the Cherkess and Cossack leaders had called for a boycott. But although open conflict was avoided, the discontents within Karachai-Cherkess remain. There is also scope for conflict in the republic's neighbour and twin, Kabardino-Balkar, in which the dissimilar Balkar and Kabardins have been combined in similar circumstances. The Adygs too share the Karachai problem of becoming a minority on their own lands in their republic near Krasnodar.

Aside from illustrating still further potential for violent conflict in the Caucasus, the tensions in Karachai-Cherkess reveal the frailty of the emerging nationalist movements. Kazi Tenayevitch Leipanov, the Jamagat leader, himself provides an example. His personal background demonstrates the ease with which nationalist feeling can be exploited by the former communist apparatus. Leipanov, like the other Karachai leaders, is of an older generation than the one generally coming to the fore in the 1990s. Although in his late sixties, he cuts an impressive figure. He wears the military decorations on his coat with pride and describes his war wounds with enthusiasm. His voice is confident and too loud for a sitting room. But he is less forthcoming on the reasons why he was able to escape being deported, and he has carefully crossed out the words on his business card that identify him as a lecturer in the history of the Communist Party of the Soviet Union. Within two years of its formation, the Jamagat movement had split and Leipanov and his rival were bitter enemies.

Russia's vanguard: the Cossacks

The Tsarist empire's expansion into the Caucasus was accomplished by settling communities of Cossacks in newly conquered and insecure areas. The Cossacks, who are overwhelmingly Slavic, occupy a special place in Russian history and folklore. The soldier-farmers take their name from the Turkish word for freedom, a homage to their outlaw past. The original Cossacks were peasants who escaped the serf system by fleeing to the wild hinterland of what was then Ukraine. Left alone for 200 years, they developed a communal style of living, and an egalitarian method of government. In 1654, the Cossacks acknowledged Russian sovereignty in return for a promise to respect their autonomy. From the 18th century, the Cossacks were at the forefront of the Russian expansion southwards. Their settlements, which followed the Don, Kuban and Terek rivers, helped make Tsarist military victories irreversible.

At the beginning, there was little animosity between mountaineers and the free men. The Cossacks' egalitarianism and communal system of land ownership were not so different from the customs of their Chechen neighbours. Although in Ukraine there was an emphasis on

Christianity, with Cossack recruits to the Dniepr troop made to kiss the cross, there was a certain amount of accommodation with local Muslims. Over the years, the Cossacks opened their *stanitsy*, or fortified villages, to the locals, and took Chechen women as their wives. The Cossacks' famed dress code also owes a lot to the mountaineers. The fur hats, shaggy cloaks and bandoliers are still worn by villagers in the high Caucasus, and by Cossacks on ceremonial occasions.

In their *stanitsy*, the Cossacks developed traditions that revolved around their utility to the Tsarist army: taking pride in their loyalty, bravery in battle, horsemanship and physical strength. In exchange for their lands and freedom from serfdom, every Cossack male was pledged to present himself with sword and horse to the Russian army and to serve for twenty-five years. They ruled themselves through elected leaders or *atamans*, and according to their own codes. Today, the descendants of the Cossacks in the northern Caucasus number 600,000, compared to 4 million in the former Soviet Union. But their leaders argue that this is a fraction of what the population might have been if not for the persecution during the communist era.

More than one million Cossacks were killed during the civil war, in which they fought predominantly on the side of the anti-Bolshevik White Armies. Others were deported. Tens of thousands more died during the famine that resulted from collectivisation in the early 1930s and in the terror later that decade. During the war, some Cossacks were sympathetic to the Nazi invaders and 30,000 of them accompanied the German retreat. They were repatriated by the British at the end of the war, and most of the Cossacks died later in Soviet prison camps. There was a further repression in 1957. Throughout the Soviet era, all mention of the Cossacks was frowned upon, and the word *ataman* stayed in use as a synonym for gangland boss.

The situation changed in 1990. The rehabilitation of the Cossacks heralded a new assertiveness among the descendants of Cossacks. In Russian liberal circles, the Cossacks became fashionable, and their efforts to carve out a role in the new Russia were treated with some sympathy. This fact was recognised by Yeltsin in June 1992, when he signed a decree rehabilitating Cossacks and authorising the revival of their traditions.

But even before that official sanction, the descendants of Cossacks in the former centres of Krasnodar, Rostov and Vladikavkaz had elected *atamans* and governing councils. Aside from a romantic interest in the costumes or folklore of a bygone era, the Cossacks took political positions. They began to demand that their own claims be recognised in a region which they have occupied for several centuries.

Vladimir Gromov, who was elected *ataman* of the Kuban river

Cossacks in the Krasnodar area in 1991, embodies both tendencies. A pudgy and jovial man who clearly enjoys the costumes and ceremony that accompany the post, he nonetheless has a rigid outlook towards his Caucasian neighbours: 'We are ready to live with everyone if they came to our place, they must live according to our traditions, because they are very good.' Mr Gromov, a history professor, is no doubt aware of the identity of the original inhabitants of the Krasnodar region.

Aside from an increase in bigotry, the new Cossack assertiveness presents the Russian authorities with a very real security threat. Many of the young men expressing interest in old traditions have undergone military training, while waiting for their call-up into the Russian army. There are large numbers of Cossacks in the police force, despite bans on political activity. Such membership has transformed the Cossack bodies from mere repositories of tradition into organisations that in some ways are reverting to their original purpose. As before, the Don Cossacks are the most numerous, organised and militant group currently active, followed by the Kuban Cossacks based around Krasnodar. There is also rising militancy among the Cossacks of the Terek river in Vladikavkaz, as well as in the new grouping at Stavropol.

This serious approach to the old Cossack duty of defending Russia's borders has led to friction in areas other than Karachai-Cherkess. Cossacks in independent Chechnya became determined to resort to arms if Grozny's independent government tried to compel them to hand over four villages they have occupied since the Chechens were sent into exile. The militant Don Cossacks were at the forefront of unrest involving ethnic Russians in other parts of the former Soviet Union. The Don and Kuban *atamans* each admitted to sending at least a hundred men, as well as weapons, to fight alongside Russians in the Trans-Dnestr republic of Moldova. In the Adygeya republic near Krasnodar, demands for more autonomy similar to those of the Karachai resulted in clashes between Cossacks and Caucasians. Cossacks were also involved in clashes with Armenians and Azerbaijanis in Krasnodar itself, which is home to more than a hundred different nationalities. In fact, Armenians in the region number 120,000, more than the indigenous Adygeya.

The competing demands of non-Russian nationalities have spawned and fed a new and militant Cossack revival. The popularity of Cossack organisations was in part a result of a collective memory of deeply conservative values and a conviction that Russia was indivisible. 'When the movements for sovereignty started, Cossack rights were taken away. Cossacks fear that young people will leave the autonomous republics because of a feeling of repression, leaving only old people behind', explained the Stavropol *ataman* Piotr Stefanovitch Fedosov.

But at a time of widespread concern about crime and unrest through-out the former Soviet Union, the Cossack image of stability had broader appeal. In other cities, where traditional guarantors of law and order no longer seemed reliable, Cossacks managed to carve out an admin-istrative role. Such involvement was also good public relations for the rehabilitation campaign. It was a fact recognised early on by some of the more organised *atamans*, such as Stavropol's Piotr Stefanovich Fedosov, commander of 40,000 Cossacks:

> We don't want to only talk on national problems because the Caucasus is like a tinder-box stuck between a bomb on one side and a canister of petrol on the other. If we are not careful catastrophe can strike on either side. We must be involved in stabilising the situation.

In Krasnodar, which was founded on land granted to the Cossacks in 1793 by Catherine II, the Kuban Cossacks won permission from local authorities to patrol railway stations in the winter of 1991–2. They were empowered to join police in stopping and searching pas-sengers to prevent smugglers from exporting large quantities of food from the agriculturally rich region. At the same time, the Cossacks took it upon themselves to force local authorities to prohibit Meskhetian Turk refugees from doing fieldwork in the Krasnodar area. The Meskhetians, who fled pogroms in Uzbekistan in 1989, had been living in the area without residence permits, and so were ineligible for permanent jobs. Cossacks from the Sochi region, too, have taken on policing functions on the Russian–Georgian border to prevent arms and food smuggling. In January 1993, the Russian army proposed to create special units of Cossack soldiers to serve with the Don and Kuban regiments.

The frontier

Although the Cossacks have been at the vanguard of nationalist ex-pression, their concerns were little different from those of ordinary Russians in the towns of southern Russia. With the demise of the Soviet Union, these once again became the Russian frontier. Among the cities where there was grave concern at the explosion of nationalist sentiment among non-Russian minorities were Stavropol and Kras-nodar. Both are solid provincial cities, relying on the surrounding fertile lands for their relative prosperity and stability. Both were founded by Cossacks in the late 18th century as forts, points along the Russian line that constituted the empire's defence. Stavropol was also a strate-gic position after the revolution as the seat of the Kavburo, the section of the Russian Communist Party that oversaw policy in the Caucasus.

This frontier heritage became relevant again as the Caucasian nations began to voice their demands for independence. Ethnic consciousness in non-Russians has contributed to a feeling among Russians of being under siege, a sentiment that belies Stavropol's quintessentially Russian character.

Emerging from the wisps of cloud that cover the steppes, Stavropol's pastel yellow and blue buildings are similar to the 19th-century architecture of other Russian provincial towns. Stavropol, or 'city of the cross', seems a solid and prosperous town, with few visual references to the dangers of an imperial outpost. Several of the exhibits – such as the ancient crosses – in Stavropol's museum speak of early Christian settlements in the area, as if the curators are trying to establish Stavropol's past links with the Russian world. Unusually for Russia, nowadays, the museum has photographs with charitable descriptions of Mikhail Gorbachev. Gorbachev, along with Alexander Solzhenitsyn, is one of Stavropol district's most famous sons. The last president of the Soviet Union stands in the middle of the picture behind a woman with a large bouquet presented in 1967 to mark the fiftieth anniversary of the revolution. His face looks quite square beneath a full head of dark hair.

For all its proximity to a region of nationalist upheaval, the population of Stavropol district is overwhelmingly Russian. According to the 1989 census, 2.3 million of its 2.9 million inhabitants were Russian. There has not been the flood of local Caucasians that its Russian residents feared. However, Stavropol's demographics did change in the decade from 1979 to 1989 because of an influx of Armenians, refugees from Azerbaijan and Nagorno-Karabakh. The Armenian population nearly doubled to 72,000 in that time span. There has also been an influx of Russians from the autonomous republics, mainly Chechnya, thought to number in the tens of thousands.

There are no signs as yet of serious ethnic unrest in Stavropol or Krasnodar, or of the new strategic importance these cities may assume. The most apocalyptic vision among Russians foresees a repetition of history in a new Caucasian war in which Stavropol and Krasnodar will serve as bulwarks against a Muslim invasion. But what has become evident is a feeling of insecurity among Russians that had hitherto been limited to the other republics of the Soviet Union, or the autonomous republics. The fear voiced by the intelligentsia in Stavropol and Krasnodar during the winter of 1991–2 marked the first time that the nationality question had repercussions within Russia proper. In Stavropol, anxiety among Russians had become so acute that, absurd as it may seem, it became a popular analogy to compare the situation of Russia, vast and heavily defended, to that of Israel. The reasoning

was based on the fact that both were surrounded by and at the mercy
of hostile Muslim nations.

This unease among ordinary Russian civilians and the growing
militancy among Cossacks are the two popular responses to the challenge that emerging nationalism in the north Caucasus poses to Moscow.
Ethnic consciousness among the Karachai and other peoples has yet
to transcend concerns about compensation for the wrongs suffered
during the Stalinist eras. The renewed interest in Islam, far removed
from the fundamentalist brands of the Middle East, is also part of the
process of asserting national identities among the north Caucasians. As
yet, Dudayev's Chechnya is alone in flying the flag of seccession. Old
grudges over territory threaten the stability of Daghestan and Ingushetia.
No solutions have been proposed for allowing threatened and outnumbered nations such as the Adyg to reclaim their birthrights. But
in the Confederation of Mountain People are the seeds of an organisation that could make independence a reality for Caucasian peoples,
united and acting as one. Moscow will be looking closely, and with
trepidation, at its southern flank.

Notes

1. Conquest, Robert (1978), *The Nation Killers: The Soviet deportation of
nationalities*, Macmillan, London, p. 37.

2. Fuller, Elizabeth (1992), 'Caucasus: The Lezgin Campaign for Autonomy',
Radio Liberty, *Report on the USSR*, 16 October.

3. Broxup, Marie Bennigsen (ed.) (1992), *The North Caucasus Barrier: The
Russian Advance towards the Muslim World*, Hurst & Co., London, p. 219.

4. Ibid., p. 234.

5. *Express Chronicle*, 46, 10–16 November 1992, p. 2.

6. Bennigsen, Alexandre and Wimbush, S. Enders (1985), *Mystics and
Commissars: Sufism in the Soviet Union*, C. Hurst and Co., London, p. 14.

7. Ibid., p. 29.

8. Conquest, Robert, op. cit., p. 160.

9. Ibid., p. 90.

10. Sheehy, Ann (1990), 'Justice at last for the Karachai', Radio Liberty
Report on the USSR, 28 December.

11. Ibid.

10

Milestones

'Long live the Communist Party.'
'Let the nation be free and independent.'
'If there is no traitor in the nation then the
nation can overcome all of its problems.'

The slogans are familiar enough. Patriotic roadsigns abound in the
Caucasus – there is one sliced into a cliff near Goris, Armenia, dedicated to 'our great and supremely talented nation'. But these are in
Azerbaijan, within a few hundreds yards of each other, the one in
praise of party loyalty more faded than the rest, on the road to despair.
On one side lies the Iranian border, and on the other sodden tents.
The camps are for refugees from Karabakh. Robbed of their past and
their illusions, they have arrived in a place where everything seems
washed in rain or mud. Occasionally, a shepherd appears and the road
turns into a sea of sheep.

In such a featureless landscape, signs become omens. Communism,
independence, conflict and reprisal – the struggle against a resilient old
order is on display here in the flat borderlands. As yet it is impossible
to guess what the outcome will be, but most of the developments have
been disturbing.

So where are things heading? After the first years of independence,
normal life in the Caucasus has broken down completely. Although it
scarcely seems possible, things have got worse, and here it is difficult
to find any traces of positive change. The descent is painfully obvious
in the refugee camps of Azerbaijan, and the blackened bombed-out
shell of the Abkhazian capital, Sukhumi. The tented camps along the
Azeri–Iranian border house about 40,000 people, still only a fraction
of the refugees from Karabakh. They are waterlogged, the tents are
cold to the touch, and some of the children run about in rubber
galoshes and no socks. But miserable as they are, the camps, which
were built by the Iranian Red Crescent, are the most visible sign of
foreign assistance to the one million Azeris displaced by the war. In

Abkhazia, destruction has been followed by cold-blooded revenge. First there was the senseless bombardment of the legislature and a year-long occupation by Georgian forces who terrorised the population. And then, after the Abkhazian victory, came the reprisals: an orgy of killing and looting that took the Abkhazian authorities weeks to contain. Memories of the violence refused to fade. They were everywhere: in the greying missing persons posters with their fuzzy school photographs and in the buildings which have been branded with the names of the new, and invariably Abkhazian, owners. The Georgian community vanished, as did the young of all nationalities. Sukhumi became the preserve of those too old to flee, a mockery of the pleasure-seeking haven it used to be.

Elsewhere, the process has been less spectacular, but no less ruinous. Societies which valued courtliness have been reduced to heaving, angry crowds. Ordinary encounters are redolent with anger and frustration, and the possibility of violence. In Tbilisi, petrol shortages have made the transport crisis so acute that fist fights break out in the doorways of the metro. Old people who complain that they are being trampled on are met with jeers and more shoving, this time intentional. Men have been known to avenge imagined insults by shooting their opponents in broad daylight. There is little chance of being arrested. Few people go out after dark, when there is nearly always the sound of gunfire. In Yerevan, wretched old women beg on street corners. In Baku, a whole generation has been put on hold. The schools and universities have been shut for months because they were full of refugees; the government argued that it could not conclude the oil deals that would secure its future so long as parts of the country remained under occupation.

Amid such upheaval, only a few things can be taken for granted: among them war, privation, crime and Russia. The breakdown of public life began with the events that presaged the death of the Soviet Union: economic collapse and demands for democratic change. But throughout the Caucasus concerns about human rights and ecology soon took second place to an unyielding nationalism. For all their differences and mutual animosities, the peoples of the region have shared a sense of ethnic destiny divorced from economic and geographic reality. And this has contributed overwhelmingly to their fate. The magnitude of the crisis facing the entire region is such that concerns about human rights and democratic institutions are seen as unworthy of immediate consideration. There is no energy left for the debates about economic reform that have been taking place in Russia and other, more stable, republics. The changes taking place in the Caucasus have created emergency situations where familiar standards no longer apply. Human rights norms are routinely violated. There are varying degrees of censorship and political intimidation in all three countries.

It is the tragedy of the Caucasus that nationalism is inseparable from territory. The connection was the basis on which life in the Soviet republics was organised. Almost every nation and ethnic group was allotted a titular territory with limited language and cultural rights. But such provisions were uneven, particularly for minorities within each national republic. In theory, their rights were protected: geographical areas were set aside in their name where they enjoyed some measure of autonomy. Yet the minorities never enjoyed the same freedoms as the majority community, and their regions suffered from economic neglect. The grievances this produced were amplified during the Stalinist period, when borders were redrawn and peoples wantonly suppressed. As a result, minority communities such as the Abkhazians and Ossetians in Georgia and the Armenians in Azerbaijan found their interests in direct conflict with republican as well as Soviet authorities. The autonomous areas in which they were organised had helped to preserve their identity, but they were barred from expressing it fully. In many instances, it was these conflicts as much as resentment of Russian overlords which fuelled the nationalist movements of the late 1980s. In such a way, demands for democracy and independence became bloodied with ethnic conflict.

Each nation can count in its recent annals a cataclysmic event which transformed unfocused yearnings for cultural expression into a struggle for outright independence. The pace of events thereafter was so rapid that it ruled out the sorts of compacts with the communist authorities that ensued in the Baltic and other republics. It also stunted the development of political parties as they would be understood in the West. Alliances were shifting and temporary and subservient to personality. Strength was valued above all, a predilection that encouraged ever more extreme positions. For Armenia and Nagorno-Karabakh, the moment arrived in February 1988 with the demonstrations in front of Yerevan's opera house demanding reunification of Armenian-populated lands. For Georgia, and indirectly Abkhazia, it was the brutal crushing of the 9 April 1989 demonstrations in Tbilisi. For Azerbaijan, it was the deployment in January 1990 of Soviet troops in Baku against pro-democracy protesters – and ostensibly the organisers of anti-Armenian pogroms. And for Chechnya, it was the failed putsch in Moscow on 19 August 1991. Each of these events was a watershed, marking a departure from a time when it was believed that conflicts could be resolved peacefully within the structure of the Soviet Union. They signified the death of Mikhail Gorbachev's perestroika as far as nationalist leaders in the Caucasus were concerned.

The heavy-handed reaction of the authorities in Moscow to early expressions of nationalism established a climate in which compromise no longer seemed desirable – either with Russia or with local authorities. Although Armenia never entirely abandoned its allegiance to Moscow, Georgia and Azerbaijan entered into independence determined to reject any Russian influence. Only in time, and after great sacrifice, did it become apparent just how unrealistic this was. By then the consequences of greatly polarised societies were evident. The disputes which had become active in perestroika had reached their logical conclusion. Nagorno-Karabakh, Abkhazia and Ingushetia achieved a state of balance – but only through the use of force.

In Karabakh, Azerbaijanis were driven from the enclave and several districts of adjoining land, resolving momentarily the question of its jurisdiction by leaving the Armenians in total control. In Abkhazia, the Georgians – the largest population – fled, removing the biggest obstacle to the demands of the Abkhazian minority. In North Ossetia, Ingush claims to ancestral lands were silenced by their forced exodus. The apparent success of forceful methods has been crucial in the erosion of faith in negotiation. International mediation in Karabakh and Abkhazia has served the interests of the side which has been stronger militarily.

The Minsk group, representing eleven countries of the Conference on Security and Co-operation in Europe including Armenia and Azerbaijan, has been the main vehicle for negotiation in Karabakh. But it was paralysed for more than a year by a debate over whether the final status of the enclave (i.e. whether it was part of Azerbaijan or not) should be discussed from the outset or only after a ceasefire had been reached. Although the CSCE eventually concluded a preliminary settlement and ceasefire in 1993, it has lacked the means to ensure that the Armenian Karabakhi forces respect them. While Azerbaijanis have looked on aghast, their opponents have used their participation in the CSCE process as a cover for a second and purely military strategy. The Armenian forces seem intent on punishing Azerbaijan with a series of defeats until it is forced to yield up Karabakh.

The failure of United Nations efforts in the region has been even more spectacular. By the time the Security Council had agreed to the despatch of eighty-eight military observers to Abkhazia in the summer of 1993 the Abkhazian forces were already poised for their final offensive. Only five observers managed to reach Sukhumi before its fall in September. Negotiations resumed only in December 1993, when an agreement on repatriation of refugees was reached in Geneva.

Not least among the obstacles for negotiators has been the confusion surrounding the aims of the combatants. While the original goal of the Armenian Karabakhis was unification with Armenia, that option has now been set aside in favour of outright independence. It is similarly unclear whether the Ossetian and Abkhazian militants desire a federation within Georgia, attachment to Russia or full independence. In this depressing scenario only South Ossetia remains a relative success, thanks to the efforts of a Russian-Georgian–Ossetian peace-keeping force which was set up in June 1992. But mediators from the Conference on Security and Co-operation in Europe have been frustrated in their efforts to transform this ceasefire into a broader, more permanent settlement.

Seen against the failure of local and international efforts at mediation, military might has proved effective in deciding between competing claims – if only for the short term. This validation of the use of force speaks badly, not only for the future of the conflicts themselves but for continuing efforts to create more civilised societies. Despite the unavailability of the most basic food staples, of petrol, or of heating oil, there is no shortage of arms in the Caucasus. It has been a feature of the ethnic conflicts that what started as small-scale skirmishes have escalated uncontrollably, unleashing a hunger for new and ever more deadly weapons. In the absence of established regular armies, the conflicts have put paramilitaries at the centre of political life.

It has thus seemed prudent for political leaders to retain the services of notoriously undisciplined forces because they represent the only guarantors of their regimes. In Chechnya, General Dzhokar Dudayev has been unable to disarm the militias which rushed to the republic's defence against Russia in the autumn of 1991, although they were widely held to be doing double duty for gangland mafias. In Georgia, Eduard Shevardnadze has never felt secure enough to cut his ties to the Mekhedrioni paramilitary in case its commander, Dzhaba Ioseliani, turns against him. In strictly military terms, the Mekhedrioni has proved a far more motivated force than the official National Guard, forcing Shevardnadze to rely more on Ioseliani than on the man he chose personally as defence minister. Shevardnadze has turned a blind eye to some of the worst excesses of the paramilitary, including a penchant for drunkenness and car theft. The latitude granted to the Mekhedrioni has extended to other armed groups, some with purely criminal aspirations. Highwaymen operate with impunity on roads and railway lines. In Azerbaijan, Suret Husseinov preserved his personal army of 4,000 even after becoming prime minister in the summer of 1993. Exempt from the fighting in Karabakh, the men sat out the war in Gyandzha, their presence shoring up Husseinov's position.

Meanwhile, Azerbaijan was reduced to rounding up teenagers on the streets of Baku to send to the front line in Karabakh. While mainland Armenia is much less militarised than either of its neighbours, that is not the case in Karabakh. There the military clearly outweighs the political leadership, although in some instances the two are indistinguishable. There has also been a traffic in personnel between Armenia and the enclave. Commanders imported from Karabakh have taken up posts in the defence ministry in Yerevan.

There is a glimmer of hope that the perils of earlier, ruthlessly nationalistic, attitudes have begun to be recognised – at least in Azerbaijan and Georgia, where they have proved so disastrous. In Armenia, an extreme nationalist policy has paid dividends in the victory in Karabakh. If anything, it has whetted the appetite for military confrontation and made negotiations look even more unappealing. In October 1993, while Armenian forces were driving out the last civilians who stood between the enclave and a hundred-mile swathe of the Iranian–Azeri frontier, the fighting rated barely a mention in the Armenian press. It was impossible to detect any public disquiet about the offensive, and about the transformation of the Armenians from a nation of noble victims into aggressors.

The military successes in Karabakh have been a counterpoint to the dire state of the economy within Armenia. While the government of Levon Ter-Petrosian has been anxious to distance itself from the aggressive postures adopted by the authorities in Karabakh, it has been unable to silence internal critics of his moderate policies. The opposition in Armenia has taken a much harder line on national questions than its counterparts in Georgia or Azerbaijan. There, people appear to have become more or less reconciled to the departure of once hugely popular nationalist leaders. In Azerbaijan, arrests of political opponents have reduced the clamour for the return of the elected leader, Abulfaz Elchibey, who remains a fugitive in Nakhichevan. In Georgia, the overthrow of Zviad Gamsakhurdia in January 1992 continues to be contested. While the majority of the population appears to have accepted Shevardnadze, there is still a segment of the population, notably in the western region of Mingrelia, unwilling to make the break with the past. But the most ardent nationalists are now in the minority in both countries. Although Shevardnadze and Aliyev are closely associated with the corrupt Brezhnev age by virtue of their long tenures as Republican Party first secretaries, they are accepted as patriots.

However, both men have found it difficult to fulfil the hopes invested in them. They promised stability, and instead presided over military catastrophes. Few of the critics of Shevardnadze and Aliyev would actually like to take on the mantle of leadership, given the pitfalls that lie in wait. But they have been able to cast doubts on the competence of both leaders to adjust to the problems of a post-communist society. 'If you watch TV and forget to look at the calendar and just listen to Aliyev's speeches, you could be living twenty-five years in the past,' according to one critic of the Azerbaijani president. The debate over competence is worlds away from the fiery nationalist rhetoric of the 1980s. Even Gamsakhurdia, before his death in December 1993, spoke of accommodation with Russia and with Georgia's minorities. These suggestions of a new, more sober approach must be viewed in the context of the rewards offered for scaling down the ambitions of independence.

In all three countries now there is an unshakeable belief that Caucasians no longer control their own destiny. Only Moscow can save them – first by ending the wars that have mortgaged their future, and then by restoring the supply lines so that their economies can function in the present. These high expectations are no indication of trust, but a tacit recognition of Moscow's enduring strategic interests in the region. Few people in the Caucasus doubt that forces in Moscow were involved in the removal of Gamsakhurdia and Elchibey. But they accept that without compromise with Russia, there will be no reining in of the malicious influences of what is known as the 'third force'.

This reappraisal of Russia's role in the Caucasus follows two years in which both Georgia and Azerbaijan tried to assert their independence outside of the Commonwealth of Independent States (CIS) which succeeded the Soviet Union. Azerbaijanis were flattered by the interest expressed in their country by Turkey and Iran, while Georgians imagined that Shevardnadze's prestige in the West would translate into concrete expressions of support. But all the goodwill which Shevardnadze had earned in Western Europe came to nothing. The West barely considered Georgia's plans to join Nato, and Germany categorically ruled out any prospect of military aid in the Abkhazian war. Azerbaijan discovered too late that Ankara's ideal of a great Turkic-speaking alliance was not backed up by its purse. The large investment that had been promised did not materialise. Turkey also confined its help in the war to military advisers and diplomatic interventions. In contrast, Iran may have marginally improved its position in the region. After being shunned by the first two leaders of Azerbaijan, Iran has earned the gratitude of Aliyev and civilians by its practical efforts on behalf of the refugees.

But this is an exception. The prevailing wisdom in the Caucasus is that it was naive to expect to be fully integrated into the international community. So far as Europe and America are concerned, the region remains of secondary importance and no steps can be taken that would risk alienating Russia. The resulting sense of disillusion in the Caucasus has become overwhelming, and contains no small degree of accusation. 'What can you do for us in the West?' asked Tedo Japaridze, Shevardnadze's national security adviser. 'You can do nothing but give us aid. But only to a few of us; you cannot feed us all.'

There was thus a sense of inevitability in the autumn of 1993 when, defeated in war and worn down by poverty, Azerbaijan and Georgia announced their readiness to enter the CIS. Uppermost in the minds of both Shevardnadze and Aliyev was the hope that Moscow would stop aiding their enemies. But economic necessity was an equally compelling reason for the embrace of the CIS. Azerbaijan's flirtation with Turkey and Georgia's war in Abkhazia had highlighted both countries' dependence on Russian materials and transport links. It became obvious that unless links with Russia were restored, there was little chance that the countries of the Caucasus would be able to escape their economic crisis. The first steps to do so ended badly. The new currencies introduced in 1992 and 1993 – the dram in Armenia, the manat in Azerbaijan and the simply named coupon in Georgia – were undermined by high rates of inflation and reduced salaries to laughable amounts. Foreign investors steered clear of such an unstable region. They were unimpressed by the quality of local manufacture. Even those sectors of the economy which had remained relatively productive, such as Azerbaijan's cotton industry, could find no markets. As for Azerbaijan's oil wealth, the development of the offshore fields became prey to the power struggles between Moscow and Elchibey, and to Aliyev's distrust of his own ministers. The result for the foreign oil companies ready to invest in Azerbaijan has meant endless negotiations of contracts with successive governments that can still be set aside at Aliyev's whim.

For ordinary people, the rupture with Russia has proved devastating. In all three countries, economic chaos and the growth of refugee populations have brought a return to diseases which were thought to have been eradicated. The new illnesses bear all the hallmarks of poverty: tuberculosis and diseases associated with chronic malnutrition, and even a few instances of cholera. Most food staples are outside the reach of people on fixed incomes. Pensions have shrunk through inflation to two or three dollars a month. Very often people have gone unpaid for months because government coffers are empty. Armenia, which remained one of the last Soviet republics to continue using the pre-1993 roubles discarded by Russia, sustained inflation rates of 7 per cent a day. The consequences were horrifying. According to medical officers in Yerevan, some pensioners were losing three kilograms in weight every two weeks, and babies had been admitted to hospital with bloated stomachs. The lack of fuel and electricity has exacerbated a situation so desperate that almost all who can do so, leave. Yerevan has now been transformed into a sort of summer capital for the Armenian diaspora. With all their good intentions, the volunteers from the West are unable to put up with a winter under Azeri blockade. With each November, the doctors, nurses and engineers pack their bags to return home. Native Armenians with relatives in Russia or elsewhere have also become seasonal residents. Of course, those who find work elsewhere may never return. The situation in Georgia is little better. The drop in living standards from the days of wine and plenty during the Soviet era has been drastic. In Tbilisi, the government was forced to deploy troops outside bakeries after people were beaten to death on the bread-line. Azerbaijanis have also suffered from rising prices and, in a country with oil reserves to rival Kuwait's, the ridiculous problem of petrol shortages.

These crises have not gone unnoticed in the West, despite the complaints of government officials. Within a year of independence, the Red Cross, the United Nations High Commissioner for Refugees and the main international aid agencies set up offices in the three Caucasian capitals. Government aid also arrived. In 1992, the US donated $188 million to Armenia, the largest aid spending in the former Soviet Union after Russia. But the crisis engulfing the Caucasus is of such magnitude that these efforts can have little impact. Without the international assistance tens of thousands of people would go hungry. A rough estimate reveals that the Red Cross is providing food parcels to more than 20 per cent of the Armenian population; thousands more families are relying on US government aid to adapt their homes for the winter. Armenia also faces the problem of donor fatigue because the appeals for international assistance stretch back to the earthquake of December 1988. All these factors reveal the inadequacy of any Western aid programme. Real salvation requires a lasting peace, and that must involve Russia.

Yet despite its primacy to their future, Moscow's real intentions towards the Caucasus remain unclear. At times, there have seemed to be two, and possibly three, distinct strands of foreign policy emanating from Russia. These have reflected the power struggles between President Boris Yeltsin and his conservative opponents in parliament, and the Russian military. The status of the 'near abroad', as Russia now calls the former republics, has been one of the most divisive issues in the struggle between conservatives and democrats. While the Russian president was stating his desire to establish better relations, the parliament – which had mobilised around the erstwhile vice-president,

Alexander Rutskoi, and the Speaker, Ruslan Khasbulatov – was determined that Russia should have absolute control over the Caucasus, even if that meant dismembering Georgia and Azerbaijan. From his corner, the defence minister, Pavel Grachev, warned that Russia had an abiding interest in the region. He infuriated Georgians in particular by reminding them that Russia still had a role to play in the Black Sea. Nowhere were these conflicts illustrated more clearly than in Abkhazia. While Russian diplomats were actively engaged in seeking a peace accord, Russian soldiers were surreptitiously aiding the rebel forces. The duality was apparent even after the fall of Sukhumi. Russian officials roundly condemned the Abkhazian violations of the ceasefire and announced the imposition of an economic blockade. Yet there was little actual evidence of this on the Russian-Abkhazian border. Cars, buses and pedestrians continued to pass freely, bringing in petrol and food supplies as needed. After the arrest of Rutskoi and Khasbulatov and the defeat of the conservatives during the October 1993 putsch, Georgians hoped for the emergence of a more coherent foreign policy from Moscow, and one that would be less hostile to their interests. Armenians and Azerbaijanis also kept watch for a change in Russian attitude, anticipating a swing away from Yerevan and towards Baku. But two months later the success in the Russian parliamentary elections of the far right party led by Vladimir Zhirinovsky set back hopes for a coherent, non-interventionist Russian foreign policy in the 'near abroad'. Even more than the conservatives of the old parliament, Zhirinovsky has been adamant that the Caucasus remains an integral part of Russia.

In the autumn of 1993, Shevardnadze sealed his country's return to the Russian sphere of influence by pleading for, and receiving, assistance from Russian troops in fighting off a new phase in the rebellion by followers of Zviad Gamsakhurdia. The uprising had erupted in September while Georgian government forces were facing defeat in Abkhazia, and forced Shevardnadze to take seriously an opponent he had written off as spent. As the Zviadist forces advanced along the main road towards Georgia's second city of Kutaisi, a further dismemberment of the country loomed, only days after the disaster in Abkhazia. In the final days of the Abkhazian war, Shevardnadze had appealed to Grachev for assistance, but the Russian defence minister was unwilling to expose his troops to such a dangerous venture. He candidly told Shevardnadze that Georgia was bound to lose Abkhazia. Weeks later, however, Shevardnadze appealed again for assistance and this time got a positive response. By early November, Russian marines and ground forces had fanned out from the port of Poti along railway lines and bridges across western Georgia. Though expressly forbidden to take a direct role in the conflict, they freed up the Georgian paramilitaries to beat back the Zviadists.

An even more significant result of the thaw in relations with Moscow was the agreement reached in October to allow Russia a permanent military foothold in Georgia. Although it had previously been agreed that Russian troops would depart by 1995, the new agreement provided for three Russian bases: at Tbilisi, the old headquarters of the Caucasian command, at Batumi, on the Black Sea, and at Akhalkalaki, an area to the south where there is a large Armenian population. The selection of the sites for the bases makes it apparent that the Russian military continues to view the Caucasus as a bulwark against Turkey, and Georgia as the most important country within the region. Together with the installations at Goumri (formerly Leninakan) and at Gyandzha in Azerbaijan, the Akhalkalaki and Batumi bases preserve the old defensive line along the southern edges of the Caucasus. Towards the end of 1993, Russian forces resumed policing the Azerbaijani–Iranian frontier, a task that had been entrusted to Azeri forces earlier.

Russia's interest in the Caucasus has remained strategic. Although reliable statistics are not available, anecdotal evidence suggests an exodus of ethnic Russians from the Caucasus, especially Georgia. Alexandrov's Gardens, a park in Tbilisi, has become an unofficial exchange for people seeking flats in Russia, and there are long queues outside the Russian embassy. But these developments are peripheral to Russian concerns about its security *vis-à-vis* the Muslim world beyond, and within its own frontiers. After a two-year stand-off with Chechnya, Moscow has begun to seek some sort of accommodation with Dudayev that would ensure that the rest of the North Caucasus does not become dangerously restive. It is in this northern part of the region, with its large populations of settlers, that Russian policy is motivated also by concern for ethnic Russians.

A common forecast has predicted a conflagration affecting all of the North Caucasus after the various small conflicts explode. This has not happened, but the region remains unstable. The involvement of Chechen, Kabardian and other irregulars from the North Caucasus in the Abkhazian war has doubtless prompted Russian strategists to renew their efforts to seek an accord with Chechnya. From the Russian viewpoint, there is a delicate balance to be maintained between rendering the Caucasus weak and unstable and stirring up conflict to such levels that it spills over into its own backyard.

The past two years have proved revelatory. There has been no change in the weakness of democratic institutions, and the inability of governments to resist malevolent forces. The long years of communism, during which party first secretaries ruled for long stretches and surrounded themselves with acolytes, created a tolerance for corruption which has proved difficult to overcome. And yet the public remains forgiving of its leaders. This is largely because they fear a further decline in living standards. It is popularly held that there is little alternative to the present leadership in all three countries. Although the Elchibey and Gamsakhurdia administrations undoubtedly suffered from inexperience, they fell because of their approach to the nationalities question. Their competence became an issue only belatedly. The Armenian government, for all its failings, is still seen as the best bet for a country in the grip of crisis. While the peoples of the Caucasus cannot be satisfied with their leaders so long as daily life is such a struggle, there is little stomach for the upheaval that would be required to change them.

The countries of the Caucasus have suffered the same economic dislocation as the other newly independent republics. The regimes all lack the expertise needed for the transitions to market economies and party democracies. But what makes the road ahead so perilous for the Caucasus is a geographical and administrative make-up which has made it especially susceptible to ethnic conflict. As at the dawn of independence, the expression of national identity is the most important issue for the Caucasus. Unfortunately, there has been little variation in the forms this has taken, and the result is the wars that have halted economic and political modernisation in each country. The pace of events leading up to independence blocked the development of a genuine political discourse in which questions of language and cultural rights could be addressed. Once war had broken out, the apparent ineffectiveness of the negotiating process further legitimised the use of force.

What must now follow is a re-examination of the principles on which independence was fought and won. The wars in South Ossetia, Abkhazia and Nagorno-Karabakh are inextricable from the processes which brought party politics to all three countries. All three ethnic conflicts began with demands for redress following years of cultural suppression. There is no question that minorities in all three countries did suffer discrimination in the communist era, and their struggles have received broad support in the West. Such sympathies were only natural in a world which generally has accepted the right of a people to self-determination. But it has become readily apparent since the fall of communism that the equation of territory and national rights is a lethal one.

Many would now argue that the disputes in the Caucasus have gone too far for communities to live together as they did before. But the experience of the past years has shown that separation is no solution. Economic life cannot resume when the region is broken down into a patchwork of armed camps. The future now lies in modifying the basis on which the Soviet republics and their successor states were founded. Just as in Russia, where President Boris Yeltsin has been forced to acknowledge the desires of non-Russians in forging a new constitution, so the Caucasus must find some way in which cultural rights and a meaningful autonomy can be accommodated within existing boundaries. This task is made even more fraught by the pattern of Russian interference in the region. Moscow has been all too ready to encourage the demands of smaller nations such as the Abkhazians as a way of keeping the larger nations in check. The effect has been to compound the suspicion with which Georgians and Azerbaijanis already view minority aspirations.

If the peoples of the Caucasus are ever to have a secure future these conflicts must come to an end, and meaningful settlements put in place. The international community has already taken a role in mediation; it must have the resources to enforce ceasefires and structures that would speed up the process of negotiation. There must also be early measures to demilitarise a region that begins to rival the Balkans in terms of weaponry. Only after that can the long and hard process of constructing societies in which the aspirations of all nationalities can be addressed begin. The Caucasus faces a perilous journey: there are few signposts ahead, and few routes to choose from.

Index

43, 44, 46, 47, 48, 49, 50, 51,
52, 53, 55, 57, 58, 59, 62, 64,
65, 66, 68, 71, 72, 73, 75,
77–80, 115–31, 133, 135, 148,
149, 150, 151, 176, 182, 211,
213, 215, 216, 218, 219, 222
Azerbaijani Social Democratic
Group, 118
Azerbaijani Society for Cultural
Relations with Countrymen
Abroad, 135
Azerbaijanis, 4, 5, 11, 22, 23, 31,
35, 41, 42, 54, 56, 60, 65, 67,
93, 101, 134, 154, 157, 161, 164,
165, 166, 209, 216, 225
Azeris, 29, 50, 56, 65, 155, 213,
223; pogroms against, 33
Aznavour, Charles, 67

Baburyan, Karen, 171
Bagratian, Grant, 149
Baichorova, Maria Osmanova, 195,
196
Bakradze, Akaki, 92, 95, 98
Baku Commune, 33, 37, 160
Balayan, Zori, 162
Balkars, 3, 8, 177, 178, 180, 192,
194, 195, 197, 198
Belgium, 28
Beria, Lavrentii, 6, 40, 86, 89
Berlin, Treaty of, 20
Black Hundreds gangs, 26
black market, 65, 70
Black Sea Economic Co-operation
project, 50, 63, 68
Bolshevik Party, 25, 32, 33, 34, 35,
36, 37, 38, 39, 40, 46, 53, 119,
136, 159, 160, 179, 192, 197,
206
Bosnia, 49, 51
Boutros-Ghali, Boutros, 112
Brest-Litovsk, Treaty of, 32
Brezhnev, Leonid, 43, 115, 122,
218
Bush, George, 169

Caspian Sea Co-operation Zone, 58

Catherine II, 18, 210
Caucasus, North, 174–212
censorship, 85, 87, 128, 129, 215
Chanturia, Giorgi, 95, 96, 97, 111
Charents, Yeghishe, 40
Chavchavadze, Ilia, 24
Chechens, 3, 6, 7, 8, 20, 21, 22, 41,
42, 65, 66, 67, 108, 111, 175,
178, 180, 182, 183, 191, 192,
194, 195, 197, 198, 199, 223
Chechnya, 56, 66, 73, 86, 134, 174,
176, 183–90, 199–200, 212, 215,
217, 223
Cher, 67
Cherkess, 3, 180, 192, 205, 206
Christianity, 1, 2, 4, 5, 13, 15, 16,
27, 31, 49, 56, 62, 63, 95, 153,
155, 156, 157, 175, 177, 190,
208
Church, 14, 15; Armenian, 27, 134,
158; Georgian, 13, 18, 19, 89,
90, 91, 94, 95, 96, 102, 110;
Orthodox, 13, 51
Ciller, Tansu, 54
Circassians, 3, 5, 8, 19, 20, 21, 26
Cold War, 48, 135, 136, 137, 140,
172
collectivisation, 39; forced, 41
Committee for Union and Progress,
30
Commonwealth of Independent
States (CIS), 47, 58, 59–63, 93,
101, 107, 119, 120, 130, 166,
168, 179, 219, 220
communism, 121, 191, 208, 213,
223
Communist Party, 43, 122, 138,
175, 176, 181, 203; of Armenia,
36, 37, 40, 142, 143, 145, 163;
of Azerbaijan, 117, 122, 163; of
Georgia, 88–92, 98–9; of USSR,
37, 94, 207, 210
Confederation of Mountain
Peoples, 108, 181, 187, 212
corruption, 43, 91, 142, 203
Cossacks, 1, 8, 18, 21, 26, 39, 176,
196, 206, 207–10